THE BRITISH
IN MALAYA

The Association for Asian Studies: Monographs and Papers XVIII

THE BRITISH IN MALAYA
The First Forty Years
1786-1826

K. C. Tregonning

Published for the Association for Asian Studies by
The University of Arizona Press   Tucson   1965

The publication of this volume has been made possible by a generous grant to The Association For Asian Studies by the Ford Foundation.

To My Mother and the Memory of
My Father

CONTENTS

INTRODUCTION

There are two threads that run through this narrative, the British in Malaya and the influence of British trade with China. For over forty years the two were linked together, the latter almost invariably playing some part in the activities of the former. The movement of the British eastwards from India to the Malay Peninsula, the impulse that led to the foundation of Penang in 1786, to Singapore in 1819 (and the onward movement to Hong Kong in 1842), represented above all the British desire to strengthen trade with China. Implied if not stated, the influence of this Chinese trade on the British in Malaya is present throughout the book.

In essence, the theme throughout this study, although for the most part Penang assumes the center of the stage, is the role of China. It is the pull of China which makes difficult any parochial study of Penang, for China is an influence which necessarily diverts our attention, time and again, from the narrow affairs of the peninsula. Thus although some space is given to a study of Malayan history, it is also an indication to those interested in Malaya (and indeed to those interested in Southeast Asia as a whole) that the history of this region can not be taken in isolation.

This book began as part of a thesis presented to the University of Malaya. The research was conducted in Singapore, Penang, Malacca, Balambangan, and elsewhere in Malaysia. Field work in the area, combined with the microfilm library facilities in Singapore, compensate, I hope, for the lack of access to other material in Europe. C. Northcote Parkinson, who is former Raffles Professor at the University of Malaya, assisted me in this research, as did Dr. Eric Stokes, now professor of history at the University of Southern Rhodesia. I am indebted also to the University of Singapore for liberal financial assistance. To my graduate students, G. Krishna Iyer, Lee Chye Hooi, C. C. Rajarao, and Saw Chee Leng, who worked with me on various aspects of early Penang, and to the students who, as members of the University Archaeological Society, scrambled on the banks of the Merbok and Muda rivers to find traces of an ancient Indianized settlement, I owe a special debt of gratitude.

K. G. Tregonning
Singapore 1964

I
THE PROBLEM

The Malay Peninsula today is one of the more prosperous and stable areas of Southeast Asia. A mixed population of over seven million Malays, Chinese, Indians, and Europeans work rubber estates, mine tin, and carry on active trading with Europe and the rest of Asia. A network of roads, railroads, airlines, and shipping services functions under an efficient independent government and for an educated citizenry.

The first steps towards the modernization of this peninsula began in the late eighteenth century, at a time when almost the only inhabitants were small groups of Malays, living a traditional life that scarcely changed from one generation to the next. For most of its history the Malay Peninsula has been on the flank of greater empires, either in Southeast Asia itself (empires which have controlled it) or in India and China (empires which have influenced it). Denied the ample flat land a great civilization demands, the Malay Peninsula has been, almost invariably, a subsidiary of greater empires elsewhere in Asia.

From the late eighteenth century onwards, the peninsula was to fall under the domination of none of these Asian empires, but of the British. The British in India, attracted to China, moved east, and established settlements in the Straits of Malacca, "Straits Settlements" as they were called, at Penang and then at Singapore, to assist that movement. British ability to move east of India and to create the nucleus of a new Malaya on the island of Penang was due to British control of the sea, and Britain became yet another nation to prove that who controls the sea-ways controls mainland and island Malaysia.

Among the first to prove this had been the Indian traders of the early centuries A.D. Attracted to China as a place where their peppers and pearls would sell well, they left on their way a few of their number in small riverine settlements, throughout Southeast Asia. These in time, with the blend of Indian and indigenous genius, grew into states; a few expanded into empires.

The earliest of these empires to dominate at least part of the waterways of Southeast Asia had been Funan, on the bulge of Indo-China. For several early centuries Funan controlled, amongst other places, the small east-coast river states of the Malay peninsula. Later, the east coast from the third century onwards, was to fall under the control of another Indo-Chinese maritime empire, that of the Chams, similarly placed on the other side of the selfsame sea that joined the Chams, culturally and ethnologically, to the Malay Peninsula.

The east coast of the peninsula, however, is separated from the west by mountains that, running down the center, have always divided Malaya; and the western side of Malaya has had its maritime links and many of its cultural links with the power across the waters that join it to Sumatra. So it is with the rise of Sumatran Srivijaya in the seventh century A.D. that we first hear of Kedah, off which lies Penang, and it is as one of the peninsula's most valued possessions, indeed, some would claim[1] as one of its twin capitals, that Kedah passes through the succeeding six centuries.

Most of the peninsula is hilly. Kedah is almost unique, in that it possesses an area of flat land, suitable for padi growing, and in addition a good anchorage in the Merbok, a sheltered river. Hard by this anchorage is Gunong Jeraya, a mountain visible (as is the peak of Penang, a score or so miles south) from far out to sea—an ideal landfall to the weary traveler crossing the Bay of Bengal.

It is no wonder that a settlement was built by the Merbok River, on the slopes leading up to the mountain, nor that prayers were said at the top as padi was grown on the flat land at the bottom, from at least the fourth century A.D. An easy land route across the peninsula enabled the Merbok settlement to avoid the calms, currents, and *krises* of the straits to the south. With these advantages the settlement was able to revive after damaging Chola raids early in the eleventh century and to remain a prominent Southeast Asian port long after other Indian settlements such as Langkasuka, Selingsing, or Takola had faded into obscurity and legend.[2]

But with the collapse of Srivijaya in the thirteenth century, Kedah, along with much of the Malay Peninsula, fell not to the maritime successor of Sumatra, the Javanese Madjapahit, but to the land empire of Siamese Ayudhia, which, with the new vigor of the T'ai in its bloodstream, was then conquering Cambodia and moving against the states of Burma as well.

In the ill-defined and fluctuating border between Siamese overlordship and Madjapahit grew Malacca, which, with a true sense of where its greatness lay, turned instinctively to the sea. Kedah declined, while Malacca, embracing the tenets of Islam, grew to replace Kedah and more; for whereas the traders of east and west had frequented the various ports of Southeast Asia before, with little but economic impulses to guide them, now religious ties and political objections to Madjapahit pretensions dictated Malacca and Malacca alone. And despite subsequent Madjapahit collapse, neither the Portuguese nor the Dutch, nor the centuries they represented, nor even the adoption by Kedah of Islam, lost for Malacca the peninsular pre-eminence it had won.

---

[1]G. Coedes, "The Empire of the South Seas," *Journal, Thailand Research Society,* Vol. XXXV, Pt. 1, February, 1944, pp. 1-16.

[2]This is dealt with in detail by P. Wheatley, *The Golden Khersonese: An Historical Geography of Malaya 300-1400 A.D.* Malaya (U. of M. Press, 1960).

Kedah became and remained a remote outpost of the Siamese empire, virtually autonomous. Such overlordship as was exercised came but rarely from Ligor, the southern state entrusted by Ayudhia with the care of its peninsular possessions, and most infrequently from Siam itself. Thus it was a most insignificant piece of jungly coastline that towards the end of the eighteenth century witnessed the arrival of the British, and although a millennium and a half had passed since the Indians had first dropped anchor, in essentials the impulses towards settlement were the same; both Indians and British came, by virtue of their command of the seas, to secure a port convenient for the replenishment of ships from India and for the acquisition of goods suitable for sale in China.

This was not the first attempt by the British to establish a settlement or a trade post on the Malay Peninsula, nor was it the beginning of British interest in China. Both enterprises had been attempted before, but the Malay peninsula efforts, though interesting enough perhaps to the British historian searching for national beginnings to great undertakings, were puny affairs and do not warrant detailed notice.

A factory, so-called, was established in Patani, on the east coast, in 1612. Another was founded in Kedah, a very minor outpost indeed of the East India Company, in 1669. Both struggled to survive; a ship a year, perhaps two, endeavored to secure a cargo. The letters extant,[3] despite the high hopes entertained for Patani, record dismal tales of frustrated plans and failure. When the traders were withdrawn, from Patani in 1623 and from Kedah in 1676, few could have lamented their departure or mourned their passing.

A century later, however, the British came back to Kedah in strength, borne on the on-rushing tide of their trade with China. For, from the time of their first entering Southeast Asian waters, the British had attempted at intervals to reach Cathay. By one stratagem after another they had endeavored to participate in what is one of the great constants, one of the underlying economic phenomena of Southeast Asia, the trade with China.[4]

From the first British maritime contact in 1635, and thence throughout the seventeenth century, the Chinese authorities had not merely denied Europeans access to Chinese territory but had refused officially to admit the very existence of Europeans. The Chinese had so complicated and restricted European activities that the British, discouraged but not dismayed, had turned to ideas of a settlement in Southeast Asia. A settlement was envisaged as useful, not merely as a place where spices could be collected for Europe, but also as a depot where goods could be secured for China and where, with luck, Chinese, remote from imperial decrees, might feel free to trade. Thus the barbarian would be saved fruitless visits to the rocky shores of south China.

[3]See: *Records of the Relations between Siam and Foreign Countries in the 17th Century.* (Bangkok, 1915); *The English Factories in India, 1670-77*, Vol. 1. "The Western Presidency" ed., Sir Charles Fawcett (Oxford, 1936).

[4]For a detailed examination of this, see in particular Earl H. Pritchard, *Anglo-Chinese Relations During the Seventeenth and Eighteenth Centuries* (University of Illinois, 1930); and his *The Crucial Years of Early Anglo-Chinese Relations, 1750-1800*. (Washington State College, 1936).

These objectives are not necessarily complementary, and the position where a judicious balancing of them could be maintained was never achieved. But this is not to say it was not attempted, and although the various Southeast Asian settlements founded by the British in the seventeenth century were aimed largely at the spice trade, nevertheless, trade with China was an additional spur to such undertakings.

The first settlement that partly realized these aims was Bantam, in Java, established in 1603 by Lancaster, shortly after the foundation of the East India Company, but eventually Bantam was to prove too isolated. The Dutch crowded in, the British were too remote, and seventeenth-century trade with China was a weak and paltry thing. Settlements on Borneo (Soekadana, 1612-1622, and Banjermassin, 1635-1651), Cambodia, Ayuthia, Sumatra, and elsewhere assisted in no way whatever.

For the first half of the eighteenth century there were few signs, despite the amalgamation of the rival concerns trading to the East, and the formation in 1709 of "The United Company of Merchants trading to the East Indies" that the seventeenth century tale of failure would not be repeated, for while the Company strengthened its position on the flanks of India, its Southeast Asian settlements continued to wither and die. A factory established on Pulo [island of] Condore in 1701 came to an abrupt end in 1705 through the sudden revolt of the Macassarese soldiers of the Company's garrison and the massacre of sixteen Europeans. The few who escaped never returned. Borneo still beckoned, but it was the lure of a charlatan; a factory at Banjermassin, where the Chinese often called, ended almost as abruptly as that on Condore, with the swift attack of the slighted Sultan, and the expulsion of the British in 1707. Again dismayed, but not completely, and still seeking that will-o'-the-wisp, the mart whereby China could be induced to buy and sell, the British came back in 1737. A precarious existence was ended by Dutch expulsion ten years later.

But now the tempo was increasing. By the middle of the eighteenth century, four great factors had emerged which were to transform the British position in the Far East, and to lead, *inter alia,* to the settlement of Penang. We have mentioned one before, the coalescing of the two rival trading concerns and the formation of a new, more powerful East India Company. Secondly, there was the reluctant admission in 1751 by the Peking Government that foreigners existed, and that their trading could be undertaken in China itself, at Canton. In India there were the conquests of Clive, which transformed the Company from a trading concern to an administration governing vast stretches of country; and finally there was the acquisition by the great bulk of Englishmen, during the latter half of the eighteenth century, of a taste for tea.

This demand for tea changed the trade from one of luxury to commerce for a staple in great demand. Permission to land in China gave to the Company the opportunity of acquiring the tea trade, while the costs of administering its expanding Indian Empire gave it the necessity; and the eighteenth century encouraged the technological improvements in the sailing vessel that made active participation possible.

The trade in tea, then, was the basic impulse that led to the expansion of British power in the Far East, and as a corollary, in Southeast Asia as well. Throughout the latter half of the eighteenth century, the demand for tea kept rising; and because of this, the East India Company, which maintained a mono-poly of the China-to-England trade, and which exercised a complete control over the London tea sales, was able to finance its expansion in India.

But if the English wished to buy China tea, as indeed they did, they had to offer something in exchange. And here the need for a post in the islands re-mained; for while the Chinese could wait at home, as indeed they had been doing, very largely, during the preceding centuries, and sell their goods without stirring, something had to be offered in exchange. Until the nineteenth century arrived, until opium came on the scene, it was more and more obvious that the British traders had nothing that China did not already possess or was not quite prepared to do without. There were exceptions of course; there was, for example, silver bullion; no Chinese would object to that. But in this exchange, current British economic prejudice saw signs of national weakness. No bullion, or at least as little as possible, must be drained out of the country. So in addi-tion there was what? British woollen goods? The economy of eighteenth-century Britain rested on the sheep's back to an extent only parallelled in twentieth-century Australia, and wherever this economy expanded, it attempted to export its wool. However, the wool had a regrettably poor sale in the Far East; it was useless as ballast coming out, useless in India and the islands, and most definitely useless in China. But if Britain itself produced nothing of value to China and if Indian cotton was insufficient, fortunately there were a few other commodities Britain could secure in exchange for which the *towkays* of Canton would exchange their tea. Chief of these were tin and pepper. And it was largely for the acquisition of these two commodities that Britain doggedly continued its search for a Southeast Asian base.

In the sixties and seventies, tea and the other (minor) commodities that made up the trade from China were still being exchanged for little else but silver. In Europe the East India Company acquired silver from Spain; in Asia it came partly from Persia but mostly from Manila. It was acquired from that port not by the Company, which had found by the 1750's that it had lost its aptitude for specialized trading, but by country ships, vessels under the Indian flag that during the eighteenth century traded with ever increasing frequency into Southeast Asian waters. In exchange for goods from India, in particular cotton, ("piece goods" so called) they obtained the silver of Spanish America; from Madras to Manila, and thence to China where their silver was sold to the Com-pany; such was the pattern. But as the China trade increased, and as the expenses of governing India mounted, this precarious supply, dependent very largely on Anglo-Spanish relations, became insufficient, and the East India

Company turned, with mounting urgency, towards the foundation of a factory in Southeast Asia.

The decisive step was taken in 1767; in London the Court of Directors, after contemplating the steady drain of bullion and the difficulties of securing more, and aware of the increasing profits from their tea sales, decided that steps must be taken immediately and effectively to extend the trade of the Company. India must acquire more goods for sale in China.[5] From this stemmed all that followed. With the Company in India so instructed there occurred Acheh and Kedah in 1772, Balambangan in 1773, Cochin China in 1778, Rhio in 1784, and Penang in 1786, virtually a twenty-year search, pursued with a determination difficult to explain in the light of the China trade problem, and the discovery, finally, that it was unnecessary.

The determined search was found unnecessary for by the early nineteenth century the pursuit of tin and pepper had been largely abandoned. The private traders at Canton, whose presence grudgingly was accepted as necessary to the economic maneuvers of the Company and to the financial advancement of its members, had found in opium a commodity far more valuable than tin with which to trade. Opium, easier to secure and yielding greater profits, was replacing tin by the end of the eighteenth century, and it is largely the change to the Indian drug, and the abandonment of the search for the elusive metal, that explains the absence, for nearly a hundred years, of any Malayan parallel to the gradual British occupation of India. Until the Suez Canal was cut in 1869, bringing a new and strategic factor into the China trade, and until the growth of the canning industry brought a new demand for an age-old product, the Malay States remained Malay States. Penang, and a little later Singapore, became, as entrepôt ports, very useful to the private traders; but as opium replaced tin in the *godowns* of Canton, no annexation of the Malayan hinterland ensued.

In search of a late eighteenth-century base in Southeast Asia for their growing trade with China, the British were hampered by the presence of their old rivals, the Dutch. Although not territorially in occupation of much of Malaysia, the Dutch, by treaties with numerous native rulers, reinforced by a navy that maintained as a Dutch preserve the lands lapped by the Java Sea, had secured such a control that the intrusion of another power would have precipitated international repercussions of a gravity far exceeding any possible advantage.

Under normal circumstances Holland provided a very useful buffer in Europe. Britain had no quarrel with it, and an invasion of Holland's sphere of influence in Southeast Asia would have been tantamount to an act of aggression, unacceptable alike to the authorities in India and to Parliament in London. So Britain, by policy and necessity, looked for a base in an area remote from the Dutch. But it had to be not merely remote from the Dutch at Batavia or Malacca, for the factory had to fulfill a certain specific function, namely, to

[5]This is shown clearly in V. Harlow, *The Founding of the Second British Empire*. London, 1952. Vol. 1, p. 84.

assist the China trade; and in addition, it had to be safe, in an area politically stable.

These qualifications, of remoteness, utility and stability, ruled out most of the mainland of Southeast Asia. Ava, Siam, and Cochin China might possibly have been considered but although different in their national characteristics, and frequently warring with each other, each was ruled by a sovereign hostile to Britain, arrogant in attitude and unstable in manner; besides, they had no tin. No base could be considered there. Nor could it in the far southeast end of the islands, for although this location could claim remoteness from the Dutch, it was remote also from everywhere else, particularly China; and again, there was no tin. The center of the area, the Java Sea, was Dutch, and there remained but two areas, the northwest (the north of Sumatra and of the Malay Peninsula), and the northeast (North Borneo), where the qualities necessary for success of a factory might possibly exist. These were examined.

They were examined in the first instance by the Company at Madras. The British in India after Clive held three great areas, designated Presidencies, each, until the re-organization of 1784, largely independent of the other. There was Bengal, where lay the wealth, the heart of India, controlled by Fort William at Calcutta. On the west coast, the original seventeenth-century foothold at Surat had given way to Bombay, where the Company's marine was stationed. On the east coast there was Fort St. George, or Madras. Long before the arrival there of the English, Madras had looked seaward for sustenance. The links from India to Malaya, both ancient and modern, come largely from Madras, and the British when they came merely intensified but in no significant way altered the age-old trade from here into Southeast Asia.[6]

The Company itself did not participate in this trade. It had grown too big and bureaucratic. It had become a great government unable to fit into the small retail trading enterprise that had characterized it. It was too heavy, too ponderous, to effect the quick adjustments, the flexible switching, that were necessary in the risky but profitable river and coastal trade of the islands. This was a field of commerce handled with skill and acumen by the country traders, and the first attempts by the Company to take over from them, and so to secure a greater supply of goods suitable for China, met with utter failure.

In Madras in the 1770's, these country or private traders, owners or agents for ships that carried on this island trade, had not quite reached the stage of formally joining themselves together into joint-stock companies. Nor had they altogether preserved the older loose relationship of associating together for one venture only, which had been characteristic of the Company itself over a hundred years before, and which was continued by the brilliant Portuguese families who stayed on, or who strayed in, when Madras became British, and who provided the dusky and passionate background for the sober English

---

[6]The trading of the British and other Europeans in India during the eighteenth century is dealt with by Holden Furber, *John Company at Work* (Harvard, 1948).

merchants. Rather there was an arrangement somewhere between the two: an association of business men for some length of time, but without the legal clarity or commitments of a Company. One such an association in the 1760's was between Messrs. Jourdain and Sulivan, which widened with success to bring in, a decade or so later, Mr. De Souza. It was the activities of this association that, after initial failures, led the East India Company in strength back into Southeast Asia.

II

ON THE WAY TO CHINA

In 1771, the Directors in London heard with astonishment of what appeared to be the beginning of another British power in the East. From some quarter they received a garbled account of the activities of Jourdain, Sulivan and De Souza's Association in Acheh in North Sumatra, where a factory had been established and trading arrangements entered into with the Sultan. The directors expressed grave annoyance "at the intrigues of the factors, who supported by a naval force and some hundreds of Sepoys from your coast have gained such an ascendancy as to restrain the freedom of trade . . ." They mentioned the link between the factotum and the "King," warned of the "grave consequences if private persons enter into compacts and connections with any power in India, contrary to our express orders,"[1] and they called on Fort St. George for an explanation.

One was provided, a little over a year later, by Madras, who forwarded to London Jourdain's description of how in 1766 he purchased the *Indian Trader,* and despatched her, as agent for the owners, himself and Sulivan, to Acheh and the Straits of Malacca, in the hopes of a good trading profit; how Harrop, the supercargo on board, accepted the Sultan's offer of a block of land for a factory (or store shed) and half the retail trade of the country, in return for the protection of a few armed men there; and how, as a result of establishing a shore depot, policed by seventy-five Indians, the trade of Acheh steadily increased, other European ships began a trade that had almost ceased, and the town benefited accordingly. No restrictions on that trade had been imposed, no one had ever complained; and if the King had acted autocratically, the association could not be blamed, particularly as Harrop was receiving and buying goods not merely for it but for a number of other Madras merchants as well (Messrs. Savage, De Fries, Stratton and Smith in particular).

Although this explanation was forwarded to the Court, providing a rare insight into eighteenth-century "country" trade, the Directors had not waited. Following their first letter of April, 1771, they decided, early in May, to take

[1]*East India Company.* Sumatra Factory Records, Vol. 15. London to Madras, 10 April, 1771.

over whatever was in existence in Acheh and, after suitable recompense had been paid, to incorporate the factory there into the East India Company.

Some inkling of their intentions must have reached the Company officials at Madras; they were fully aware of the need for such a factory, for they had been writing since at least 1763 of the urgency to secure either more silver or some other commodity acceptable to the Chinese if the trade there was to be maintained. In 1768 they wrote, "we cannot avoid expressing our apprehensions that it will be impossible for your China trade to be any longer supported by sending specie from India; Manila used annually to afford many thousand dollars which greatly assisted, but our intercourse with the Spaniards no longer exists..."[2] As the port most intimately concerned with this trade, Madras devoted itself to seeking a remedy. Not content then with merely addressing an enquiry to Messrs. Jourdain, Sulivan and De Souza as to just what was going on in Acheh, it took the initiative itself. Madras said to London, — and note the pull of China — "it appeared to us in the course of our enquiry that a factory at Quedah would be more advantageous to the Company than one at Achin, because we conceive the great object to be the means of supplying the China market. Tin, which is a staple at Canton, is produced to a very considerable amount in the districts of Quedah, but at Achin most of the articles fit for the China market are brought there by trading vessels and bartered for the manufactures of the coast."[3] So it proceeded simultaneously with the organization of Company expeditions to Acheh and to Kedah, without waiting for the Directors' express approval from London.

Two young men, favorites it would seem, certainly without trading experience, were chosen to lead these expeditions. The Honourable Edward Monckton was appointed commander of the mission to Kedah, and Mr. Charles Desvoeux became the leader of the Acheh Mission.[4] For Kedah, the experienced Francis Light (of whom we are to hear more later), was ignored. If that is reprehensible, for he was after all only a country trader, an agent in Kedah for Jourdain, Sulivan and De Souza, for Acheh the Company completely by-passed its own officials at Bencoolen.

Bencoolen, a minute settlement on the west coast of Sumatra, was the solitary reminder during the eighteenth century that the East India Company had been formed originally to trade in the East Indies, and that it had rounded the Cape of Good Hope in search not of Indian land, or Chinese tea, but of spices. Diverted to India itself, the Company had abandoned its earlier settlements in the East Indies, and it clung to Bencoolen more through policy than through profits, for although it had hoped to make it a pepper emporium it never flour-

[2] Madras to London, 11 May, 1768. (This, and the following acknowledgements to quotations in this chapter are all taken from the Sumatra Factory Records, Volume 15, unless noted otherwise).

[3] Madras to London, 28 February, 1772.

[4] Monckton, fifth son of the first Viscount Galway, married the daughter of Lord Pigot, governor of Madras, in 1776. He was Sheriff of Madras in 1770, at the age of 26, and was succeeded in this post by C. Desvoeux, another civil servant. See H. D. Love: *Vestiges of Old Madras, 1640-1800*. (London, 1913). Vol. III, pp. 58, 556, 578.

ished. No port, throughout recorded history, has ever flourished on the west coast of Sumatra; the huge incessant swell offshore, on what is a lee shore most of the year, and the forbidding hinterland behind the rocky coast, where there are rugged mountains, make a thriving settlement impossible. But by keeping a minute force there, the Company kept its foot in a door that otherwise would have been firmly closed. It paid its annual losses with ill grace; but it paid them, and it was from here that one might have thought a representative to nearby Acheh would be selected. Sumatra at that stage produced a goodly proportion of the world's pepper, so a Bencoolen experience might have been of some assistance. It was ignored; but in any event, it is doubtful if anyone from there could have assisted Desvoeux to the extent of saving the mission, for too many factors were against it.

Desvoeux was instructed by Madras in February, 1772, to sail to Acheh, there to discourage the country traders from forming their own factories, and to take over, on behalf of the Company, the stores, sheds, and fort of Mr. Harrop. From the Sultan he was to secure the port duties, or at least the right to collect them, to meet the costs of maintaining himself and the Sepoys he was to recruit from Mr. Harrop's force. He was to exchange the cloth shipped him from the coast for tin, pepper and gold dust, for "our chief view is to provide such articles as are staple at the China market."[5] As Sulivan had estimated an annual trading profit of 30,000 *pagodas,* his expedition set sail with confidence.

Acheh is rather like an immense amphitheatre facing the sea, a broad plain encompassed by lofty ranges that cut off this northern triangle of Sumatra, effectively isolating it from the rest of the island. The main range runs from the northernmost point, Acheen Head, south and east, leaving a fertile and well-populated area of some 26,000 square miles between it and the Straits of Malacca. The chief town of the state is near to Acheen Head, standing on a river; in Desvoeux's time as today, the houses that clustered rather haphazardly together were wooden, raised on posts to keep dry from the heavy rain, with an attap roof, a porch reached by wooden steps, surrounded by shade trees — the typical dwelling place of the Malay or Indonesian, little changed in centuries. Then as now and as with Kedah across the Straits, Islam was strong, verging on the fanatical, in Acheh.

Captain Forrest, an experienced trader, when describing his visits to Acheh between 1762 and 1784, wrote:

> The country above the town is very highly cultivated and abounds with inhabitants in many small villages, and single groups of three or four houses, with white mosques interspersed. Walking that way, if after rain, is disagreeable to a European, as they have no idea of roads; but Malays do not mind walking through mud up to the knee, which however they are careful to wash off, when they come to a house, before they climb to enter it.
> The main street in the town is raised a little, and covered with sand and gravel; but

[5]Madras to C. Desvoeux, 23 February, 1772.

nowhere else are the streets raised; and even this is sometimes overflowed by the swelling of the river, by sudden rain on the hills just above the town; in which case they make use of canoes: this often happens, especially during the rainy season, (our summer); but the town, which is on the south side of the river, struggles so as not to deserve the name of the capital of a populous though small kingdom. . .

Many Maldivia boats come yearly to Acheen, and bring chiefly dried bonnetta (fish) in small pieces about two or three ounces; this is a sort of staple article of commerce, and many shops in the bazaar deal in it only, having large quantities piled up, put in matt bags. . .

The king's palace, about a hundred yards from the skirts of the town, and to which there is access by canal from the river, as well as by land, is about three quarters of a mile in circumference, is ditched round, and is also surrounded with a strong wall, but not high. A number of large venerable trees shade it, with a good many tall bamboos. It is built on higher ground than the town, so of course it is not subject to be over flowed.[6]

Ships anchored in the bay at the river's mouth. It was tolerably protected, deep close to the land, and it provided a useful rendezvous both for the numerous Sumatran vessels wishing to keep clear of the Dutch at Malacca, and to the country traders, following on the heels of Sulivan, who derived some comfort from the presence of Harrop and his contingent of Sepoys. They felt there was more hope here of trade than southward down Sumatra, for as Horsburgh was to comment in his famous sailing *Directory* over sixty years later:

The coast of Sumatra is little known; it is all low land, the trees only appearing above water, with several rivers and shoal banks stretching out a considerable way from the shore . . . The natives being perfidious, the place is seldom visited by the European.[7]

Desvoeux arrived off Acheh on 26 March, 1772. He found Harrop absent, the man he had come to replace. Harrop's deputy felt too ill to come out, and on landing, Desvoeux was told the discouraging news that a man from Fort Marlbourough (Bencoolen), had come in an effort to establish a Company outpost a few months before, had met the Sultan, and had been absolutely refused.[8]

Harrop on his return organized for Desvoeux an interview, at 1 a.m., "the time of transacting all matters of consequences in this country,"[9] with the Sultan's favourite, one Kassim, a Malabar Moslem, and this led to an audience with the Sultan himself. He felt quite unable to grant the port dues to Desvoeux, and although expressing a general desire to see the Company establish a factory, he found that he could make no contribution whatever towards its upkeep. His only reliable revenue, the port dues, had been assigned to Harrop for five years at 60,000 rupees per annum. This barely kept his head above water. He

⁶T. Forrest, *A Voyage from Calcutta to the Mergui Archipelago . . . also An Account of the Islands Jan Syl, Pulo Pinang and the Port of Queda; the present state of Acheen . . . to which are added An Account of the Island Celebes* . . . (London, 1792) p. 44.

⁷J. Horsburgh: *India Directory, etc.* 2 Vols. (London, 1817). Vol. 2. p. 155.

⁸This was Giles Holloway, the Resident of Tappanooly, an outpost of Bencoolen, who was acting for J. Herbert, the leader of the Balambangan Mission. See T. Forrest: *A Voyage from Calcutta to the Mergui Archipelago.* (London, 1792) p. 50.

⁹Desvoeux to Madras, 15 April, 1772.

gave Desvoeux the right to trade, and, subsequently, he granted him the land on which stood Harrop's factory. But that was all; and it is doubtful, in view of the divided condition of the land, and of the great chiefs hostile to, and almost as powerful as, the Sultan, whether Harrop could have done much more, even if he had been more cooperative, for his writ scarcely extended further than the bay beside which he lived.

Desvoeux inspected the factory he had acquired. It was situated on the banks of the river, some three miles from the mouth, and close to the Sultan's fort. Although it had sufficed Harrop for six years or more, Desvoeux, used perhaps to the comparative magnificence of Madras, was appalled at its inadequate defence.

The enclosure is of bamboos 8 feet high and pointed at their ends. At each angle is a very small wooden battery, the flanks of which do not project more than 8 feet, so that they are scarcely of any use, and there is not any stage or rampart within. There is no ditch, two sides indeed are secured, the north by the river and the west by a watercourse, but the other two are quite exposed and these are nearest to the Roads from whence an attack may be expected . . . We are generally once a week alarmed with reports of the Sultan's enemies coming to attack him.[10]

There were two parties that had reason to oppose the East India Company in its efforts to establish itself in Acheh. There was Harrop, acting in the interests of his principals, who feared that the Achinese, "to whom we were always obliged to sell on credit, and who were considerably indebted to us, would take advantage of the Company's intention and find means to evade payment of their just debts to us, unless compelled to."[11] The Association had been established in Acheh for some time, it was functioning profitably and without fuss, and now "The Heaven Born," the East India Company, was attempting to take over.

In addition to this possible opposition there was the enmity of the great provincial leaders. As Marsden[12] says, the history of Acheh presented a continual struggle between the monarch and the aristocracy of the country, and in 1772 the state was divided, almost to the point of anarchy, between the great chiefs, each of whom controlled a number of *mukims,* or small districts. These were united only in opposition to any increase in power to the Sultan; otherwise they acknowledged no one among them as leader, admitted only a nominal superiority to the Sultan, and rarely paid obedience to his commands.

Desvoeux was convinced by this opposition, particularly by the condition of the country, that "no advantage can possibly accrue to the Company from having a factory here which will be adequate to the expense of supporting it. If the end proposed be the provision of goods for the China market, I am sure it

[10]Desvoeux to Madras, 23 May, 1772.

[11]Jourdain and Sulivan to Madras, 17 June, 1772.

[12]W. Marsden, *The History of Sumatra.* (London, 1811) p. 401.

[13]Desvoeux to Madras, 23 May, 1772.

will never answer . . . there is no regular administration of government in any department, nor much regard paid to the Sultan."[13]

His only policy, one would have thought, would have been to support the Sultan. The period of rigid non-intervention had not dawned. He had troops, and however poor in quality they were at least an armed force commanded by a European, Lieutenant Lane, and the Sultan was not completely powerless. Together they could have secured a considerable increase to his power, and a lessening of the turmoil. Firm action however would appear a trait foreign to both Desvoeux and Monckton. As Francis Light wrote to Mr. De Souza, "you will never be able to make a settlement, in Acheen or Quedah, unless you act with spirit and authority."[14] Desvoeux had a force, but he never used it, and the Sultan was bullied into withdrawing the timid support he had extended originally, and in turning against him.

By December Desvoeux was scarcely venturing outside his factory, and the Sultan had been completely intimidated. Madras had decided in June, after receiving Desvoeux's early letters, that it seemed pointless to persist with Acheh, but that as it was advisable for the factory to be maintained until the Court in London could make a decision, Company goods should be sent for sale early in 1773, to help defray the expenses, and Desvoeux should begin trading. With the deterioration in conditions apparent by December however, it was conceded that the actual safety of the factory was in danger. It was decided to withdraw the expedition immediately. The *Cuddalore,* the trustworthy beast of burden that had been crossing and recrossing to Acheh, Kedah and Madras, set sail, and Desvoeux and his two European assistants were back in India by early 1773. So ended, most ignominiously, the Acheh expedition.

In considering Kedah, where the experience was much the same, we meet one of the main characters in our early narrative, Francis Light. Although fresh information has been revealed since Hugh Clodd[15] rescued him from oblivion, the main details of his life have been recorded already. Suffice to say that born, illegitimately, in 1740, he joined the Navy at the age of nineteen, left it in 1763, and then came out East; a typical enough move, although not for a European not employed by the East India Company; no Englishman was permitted past the Cape of Good Hope unless licensed by the Company, and although the practice was scarcely consistent with the theory, it is strange that the man largely responsible for the successful eastward move of the Company had never been, it would seem, a member of it.

His quarterdeck experience in the Navy, although slight, (he was a midshipman), was sufficient to secure him employment at Madras with Jourdain, Sulivan and De Souza as an agent; and it was as a country trader, reinforcing Harrop in 1770 at Acheh, that he first made his mark. At Acheh he soon became aware of a traditional flow of pepper, tin, and other goods across from

[14]F. Light to De Souza, 25 November, 1771.

[15]H. Clodd, *Malaya's First British Pioneer* (London, 1948).

East Sumatra to Kedah. Many Sumatran *prahus* then as now found it an easier passage, with the northerly winds, than one up the straits into the teeth of the wind to Acheh. In early 1771 he followed this trade to Kedah, there to write to his employers, in August 1771, that the Sultan had granted to them the port at the mouth of the river, commanded by a fort, in return for assistance against the southerly state of Selangor, which, dominated by Bugis adventurers, had raided Kedah the previous year. A few months later, as fear of the Selangor Bugis increased, the Sultan ceded the entire coastline, the danger area, stretching from the Kedah river southwards to the island of Penang. Light had come ashore, was residing in the old fort, and was conducting a profitable business, particularly in sales of opium at $800 a chest.

He wrote to Jourdain in November that "there is more pepper and beetlenut brought to this port from the coast of Pedir [East Sumatra] than is carried to Acheen, and with that, tin and dammar, I will engage to load any two of your vessels from this port by 1 January;" and in a letter to De Souza we have our first specific reference to Penang as a suitable place for a settlement for the Company. "Withinside of Pulo Pinang is a fine clear channel of 7 and 14 fathoms through which a ship may work any time. I remember it was once your opinion that a House upon Pulo Pinang would be very useful; it would be extremely so because the Europe ships[16] can easily stop there. There is plenty of wood, water and provisions there, they may be supplied with tin, pepper, beetlenut, rattans and birdsnests, and the Macao ships will be glad to stop there, and all other vessels passing through the Straits may be as easily supplied as at Malacca. Whether this would not suit the Company better than our Association I leave you to judge. . ."[17]

These letters were supplied to the authorities at Fort St. George when they asked the Association in January, 1772 to explain its activities. They were instrumental in deciding Madras to send an expedition to Kedah as well as to Acheh, particularly as the Sultan himself had written in March, 1771 after the Bugis had devastated his lands, intimating a willingness to receive the Company. The Honorable Mr. Monckton then was selected, and instructed to offer protection to the Sultan against Selangor. In return he was to secure if possible the port customs of Kedah, or failing that at least the right to collect it, that the costs of the troops might be met. Also he was to obtain a site for a factory, from which the Sultan was to take each year goods at fixed prices, and to offer in return "tin, wax, pepper, and elephants teeth, or other staple articles for the China market . . . the great object is trade and barter."[18] Monckton was even more optimistic than Desvoeux, for the estimated annual trade of Kedah was over 130,000 *pagodas*, and a profit seemed possible of at least 45,000 *pagodas*, greater than that of Acheh. Leading an expedition of two ships and a force of

---

[16]That is, the East Indiamen from Europe bound for China.
[17]Light to De Souza, 25 November, 1771.
[18]Madras to Monckton, 23 February, 1772.

artillery, lascars and Sepoys under the command of Lieutenant D. McClintock, Monckton set sail for Kedah.

Until it was developed in the twentieth century, Kedah consisted in effect of a number of rivers flowing westwards through thick jungle. All movement was by boat, whether eastwards inland to the mountain backbone of the peninsula or along the coast. Of these rivers the most important were the Muda, in the south near Penang Island; the Merbok, where the ancient Indian settlement lay buried and forgotten by the slopes of Gunong Jeraya; and the Kedah River itself, a further forty miles north. By the banks of these rivers, padi was grown. In modern times Kedah was to become the rice bowl of Malaya, for it is the one sizeable area of flat land in the peninsula. It explains perhaps Siam's long interest in it, and how it was that a large proportion of the Malays inland from the Islamic fringe on the coast spoke a Malay-Siamese dialect, and worshipped Buddha. Kedah was in the uncertain position of straddling a great cultural division, and the wonder is that it managed to survive and emerge as a strong, self-sufficient state, culturally homogeneous. But that emergence lay in the distant future; when Monckton appeared, it was badly mutilated, its coastal villages at the river mouths defeated, and although the capital, Alor Star, had survived, owing to its strategic position, well up river, Kedah's Sultan was virtually a refugee, residing in the far north, sheltering in the pocket principality of Perlis, as far from the Selangor Bugis as he could put himself with safety.

Francis Light met Monckton when he landed at the river mouth. As had Harrop, he made some initial attempts to help the Company representative. Both men subsequently appear to have been ignored and to have withdrawn from the scene. Light and the Laxsamana, that is, the official in charge of the Sultan's navy and things maritime, who was the father-in-law of the Sultan's eldest son, dispatched messages to the Sultan at Perlis, as did Monckton himself. Replies came to Light and the Laxsamana, asking for advice; Monckton was ignored: an ominous beginning.

Without waiting for an invitation, Monckton set out to visit the Sultan. He took a dozen artillerymen, eighteen Sepoys and an interpreter, Mr. Mallow. Mr. Light accompanied them. The small force in a long-boat and two prahus sailed and rowed all day past the coastal mangrove to the Perlis river. There it was received in audience by the Sultan the following morning. Monckton insisted on a salute at his entering, another at the delivery of his present, and another at his departure, but when he intimated the willingness of the Company to establish a factory, provided that the costs of maintenance were defrayed by the customs revenue, and that the Sultan should buy piece goods and opium in exchange for tin and pepper, he received a very lukewarm reply indeed.

The Sultan maintained that he had never written for assistance and that he was too old to bustle and make contracts for purchasing large quantities of opium. He insisted that he could not make any grant of land or privileges unless he was assisted by an attack against Selangor. At this point the conference broke down. Monckton could not agree to aggressive southward action; the Sultan would yield nothing unless it was promised.

Monckton made no further attempt, and throwing in his hand, returned to Kedah the next day. He did not see the Sultan again for four months. Light, however, had visited the Sultan after the break-up of the one and only conference, and had diplomatically retrieved the situation. The Sultan granted to the Company a large stretch of land where a factory could be built at the entrance to the Kedah river, gave an option to the Company on all tin to be exported, and made a ruling that the Company alone could purchase black pepper and elephants' teeth. The customs duties on foreign vessels also were granted to the Company with half to be paid to the Sultan, on condition that should Selangor invade Kedah, the Company would send a vessel to attack them.

Here, it would appear, is all that Monckton asked for, secured by Light in a few minutes conversation after Monckton had stumbled with his interpreter unavailingly for hours. Monckton was quite unappreciative, informing Madras that "Mr. Light secured a grant, not near as full and clear as I would wish, but still something."[19] One cannot help thinking, on reading the original correspondence, that Monckton's mission was mishandled, not the least by this precipitous swoop on the Sultan, the immediate presentation, through an interpreter, of demands, and the abrupt return to Kedah. As Light no doubt could have told him, one does not do business like that with the Malays; if one attempts it, failure is the result. They are gentle people, patient and courteous, prepared in negotiation for a long exchange of pleasantries, whereby an arrangement is concluded as among friends, after much discussion. To arrive swiftly at the point is anathema.

Monckton had added insult to injury by rowing up river to Alor Star, the capital, where dwelt the two sons of the Sultan. The eldest was administering the state in his father's absence, and would have provided Monckton with a valuable ally. Light, spurned by Monckton, had washed his hands of the project, and had left Kedah to open a trading post in Junk Ceylon, an island to the north, and Monckton went without him. He was received civilly, but without ceremony, for astonishingly he had brought no present. He won no friends there, and by his other actions he seriously alarmed his superiors in Madras. He wrote to Fort St. George:

I have wrote Amoy by a large China junk that is here, to encourage the Chinese to come and settle here. The Dutch make the junks pay $4,000 for liberty to pass (Malacca), and I therefore gave the Junk an English Jack and a certificate that she was freighted by me, promising that you would send to the supracargoes at Canton a Passport to go from Quedah to Amoy and back. The passport must be made out for Toei Veng, and he will send to Canton for it, we must hereafter make use of the same expedient to get all the Buggesses to come here.

In addition to this, Monckton pressed the Company to ally itself with Rhio

[19]Monckton to Madras, 22 April, 1772.

and fall on Selangor.[20]

These suggestions horrified the Board at Madras. Monckton it would seem could see no further than the local scene, whereas to the Company the international repercussions with the Dutch, allied as they were to Selangor, and fearful of European intrigues in the south, accentuated concern lest the Company become involved in a local war of indefinite length. Monckton was admonished accordingly.

Reluctant to return defeated, Monckton continued to reside at the river mouth, and the Sultan stayed in Perlis. In July Monckton journeyed again to the north, and asked the Sultan to confirm the grant of the port. The Sultan again endeavored to persuade Monckton to act aggressively against Selangor, but Monckton again refused, and again the conference broke down, with the Sultan this time withdrawing his previous grant. Monckton placed the blame on the "Chuliahs" and "Malabars" (South Indian merchants), whom he alleged had intrigued against him; but it would appear as if his own insufficiency as a negotiator must have been at least partly responsible.

Monckton left Perlis on the twenty-ninth of July. "I think it lucky the King refused my settling here," he wrote to Madras, and in an effort possibly to divert attention from his failure he added that, "from the very best information I have very great reason to think a very valuable settlement may be made at Rhio and Tranganio,"[21] and there he intended to sail. He did so, in the faithful old *Cuddalore,* reaching Rhio on 29 August.

South of the mainland of the Malay Peninsula is a scattered array of islands. Very few rise over a few hundred feet. They squat on the equator, low-lying, covered by jungle, connected by shallows and coral reefs. The one broad, clear gap between them is the swath cut by the Straits of Singapore, some five miles wide, that sweeps from the south China Sea round to the Straits of Malacca. The islands lying to the north of those Straits are Singapore and its ancillaries; to the south there crowd the myriad shores of the Rhio Archipelago.

The inhabitants of the islands were few; *orang laut,* who sold their fish to ships that lay becalmed in the Straits, and Malays, slightly more advanced, who boldly attacked those selfsame ships, whenever they were guaranteed an overwhelming supremacy. It was a lawless area, with a significance to the Malay peninsula about equal to that of the Shetlands to England. And then from the Celebes in the eighteenth century came the Bugis.

The Bugis have been compared to the Norsemen in Europe, for both were adventurers who embarked on the seas, there to raid, pillage, trade, and settle. Like the Norsemen, the Bugis were possessed of an organizing power greater than their neighbors. In Europe the well-governed dukedom of Normandy rose; in the East the Bugis, moving out of the Celebes at the beginning of their confused century of conquest, settled in numbers at the Klang and Sel-

[20]Monckton to Madras, 22 April, 1772.
[21]Monckton to Madras, 13 August, 1772.

angor estuaries, there to create a Bugis state by 1710, and to establish them-selves in Rhio as well by 1722. Here grew two powerful and aggressive states.

By the middle of the eighteenth century, Bugis power was effective over most of the Malay Peninsula. The Dutch had not ventured to check this power, and they had seen their sea authority severely weakened. The only repulse the Bugis had suffered had been at the hands of the Minangkabau, seventeenth-century migrants to Malaya from Sumatra, who had moved into the vacant lands behind Malacca between 1650 and 1700. They were hard-working peas-ants, matrilineal agriculturalists; and peasants, as both Rome and Russia have shown, make good fighters. This too the Bugis discovered, their pressure between 1760 and 1770 being completely ineffective. But elsewhere they had established a firm control. Rhio, allied to Selangor, was their Normandy, and when Monckton visited it in 1772, Daing Camboja, the famed under-king (for they never assumed the royal title, and maintained puppet Malays as Sultans, as the British did a century later), was controlling a web of trade.

Monckton mistook the facade for the reality, and called on the Sultan. He was as unreceptive as his colleague in Kedah, and in response to a request for a grant of land to the Company, Monckton was asked to wait until the nobles and the under-king met and considered the question. He sailed on instead, speeding up the east coast of the Malay Peninsula, past the rivers of Pahang, the southerly monsoon driving him so rapidly that by the third of September he was anchored over the bar in the "tringanio" (Trengganu) River. But again no offer of a grant, for the Sultan's revenue came almost entirely from the tax on the imports and exports that Monckton desired for the Company.

He returned to Kedah, firmly convinced that although there was little to offer at Trengganu, Rhio was abounding in possibilities. The Bugis were still aggressive along the arms of their web, at the extremities of their influence, but at the heart, in Rhio, there was order and administration. Fleets of their *palaris,* copies of seventeenth century Portuguese vessels, moved with the monsoon to and from their home ports in the Gulf of Boni, and to other centers free of Dutch or Malay restrictions. Besides the Bugis trade there was the Chinese. "There are a great number of fine islands at the mouth of the Straits," he wrote, in a dispatch that anticipated Singapore, " — and the Chinese are the life of trade, they swarm in the Straits like bees, a great number of them offered to go if the English would form a settlement in these parts."[22] But as he had quite failed to secure any promise of a cession, his mission was as fruitless as his experience in Kedah, and it was left to Raffles to prove him cor-rect nearly fifty years later.

Madras decided that Kedah was as useless as Acheh. Francis Light was blamed, not Monckton. "It appears that the place has been much misrepre-sented to us," Fort St. George wrote, "and little dependence is to be placed

---

[22]Monckton to Madras, 12 October, 1772.

on the representations of persons whose characters are not well known and tried. The persons employed by those concerned in the trade have as is now apparent misled them by specious representations in order to continue themselves, though ruinous to their employers."[23] Monckton was recalled to Madras. He embarked his force in the *Tankerville* on December 13, and after calling at Acheh on 26 December, where he found Desvoeux sheltering behind his coconut trees, he arrived back in India on 12 January, 1773.

Although the anarchy of Acheh from the beginning had made the mission of Desvoeux impossible, Monckton's failure in Kedah is less easy to explain away, particularly when it is compared to the success of Light in 1786. Conditions by then had changed, but not appreciably; the East India Company could have established a factory at Kedah in 1772, had the mission been better led. The failure in 1772 was the failure of Monckton; because of it the Malay Peninsula disappeared from the considerations of the Company for over a decade.

The northwest, then, had been tried and found wanting. It was remote from the Dutch, Acheh more so than Kedah, and there was tin, in Kedah far more so than in Acheh, but perhaps not quite enough available in either. And there was no security. The prospects of the northeast had still to be investigated, and although it would be incorrect to say that the Company turned from one to the other, for both areas were being considered at much the same time, the actual expedition to the northeast, to the island of Balambangan, occurred almost immediately after the failure of 1772, although the area had been under discussion for some considerable time.

It had been under discussion for at least a decade, from the time that the expanding tea trade at Canton made the need for a substantial reinforcement of the Company's purchasing power imperative. All thoughts, every action, were locked around this problem. With greater capital, greater profits could be made; and one such place where capital could be acquired, so it was reasoned, was in the northeast of Southeast Asia.

The most prominent advocate of this area as a suitable site for a trading post was Alexander Dalrymple. Born in 1737, he had secured entry into the East India Company in 1752. After the "forty five" there was need for many a Scotsman to migrate, but it was not until the time of the great Dundas, fifty years later, that waves of Dalrymple's countrymen flooded the East India Company in general and Penang in particular. He was their predecessor; he was also another who failed to find a satisfactory base for the Company in Southeast Asia.

He was stationed at Madras, the port with the traditional interest in that area, and he soon became aware of the centuries old trade. He read in the old

[23]Madras to Monckton, 5 October, 1772.

files, *Sumatra Factory Records, China Factory Records,* and *Java Factory Records* above all, of the earlier participation by the Company in this trade. He journeyed himself, as he rose in rank, throughout the island-dotted region, particularly in the *Cuddalore* between 1759 and 1764, and his reading and his interests centered more and more on the uncertain periphery of interests between the Spanish at Manila and the Dutch at Batavia; here, he felt, might be the vacuum of power where the British could move in.

In 1762, as one of the last acts of the Seven Years War in which Britain was fighting Spain (and by so fighting depriving herself of access to a vitally necessary source of silver bullion), Pitt sanctioned a two-pronged attack on Spain overseas, on Havana in Cuba and on Manila in the Philippines. Brigadier-General Draper, the commander of the small force of Sepoys and European troops from Madras that captured the latter port almost without loss, gave his protection to the aged Sultan of Sulu, who had escaped from his Spanish imprisonment in the town. In return for that protection, and for the Sultan's safe delivery back to his archipelago, Draper (and Dalrymple, who was with the expedition) secured from the Sultan the cession in 1764 of a large part of North Borneo. Although the northwest coast of that island was not his to give, for it lay firmly within the territories of the Sultanate of Brunei, the northeast coast was Sulu territory; indeed the Sulu archipelago ran across the sea almost to touch it, a coast remote from European and native control. Ideal, thought Dalrymple, for the Company.

He now attempted to persuade the Company that here was its base. It was unconvinced. A few years earlier Dalrymple, always a student of ships' logs, had deduced that the traditional passage to China, via the South China Sea with the southwest monsoon, was not the only route. The great disadvantage of this route lay in the fact that this monsoon blew for six months only, from May until September; miss the monsoon and you lost at least half a year. Dalrymple had suggested an alternative route, valid even when the northeast monsoon blew down from China. Ignore the China Sea and the Dutch, he said, sail through the Sunda Straits and then eastward between Borneo and the Celebes into the Pacific; and then head northwest for Canton. By 1764 this was an accepted course for the Company ships that arrived at the entrance to the Indonesian Archipelago too late for the more direct route, and Dalrymple urged that an obvious site for a factory was somewhere along this new track.

He returned to London to press his claims, which for some time were viewed with indifference. "We caution you to be careful that you do not by any act or otherwise renounce any right which the Company might derive from the grants to the Sultan of Xolo to settle on Borneo"[24] . . . so the Company directors in London wrote to their subordinates in Madras. They made no effort, however, to benefit from those rights. Silver might be short, the tea trade might be pre-

---

[24]London to Madras, 19 February, 1766; quoted in J. Willi: *The Early Relations of England with Borneo.* (Langensalza, 1922), p. 58, which deals with this North Borneo venture in detail.

carious, but was Sulu the answer? Dalrymple, who by this time had acquired a national reputation through the publication of his beautifully compiled charts and maps and through his learned researches into early discoveries, was sure Sulu was the answer. But where was the tin or the pepper that would sell in China? Where was the market for Indian cloth? Where was the security? Dalrymple continued to press the assets of his cession, in particular of the uninhabited island of Balambangan, a few miles off North Borneo, ideal so he said as a site for a new factory. It would become attractive immediately to natives from the surrounding islands, so he urged, and to the Chinese carrying on a traditional trade with Manila. In addition it lay near to the track of either passage to China, and would be convenient for ships.

Dalrymple carried much weight by his great knowledge, and gradually created an atmosphere favorable to his foolish scheme. When the Directors decided, in 1767, that they must most actively pursue a trading policy in Southeast Asia, they had before them Dalrymple's well-prepared and publicized plan for Balambangan. It was the only plan; it was adopted.

The decision to establish a base on Balambangan was made in 1768; the actual foundation did not occur for another five years, in 1773, and in between Dalrymple suffered two crippling reverses. He was a stubborn man, arrogant and petulant; his face portrays his character,[25] and his stubbornness lost him two chances of fame. The first chance was in 1768, when the Royal Society, on the strength of his writings and knowledge of the South Seas, invited him to lead a proposed expedition to the Pacific, there to observe the transit of the planet Venus, and to explore the area more fully. He demanded command of the ship in addition to leading the expedition; but it was a Royal Navy vessel, and no one not a member of that service could be considered as captain. He was refused, he persisted, and the Society, faced with the withdrawal of Admiralty support, accepted its suggestion that an outstanding naval hydrographer, Lieutenant J. Cook, be appointed to the joint command. So the expedition set sail, led by a farm labourer's son, a genius who had begun his nautical career as a sculley on a Whitby coal barge, and who now, because of Dalrymple's absurd demands, was given the chance of discovering the east coast of Australia and of making some of the greatest voyages in the history of maritime exploration.

The second failure of Dalrymple was to lose the command of the Balambangan expedition. In 1768 the Company had addressed the Crown. The four reasons it gave for the annexation of the island bear close resemblance to the reasons for the settlement on Penang eighteen years later. It hoped first to divert the Chinese trade of the Philippines to the island by inducing Chinese to settle and by inviting Chinese junks to call; second to promote the sale of British goods, in particular its woollens; third to open a market for the produce

[25]For example in the *European Magazine*, London, November, 1802.

of India; and fourth to extend the Company's trade in unfrequented parts.[26] Laudatory though these objectives were, the Company encountered an unexpected stumbling block in the Crown. Kings had not then grown accustomed to reigning but not to ruling. Unfortunately for the directors, this request for royal sanction to a *fait accompli,* this request for protection to an island already acquired, came out of the blue. George III knew nothing of what had gone on before, he knew nothing of the circumstances preceding this request, and he decided that before he gave his approval to the establishment of a factory he would study all the relevant papers and reports.

The Company reconciled itself to the delay with good grace, and went ahead in making all necessary arrangements. Dalrymple again turned mulish. Offered the command, he laid down his conditions. These included command of the ship, choice of the crew; all expenses paid and a commission of four per cent on all cargoes bought and sold at Balambangan; the governorship of the island; the sum of £8,000 after three years service there, and if the expedition should fail, another £8,000. Throughout 1769 he continued to demand an absolute management without control, while the Court insisted on its right to appoint all officers and to establish a Council. At the end of the year, the Crown, which had assigned a Royal Navy vessel to the expedition, experienced fresh suspicions as to the international implications of annexing Balambangan, and withdrew its support. It was secured again in 1770, but by now Dalrymple was arguing with the Company in a virulent manner on petty points concerning the crew and victualling and other matters, and when early in 1771 he demanded his full pay as governor of Balambangan, and that it be back-dated six months, although he had not sailed from London, he was dismissed from the service.

Subsequently however, as he continued with his writings and chart publications, he became the Company's and then the Navy's hydrographer, the first ever; he had much learning but little wisdom, and was better suited for the academic pursuits of research and study than for practical work among men and ships. The expedition was entrusted to John Herbert, an avaricious villain of the Company at Fort Marlborough (or Bencoolen), on Sumatra. By his selection the Company made sure, as it did with Monckton and Desvoeux, that the settlement would fail.

The expedition's vessel, the *Britannia,* left England in the summer of 1771, reached Bombay in January 1772, where it took on stores, and arrived at Madras on 26 May. The Acheh and Kedah missions had sailed a little over a month previously, but the *Britannia,* fully provisioned and ready for sea, had to wait until August for Herbert to arrive from Bencoolen. He sailed a month later, returning in his new command to Fort Marlborough, there to buy, in his capacity as Company servant, the contents of a vessel he owned in his private role as a trader. Having begun the voyage by making an excellent profit, he

[26]Home Misc. Series 771. Court to Lord Weymouth, 28 October, 1768; in *WILLI,* p. 63.

continued on his way, pausing for months at Pasir and Sulu, arriving at last at Balambangan on 12 December, 1773. It had taken the *Britannia* two and a half years to sail from London to the island. Already the directors were seriously alarmed at the conduct of the expedition.

Balambangan is a delightful little island, lying snugly alongside the protecting bulk of Banggi, its big neighbour. It has a sparkling blue bay facing Banggi, protected from all winds, sheltered from the ocean swell, and three fathoms deep to close inshore. A crisp white beach, overhung by shady *casuarina* trees, it is a little-seen tourists' delight; but it is uninhabited, unproductive, and remote from any sizeable market. Up the nearby Borneo rivers, and on the numerous little Sulu or Filipino islands are small numbers of primitive peoples, then as now with few wants and fewer demands. Acheh had pepper, and tin was nearby, Kedah had tin, padi and the Sumatran trade, while both had a considerable population; Balambangan had nothing. It was a green desert.

Herbert did the best for himself with what he had. Ships began to call, on instructions from Madras and London, to off-load a portion of their cargoes of piece goods and opium. Herbert could give nothing in exchange but bills on the Company. Gradually the goods so acquired were sold, either to the occasional junk or to the Suluk and Bajau *prahus* that ran up the sandy beach. The proceeds went into the pockets of Herbert and his friends; little or nothing was remitted to the Company except bills and requests for more goods.

While a stockade was built inland from the beach, and a few go-downs and huts were erected (the scrubby jungle being cleared with difficulty), Herbert dispatched representatives on exploratory missions in search of customers, and established minor posts on Palawan, Sulu and down south at Brunei, where a steady trade with China in pepper had long been in operation. But as unexpected expenses continued to be booked by Madras and London and no income was entered, the directors decided to withdraw the establishment and to carry out an investigation into the details of administration there. They were too late.

Herbert had attracted not merely the envy of the surrounding island people but their dislike as well. Go-downs filled with piece goods combined with untactful handling had created an explosive situation. "Commerce" and "piracy" are closely linked even today, in these waters; two hundred years ago they were indistinguishable, particularly to the Suluks. Herbert had insulted the Sultan and abused a prominent *Datu,* or chief, Teting. On 26 February, Teting and his men, who had crossed into Balambangan by night to hide inland, rushed the small settlement. The Europeans escaped to their anchored craft, the few Sepoy troops were killed or taken into slavery, and the merchandise was thoroughly looted.

Herbert lived along the bay, some distance from the factory. It was an odd arrangement, for his hut was completely isolated and unprotected. Although it was not burnt until the afternoon, he escaped without any of the books, diaries, or commercial papers that one might have hoped he would have endeavored to secure; so there vanished in flames the details of his criminal frauds, although enough remained, in Madras and London, to substantiate a lengthy enquiry. Herbert, Edward Coles (second in command), and Palmer, the other European, fled to Brunei. Here John Jesse, their representative, had been managing a profitable little agency; but on the arrival of a Madras ship in November, 1775, (sent to replace Herbert) the whole lot were withdrawn to India, and the scheme abandoned. Captain Thomas Forrest, a level-headed country trader, who had been sent on a search for spices far to the southeast, returned in 1776 to find a scene of desolation.

III

THE SEARCH CONTINUES

Thomas Forrest, a senior captain in the East India Company's Marine, alone of those who had participated in the Balambangan debacle, had earned the respect of his superiors. His brilliant act of seamanship, when he sailed a small Suluk *prahu* far to the eastwards on a voyage of discovery to New Guinea, through twenty months of uncharted islands, reefs and shoals, bears comparison to the better-known small boat epic of CaptainWilliam Bligh,R.N. Forrest had been attached to Bencoolen for many years, and his knowledge of eastern waters in which he had traded since 1751 rivalled that of his friend Dalrymple. He knew Acheh well, and was on friendly terms with the ruler, who in 1784 decorated him with the order of the golden sword. And he had traded with Kedah too, and with other Malay states. He appears to have been a sensible, unassuming, and extremely capable ship's captain of long experience, and when the Company decided in 1784 to make the next attempt at a settlement in Southeast Asia the responsibility was vested in him.[1]

By 1784 much had happened; in particular there had been a great increase in the trade with China. Although this had led to a resultant increase in the country trade, it still left the Company more desperate than ever for funds with which to support its investment at Canton. Silver bullion, of which more and more was needed, became virtually unobtainable when Spain followed France into the American War of Independence. Between 1779 and 1785 not a dollar was sent from England to China, and the supply secured by the country traders from Manila was most insufficient. As a result, ever increasing difficulty was found in providing payment for the China trade.

Even after the resumption of shipments of silver bullion, the demand for tea increased more rapidly than the flow of dollars. This demand had led, in 1770, to the permanent establishment at Canton of the buyers, who previously had journeyed backwards and forwards (as supercargoes) on the tea ships, and

---

[1]For a study of Forrest, see D. K. Bassett: *Thomas Forrest, An Eighteenth Century Mariner. JMBRAS*. Vol. XXXIV. Pt. 2 (1961) pp. 106-121. Also C. Gibson-Hill: *Raffles, Acheh, and the Order of the Golden Sword. JMBRAS*. Vol. XXIX Pt. 1 (May, 1956) pp. 1-4.

had endeavoured hastily to conclude all their business while their vessel was in port. This new arrangement was adopted also by the private traders from the country ships, who clung on in the face of the disapproval of the East India Company. Although they undermined slowly the monopoly of the Company, their presence, as with the representatives of the Company, greatly aided the Canton trade.

This same demand induced Pitt to introduce his Commutation Act in 1784, whereby the widely evaded conglomeration of duties, imposts and surtaxes on tea, which had risen to over 100 per cent, was reduced to a simple duty of 12 per cent on the gross amount realized from the Company's sales. This led to a rapid increase in tea exports from Canton. They rose from 698,579 *piculs* in the years 1776-1780, to 1,148,645 piculs in the years 1786-1790.[2]

The constant cry of the Canton supercargoes for more and more goods or bullion with which to pay for their purchases of tea acted as a tremendous stimulant to the country trade, of which the British, by the fortunes of war, secured the paramount share. Previous to 1780, the Dutch port of Negapatam on the Bay of Bengal had been a most active center of this trade, and the English Company had been unable to utilize a considerable portion of the profits of the private traders. In that year, however, Holland having joined France in war with Britain, Negapatam fell into British hands and became linked with Madras in the trade triangle of India—China—London. Country shipping, spurred by Canton, increased tremendously. English country tonnage alone, which had stood at 4,000 in 1780, reached 25,000 by 1790, having been stimulated by the European peace (the treaty of Versailles was in 1784) and by Pitt's Commutation Act of the same year.[3] With the Company relying very largely on the country trade for the funds with which to support its tea purchases in China, "the country trade had become the keystone of the whole structure."[4]

This keystone, however, was held up in a most unstable manner. It was supported not by any solid land-based Company factory, but by the shifting decks of individual private traders. It was not very difficult for the Company to realize that a stable bazaar was needed, that the China trade might benefit immeasurably from the establishment of a post in Southeast Asia, but the difficulty lay in deciding where. Hastings, who had come back to India as Governor General in 1774, was like a blind dog in a meat shop; he could smell it but he could not find it, as, well aware of the paramount importance of assisting the China trade, whose profits sustained him, his missions one after the other blundered unavailingly into the waters of Southeast Asia.

[2]H. B. Morse: *The Chronicles of the East India Company trading to China, 1635-1834.* (Oxford, 1926) Vol. 2 pp. 114-117.

[3]For details of this, see H. Furber: *John Company at Work.* (London, 1851). pp. 174-175.

[4]M. Greenberg. *British Trade and the Opening of China, 1800-1842* (London, 1951). p. 16; See also *Furber* pp. 3-31, 160-190.

Previously, when governor of Bengal, Hastings had attempted to find an answer to the problem of the Canton trade by developing the flow of gold from Tibet. There was a favourable balance of trade with this country, which exchanged its gold for the British woollen goods so unappreciated in South China. When Hastings (and the Company in London) realized that not only did the trade with Tibet provide a source of specie in India which might be offset against the drain of the tea trade, but also that across the Himalayas there might be found a route for the introduction of British woollen textiles into the Chinese Empire, attempts were made to make more normal and more extensive this flimsy barter trade carried on in the wild Nepalese passes. "We desire you will obtain the best intelligence you can," wrote London to Bengal, "whether trade can be opened with Napaul, and whether cloth and other European commodities may not find their way from thence to Tibet and the Western parts of China."[5] In 1774 Hastings dispatched into Tibet a small mission, led by George Bogle, who discovered that the Panchen Lama, the most important man in Tibet, exerted a great influence at the Court of Peking. He was favorably inclined to the British, and Bogle urged that his good offices be made use of, particularly as "the Company's business (at Canton) is often harassed and oppressed, and its conductors are entirely without any channel of communication or representation to the Court of Peking."[6]

Hastings snatched at the straw, and accepted Bogle's ideas of using Tibet as the back door to China. But it came to naught. In 1780 the Panchen Lama died in Peking before he had secured any concessions for his friend Bogle, who himself died in the following year. In 1784 another British mission returned from Tibet, and Indo-Tibetan trade increased, but the idea of improving Anglo-Chinese relations by encouraging this trade died with the departure of Hastings in 1785. The invasion of Tibet by the Ghurkas in 1788 and 1791 killed the trade as well as the idea, and no succor for the Company at Canton was possible.[7]

Another failure was Hastings' attempt to open a factory in 1778 in Cochin China. The *Rumbold,* a country ship returning from Canton, had put into the Bay of Tourane on the Annam coast. Here French influence, in the shape of Jesuit missionaries, was becoming established. Although country traders frequented the bay, with its safe harbor and its trade with China, it had never been considered by the East India Company as a site for a settlement since the seventeenth century. The *Rumbold,* however, gave passage to a Jesuit and two Annamite government officials, mandarins, south to Cambodia. The fierceness of the northerly monsoon swept them past, there was no beating back and

[5]Home Misc. Series. Vol. 219. Court of Directors to Bengal, 16 February, 1768.

[6]C. R. Markham: *Narratives of the Mission of George Bogle to Tibet, and of the Journey of Thomas Manning to Lhasa.* (London, 1876). pp. 207-210.

[7]For some description of this, see A. Lamb. *Tibet in Anglo-Chinese Relations, 1767-1842. Journal,* Royal Asiatic Society. 1957. Parts 3 & 4. pp. 161-176.

there was no intermediate port where the *Rumbold* cared to stop; with a rush they were carried to Calcutta.

Here Hastings met them, hospitality was lavished upon them, and it was decided that as the country traders did well out of Tourane so should the Company. A Bengal official was deputed by Hastings to return with the mandarins and to secure from the ruler permission for a factory. Hastings felt that British cloth and other goods would sell well there, and that, as seventy or eighty Chinese junks visited each year, trade with China would develop. "The Company have always had in view the encouraging of a trade with the China junks. This was Mr. Dalrymple's object when he proposed the settlement at Balambangan."[8]

Balambangan was an ominous example and Cochin China was no more successful. Charles Chapman, a Company official in Fort William, without knowledge or experience of the region (another Monckton or Desvoeux as it were), was given a vessel and a cargo of goods and with the two mandarins safely on board he sailed in April, 1778. On arrival at Annam he found a civil war in progress, the land devastated, the mandarin unwelcome (one had died on the voyage), and his presence useless. There was no security there, nor was there to be any until Nguyen Ann finally established his empire in 1802; and as there was neither tin nor pepper, and as he could not secure permission to establish a factory, as soon as possible he returned to Calcutta. The expedition had been a complete failure.

There remained the islands. These had been the preserve, very largely, of the ships sailing from Madras, but now with Hastings Calcutta played the more important role. Four separate ventures were sponsored by Hastings from Calcutta into these waters between 1782 and 1786, and although the mission to the Celebes in 1782 was scarcely connected to the China trade, and is best considered as an aggressive move against Britain's attacking enemies, the others, to Rhio, to Acheh and to Penang, when the Company was at last successful, all reflect the determination of the Company, war or no war, to advance their investment at Canton.

The Celebes mission had originated in 1780 as a decision by Crown and Company to attack Manila and Macassar, as part of a worldwide campaign conceived in London to weaken Spain by attacking the Spanish colonies. The original intent of the Crown had been to capture Manila; this the Company supported (and regretted that it had been forced to relinquish possession of it after the Seven Years War in 1763), but maintained that for Manila to be reached, a line of communication from Calcutta had to be made secure. The occupation of Macassar and the control of the eastern or outer passage between Borneo and the Celebes up to the Philippines was necessary. This strategy was accepted. Four thousand troops were assigned to it, and both

---

[8]*Bengal General Consultations.* Hastings' Memorandum, 30 March, 1778; in *HARLOW*, p. 98. For this mission see A. Lamb: *British Missions to Cochin China, 1778-1822. (JMBRAS.* Vol. XXXIV, Pt. 3 & 4. 1961).

principals were delighted with the project; but by 1781 India itself was threatened, and the realities of the situation forced Hastings to cancel the attack, despite the revelation of Dutch Indies weakness shown the previous year, when six Company captains seized without incident the crumbling posts on west Sumatra.

In place of the attack Hastings sent Thomas Forrest in the *Fly* in April, 1782. The hope was to induce the Bugis to drive out the Dutch from Menado in the far north (Fort Amsterdam), from Macassar, the seat of government (Fort Rotterdam), and from the small outposts at Bonthaim and Bulo Combo, in the extreme southwest. With the Dutch gone a British trading factory might then be established. But the Bugis were divided into six great and hostile fraternities, democratic and aggressive; they fought one another as often as they fought the Dutch. Thomas Forrest was too sensible to venture into this beehive, particularly as in addition the French were active in the waters behind him. He gathered information from Bugis traders at Kedah, at Rhio, and at islands close to the Celebes, but his expedition was no more successful than that despatched to Cochin China. No British settlement on the Celebes ensued.

The 1784 mission to Acheh is perhaps another diversion from the theme of trade with China, forced on Hastings by the French successes in the Bay of Bengal during the Anglo-French 1780-1783 war. De Suffren, the French admiral in the East, fought four brilliant actions in 1782 in which victory was only denied him by the blunderings of his ill-trained subordinates and the broken-down units of the fleet that was his instrument of attack. With October, and the onset of the northeast monsoon that made the west coast of the Bay a lee shore, de Suffren took his fleet to safety. He sailed however not back to the French base at Mauritius, far to the southwest (nor to the recently captured but ill supplied Trincomali), but windward to Acheh in the southeast. Hughes, his British opponent, begged by terrified Madras to remain,[9] stayed off the lee shore. He was struck in October by a full gale, and nearly lost a ship as he clawed his way out to sea, while some 150 merchant sail were driven ashore. Before Hughes could beat back to Madras from Bombay (he did not reach the bay again until the middle of April), de Suffren had swept all before him, British commerce had been driven from the Bay, and Calcutta was virtually besieged. An inconclusive battle and then peace saved the Company, but it had been a very disquieting experience.[10]

British control of India rested in the last instance on British control of the seas. Possession of the Bay of Bengal permitted the British slow progress up the Ganges Valley, and British expansion out from Madras. No Indian power, however formidable on land, could long check this progress, for no Indian navy of any substance existed. There remained, however, the French, as de Suffren had shown. He had demonstrated, too, a deficiency in British defence.

[9]President of the Madras Council was Lord Macartney, later leader of the first British embassy to China.
[10]For this campaign see H. Richmond: *The Navy in India, 1763-1783*. (London, 1931).

There was no British base from which the Bay could be guarded during the monsoon, a base to the eastward.

A search was instituted for such a base. It was not a very active search, for peace had been concluded, a long and expensive war was over, and economies were being effected everywhere, not the least in the Navy; thus it has been with Britain after every war. Trincomali provided perfect shelter with its land locked harbor less than 300 miles from Madras, The urgency of the naval search for a base may be gauged from the fact that Trincomali was returned to the Dutch without demur. Acheh? An agent went there in 1784, stayed, unavailingly and hopelessly, for fifteen months, and then returned.[11] After the establishment of Penang the Andaman Islands were surveyed in 1789 by Lieutenant Blair. Here a penal settlement by a commodious bay provided shelter for His Majesty's ships during the northeast monsoon, but it was a wet, wild, dreary place, and it was abandoned in 1796, with the removal of its 700 prisoners to Penang. Nothing, not even Penang, was found acceptable, and the fleet reverted to its well-established base at Bombay.

It is well to remember that to be efficient a naval base requires far more than a favorable geographical or strategic location. It needs to be able to support and supply the navy. A harbor must be more than just a harbor to become a base. There must be stores and equipment for the fleet, food and refreshment for the men, a trained labor force and at least one dock. Nothing east of India possessed these qualities, and the British were not inclined to pay for it all to begin.

The fleet guarding India continued to winter at Bombay, there to refit before returning to the Bay of Bengal. It left the Bay isolated during those months, but once the gales of October and November were past the fleet could beat back, if necessary. And Bombay was far more than a commodious harbor, as the following 1775 description shows.

> Here is a dockyard, large and well contrived with all kinds of naval stores deposited in proper warehouses, together with great quantities of timber and planks for repairing and building ships, and forges for making of anchors as well as every kind of smaller smiths work. It boasts such a dry dock as perhaps is not to be seen in any part of Europe, either for size or convenient situation. It has three divisions and three pairs of strong gates, as to be capable of receiving and repairing three ships of the line at the same or separate times . . .
>
> Near the dock is a convenient place to grave several ships at once, which is done as well and with as great expedition as in any dock in England. Near the dock is a rope walk, which for length, situation and convenience equals any in England, except that of the Kings Yard, at Portsmouth. Like that, it has a covering to shelter the workmen. Here

---

[11]It has not been possible to discover the details of this mission in Company records; it may well be that the agent was another Desvoeux, seeking commercial cessions. Hall: *History of South East Asia,* p. 429, lists him as animated by naval aspirations, whereas a contemporary work, Sir Geo. Leith's *A Short Account of Prince of Wales Island,* (London, 1804), says (pp. 1-2) that the Company "judging it necessary to establish a commercial Port in the Straits of Malacca, considered Acheen as a proper place for this purpose. Accordingly, towards the end of 1784, they sent Mr. Kinlock..."

are made cables and all sorts of lesser cordage, both for the Royal Navy, the Company's Marine, and the merchant ships which trade to these ports of India.[12]

The East India Company, when finally it established a post on Penang, did so in the hope that the Navy would come too. It sang the charms of the island so convincingly that only the most hard-hearted of lovers could have withstood them. It sang in vain. Although the Navy found the post a useful place for the collection and storing of wood and water, and established ashore an officer to tend to such naval matters, such was the limit of its expenditure.

The Navy made good use of Penang as an advanced rendezvous for the invasion of Java, in 1811, but it never became a naval base, and after 1805, after Trafalgar, there was no further need. The Navy built no dockyard, established no base east of India until finally Hong Kong was acquired, in 1842.[13]

The claim, advanced by several eminent historians,[14] that Penang was founded for reasons of maritime strategy, and that the intensive late eighteenth-century scouring of Southeast Asia was a search for a naval base and not for a site for a factory, is an incorrect interpretation of the intentions of the Company and ignores the facts of the case. Nearly all of the Company expeditions were commercial in intent and designed to assist the trade with China. They were undertaken not by the Navy, nor sponsored by Bombay, the naval center, but by Madras and Calcutta.

After his abortive mission to the Celebes in 1782, Thomas Forrest late the following year paused at Perak. Here it appears he met the Bugis Sultan of Selangor who with his uncle, Raja Hadji, the great Bugis leader of Rhio, was about to attack Dutch Malacca. With the latter Forrest opened a correspondence and on his return to Calcutta in early 1784, Forrest reported that the Company had been offered any part of Rhio that it might care to take for a factory. Here was an exceptional opportunity. The island area had developed considerably since Monckton had blundered in 1772. Raja Hadji had extended his political control to both sides of the Straits of Malacca, and a tolerable peace was maintained. Economically the previous decade had seen a large increase in country trade in the area, as the Dutch power weakened and the Bugis avoided the restrictive tyrannies of both Dutch and Malay. The *paduakans* and *palaris* from the Celebes, the *prahus* from Sumatra and Brunei, the junks from China, all sailed down the routes that led to Rhio, there to meet

---

[12]Low. Vol. 1. pp. 175-176.

[13]Although Penang possessed admirable strategic qualities for guarding or menacing the Bay of Bengal, the only power that ever made use of those inherent qualities was not Britain but Germany. In the summer of 1943, if we may conclude our naval-base digression, a submarine base was established there, German U boats were fed through to it, dockyard and repair facilities were established, and for ten consecutive months, from June 1943 until March 1944, and again in July and August 1944, the German U boats sank a larger tonnage in the Indian Ocean (half a million tons, and 78 ships), than they sank in the Atlantic, or any other area in the world. From Penang more destruction was forced on allied shipping in this period than from all the Channel ports combined. The U boats from the north of Norway to the south of France could not equal the destruction from Penang. See S. E. Morison: *History of the United States Naval Operations in World War II.* (Oxford, 1956) Vol. X, p. 274.

[14]Hall. p. 421; Parkinson, *War in the Eastern Seas,* (London, 1953), p. 12.

the Europeans, and to trade on their decks. Now the Company was offered dry land, a solid base. With the French war over, the offer was accepted.[15]

Forrest was instructed to return and to establish an Agency, to secure a spot of ground as close to the Sultan's residence as possible, and to hoist over it the British flag. "The object of your deputation is to open a free intercourse of trade, not only with the inhabitants of Rhio, but of all the neighbouring islands," Hastings told him.[16]

It might be thought that an expedition sent to Rhio was transgressing one of the basic points of policy that until now the Company always had observed; of avoiding the center of the archipelago, where the Dutch were in strength, and of restricting Company attempts at a settlement to areas remote from the Dutch, so limiting the opportunity of friction to the minimum. But by 1784 it seemed clear that in fact the Dutch were not in strength anywhere, that its East India Company was a sinking ship, kept afloat by the pumps, and that in the western sector of the archipelago at least, where Malacca alone stood, decaying, spiceless, and ignored by Batavia, the British could cruise with impunity. So when Forrest wrote of Rhio,

> I sold in one day $10,000 worth of goods and received my money the next . . . This port is frequented by praus from Borneo, Bally, [Bali], Java and all the eastern islands, likewise from Siam, Cambodja, Quinam [Annam?] and Cochin China; it is situated so well and so convenient for trade that I look upon it to be the key of the Straits and am of opinion that if there was an English flag hoisted there it would soon become a place of very extensive trade and might in a few years hurt Batavia, and it would certainly bring the China trade to it,[17]

Hastings did not hesitate. Armed with a cargo of piece goods, opium, and a present for the Sultan, in June 1784 he set sail in the *Esther*. But he was too late; the Dutch had forestalled him.

The war of 1780-1783 had brought home to Holland the glaring inadequacies of its power in the East. It had lost all its posts in India and Ceylon; it had witnessed the rolling up of its Sumatran settlements; and it had been saved from further, more vital injury only by the superb skill of de Suffren. With the peace, by a desperate tightening of the national sinews, Holland despatched to the East Indies a powerful squadron, commanded by van Braam. This arrived at Batavia to learn that the Bugis of the Rhio Archipelago were assisting their countrymen from Selangor in a ferocious attack on Malacca. Raja Hadji, the greatest of the Bugis, was there in person, fighting with his nephew, the Bugis Sultan of Selangor. Van Braam's squadron liberated Malacca, killing Raja Hadji on June 18, 1784—just as Forrest sailed from Calcutta—then went on to smash the independent archipelago south of Malacca and to send its Sultan scampering through the islands to Soekadana, in Borneo, where he

[15]*Straits Settlements (Factory) Records.* Vol. 1. Bengal to London, 23 August, 1784. See also D. K. Bassett: *Thomas Forrest*, pp. 114-117.

[16]*Straits Settlements (Factory) Records.* Vol. 1. Governor General to T. Forrest, 31 May, 1784.

[17]*S. S. (F). R. Vol. 1.* Bengal Public Consultations, 31 May, 1784.

wrote to Bengal asking for aid. Forrest, faced with this new upsurge of Dutch strength, and hearing of Raja Hadji's death while on his way down the Straits, wisely kept away, and Singapore was delayed for twenty-five years.

In the same dispatch of 23 January, 1786, in which Bengal advised London that Forrest had been sent too late, it recommended the Court to accept the offer made previously to Hastings by Captain Francis Light of the uninhabited island of Penang. And so the long search ended.

Francis Light at this time was trading from Junk Ceylon, (P'huket) an island rich in tin which lay a shallow mile off the Kra Peninsula. Since possibly the eleventh century the island had been ruled either by Ligor, the small state on the peninsula, or later by Siam, or by Ligor for Siam. From the late seventeenth century the island had been under the direct rule of Ayudhia. As the latter became more and more absorbed in its struggle with Ava, however, its control over Junk Ceylon steadily weakened. The climax to the struggle came with the war of 1764-1767, when the victorious Burmese sacked Ayudhia after a tremendous siege. It was never rebuilt. Siamese authority in the extremities of its empire vanished; both Kedah and Junk Ceylon, as well as Cambodia to the east, became *de facto* independent. The Siamese officials on Junk Ceylon feared for their lives from the rampaging warriors of Ava, and the acting governor, a good friend of Light's, in 1782 offered him the island.

Light was one of a number of Europeans who had taken up residence there, finding in its wealth of tin, in its remoteness from the Dutch and French, and in its favorable trade location, qualities rare and rewarding. It was peaceful and adequately governed, and its tolerant Buddhist people respected person and property. It had less trade, but in other ways it was more attractive than Rhio. It was divided into two traditional administrative areas, Pa'ket and C'halang, with some fifteen villages scattered over its twenty-odd miles of hilly territory. The main town was C'halang, but Tha Rua, situated a mile or so up a valley that ran down to the best anchorage of the island, was where the Europeans lived. It consisted of about eighty houses, on a plain, through which ran a pleasant brook over a gravelly bottom to the sea.

There was a large Portuguese settlement here, as well as a fine market street, composed of large brick buildings, among which rose the spacious houses belonging to the Europeans that used to reside here while their ships lay at anchor in the harbor.[18]

Junk Ceylon provided a very useful base for these traders. There was not merely the tin of the island itself convenient to hand, but on the mainland of the Kra Peninsula opposite (reached in those days by elephant at low tide) there was a track of great antiquity, which may have begun at the Takola of Ptolemy,[19] and which led across to the Gulf of Siam, where Indian piece goods

[18]Historical Notice on the Thalang, Takua-pa, Takua-thung, P'hangnga and P'huket Districts, by Nai Rok, Nai Suk and Nai Sua, Translated by G. E. Gerini: *Historical Retrospect of Junk Ceylon Island,* in *Journal, Siam Society,* (Vol. 2, 1905), p. 43.

[19]P. Wheatley, *Takola Emporium.* "The Journal of Tropical Geography," (Vol. 2. March, 1954) pp. 2-13.

had a ready sale; and there was the trade of Kedah and the other western states on the peninsula as well. Light had a good friend here, James Scott, another ex-navy country trader, who followed him to Penang. Both acquired mistresses here from the Portuguese — Eurasian community, with whom they thereafter lived. Both also were anxious that British rule should replace the rather uncertain and indefinite position into which the island had fallen.

Light transmitted the offer of the acting governor to India, sending it directly to Hastings and not to Sulivan in Madras this time, for it would appear as if he was acting as his own principal on Junk Ceylon. Previously in 1780 he had waited on the Governor-General in person to press home the advantages both of this island, and of Penang, but particularly of the former. Hastings was dubious. Without doubt Siamese officials were there, isolated from their devastated homeland no doubt, but still exercising authority, and with over a hundred retainers. European ship owners such as Forrest and Light might be welcome, as a source of income to these administrators, and traders such as Scott could live there for half a dozen years; but would the government of the East India Company be acceptable?

Between 1772 and 1786 little is known of Light. He figured briefly in the various travellers' tales, either he or his ship being mentioned when the chronicler nears Junk Ceylon,[20] but little official correspondence relating to him has been discovered. Presumably he traded, influenced by the unseen demand for tea in England that had the Company clamouring for tin in the East. Although the profits were good, and life no doubt was pleasant, the risks were considerable too.

In 1781 Britain was at war with France. The famous chronicler William Hickey, recently married, was captured on his way back to India, limping into Trincomali harbour in a damaged ship in November 1782, and unaware that the French occupied the port. Here early in January 1783 he met the French admiral, de Suffren, returning from his clashes with Admiral Hughes. "In appearance," wrote Hickey, the inveterate diarist, "he looked much more like a little fat vulgar English butcher than a Frenchman of consequence," and he proceeds to describe him minutely. He mentions in passing, but gives us no description of Francis Light, who also was present. "The same evening arrived a large grab called the *Blake,* commanded by Captain Light . . . The *Blake* had been taken by an enemy cruiser off the coast of Coromandel."[21]

We are unaware of how or when Light secured his freedom. The *Blake* was recaptured in March, but it cannot be imagined that Light was still aboard her. No doubt he was exchanged, or merely released, as neither French nor English navies retained their captives. Ships, not sailors, were their objectives, and prisoners could be expensive and inconvenient. Light had lost his ship,

---

[20]For some of this same period, (1774-1776), Horatio Nelson also was in these same waters. See C. Oman: *Nelson,* (London, 1947), pp. 19-20.

[21]*Memoirs of William Hickey.* (London, 1950), Vol. 3. pp. 108-109, 117.

however, and in 1785 a still greater misfortune befell him.

In that year Junk Ceylon was heavily attacked by a war fleet sent south by Ava. Siam was recovering from the calamitous effects of its 1764-67 war. Ayuthia was in ruins, but under Rama I (1782-1809) the founder of the present dynasty, the country had begun the long climb back. Bangkok had been founded lower down the Chao Phraya River, and Rama I had begun to consolidate and reorganize his territory. There was no valid reason for this faint heartbeat to be stopped; Ava was not menaced, and experience had shown that it could not control the vast plain of Siam. Yet Ava struck again, and this time not merely through the passes but also southward by sea as well, sending a fleet to attack the peninsula possessions, Ligor, Patani, Junk Ceylon and Kedah, claimed by Siam.

Junk Ceylon was invaded in December, 1785. Takua-pa, on the mainland nearby, had fallen already. Tha Rua was attacked and burned to the ground. Light luckily was in Calcutta, urging the annexation of either Junk Ceylon or Penang, so he was spared, but many were killed or rendered homeless and the European and Eurasian community was dispersed.

This settled the issue as far as the East India Company was concerned, and killed any further consideration of Junk Ceylon, despite its other attractions. The Company wanted no outpost in a cockpit of war. Light never returned.

Both Light and James Scott had been urging Penang as a second choice for some time. Scott had written in 1780 to Mr. George Ramsay, a most prominent and influential business man at Calcutta, describing "a harbour, safe, large and commodious, of easy access, and anchorages at 17 to 5 fathoms, where they have wood, bullocks large and fat, rice cheap and plenty,"[22] and a year later he added . . . "this is the thoroughfare of our European and Madras, Bengal, Bombay and China ships, besides a considerable number of Straits traders."[23] His arguments, and those of Light, failed to convince Bengal that the island was as useful as Rhio. It was uninhabited, it possessed no trade of its own, and the only uninhabited island that had been chosen as a factory was Balambangan, scarcely an example worth following.

By 1786, however, Rhio had been attacked by the Dutch and Junk Ceylon by the Burmese. There seemed little choice; it was Penang or nothing. As Light wrote,

The Dutch now possess both sides of the Straits of Malacca; nothing is left but the small kingdoms of Queda and Acheen. As I understand from you that it is the wish of the Government to secure some useful and convenient port for the protection of the merchants who trade with China . . . I made use of the influence and friendship I had with the King of Queda and his Minister to obtain a grant of the island Penang . . . By taking possession of the island you acquire a port at which all vessels bound to China may procure refreshments and those articles of trade which best suits the China mar-

---

[22]S. S. (F) R. Vol. 1. Capt. J. Scott to Mr. G. Ramsay, 1 Sept., 1780.
[23]S. S. (F) R. Vol. 1. Capt. J. Scott to Mr. Ramsay, 29 April, 1781.

kets, and the Malays and Bugees will have a place of safety to come and purchase opium and piece goods and Europe manufactures.[24]

Light must have been in Calcutta when he wrote this letter, for three days later it was forwarded by the Acting Governor-General, (Hastings having left India), to the all powerful Secret Committee in London, the cabinet of the Company.[25] Francis Light was referred to as "a man of excellent character and good information. He has traded to the Eastward for many years, and stands in the highest esteem with the Malay, Siamese and Pegu Chiefs."[26] It is doubtful if he stood in quite the same esteem with the Bugis, for he had recently sold them 5,000 muskets, and as they had been discarded as condemned by the Bengal military, they may have played some part in the Bugis defeat before Malacca. Scott too had been dabbling in arms, and, less successful than his colleague, was languishing in Malacca on suspicion of selling ammunition to Selangor. No matter; Light's suggestion was most opportune, and the suggestion gathered way.

In London Henry Dundas was beginning his long role as chief executive at the India House. He was well aware of the need for a base, but there were various aspects of the situation that he had to consider. With the political control of Scotland, he was the right arm of Pitt. Together the two had seen passed in 1784 the great India Act, and through the Secret Committee he endeavored to enforce one of its clauses that later was to affect particularly the Malay States; that which insisted that the Company should not become involved with its neighbours, that it should keep free of entangling alliances, that it should not enter into any political treaty that might embroil the Company in war and the annexation of more costly territory. Yet at the same time he and the other members of the Court were fully aware of the critical position of the China trade, and the need to assist it by establishing a base in Southeast Asia. In this respect an offshore island was preferable, for the possibilities of becoming a participant in mainland disputes and the necessity of having to intervene, were far less. And there remained still the Dutch, in 1786 again useful as a buffer in Europe, who must not be antagonized too far.

Leaving the details to Calcutta, "the general policy," wrote the Court to Bengal, was "that without embroiling ourselves with the Dutch, or giving them any well-founded jealousy of our intending to wrest from them or rival them in the spice trade, every practical method should be tried for extending our commerce amongst the eastern isles, and indirectly by this means to China . . . The great importance of the China trade, the necessity of extending by commercial means the Resources for our investment from that country . . . make us look with sanguine expectations to the benefit of an establishment somewhere near

[24]S. S. (F) R. Vol. 1. Capt. Light to Bengal, 23 January, 1786.

[25]For the significance of this committee see Ċ. H. Philips: "The Secret Committee of the East India Company." *Journal, School of Oriental and African Studies*. Vol. X. Parts 2-3, (London, 1940). pp. 299-315, 699-716.

[26]S. S. (F) R. Vol. 1. Bengal to Secret Committee, 26 January, 1786.

the Pitts [Malacca?] Straits."[27]

Calcutta was left with no choice. The Dutch, momentarily resurgent, restricted any selection to the northern end of the Straits of Malacca. The Burmese invasion eliminated Junk Ceylon. Acheh was a possibility but as Light said, "to form a settlement there of safety and advantage a Force sufficient to subdue all the chiefs would be necessary,"[28] and that the Company was not prepared to supply. Kedah alone remained. Was its occupation worthwhile? The previous experiment had been most unsatisfactory, and Scott told them why. The Company had taken entirely the wrong approach in its ignorance of the customs and manners of the eastern peoples. The choice of Monckton had been a mistake. Scott said that the Sultan, on meeting him, exclaimed, "has the Company nobody to send me, but a stuttering boy?" And that then the antipathy deepened as Monckton called insolent a people who had the temerity to resent his ignorance and his insults.

Nevertheless if the objective was trade with China, the Company should try again. "In 1779 we exported from the Straits of Malacca 40,000 pikuls of tin and 10,000 pikuls of pepper, four-fifths of which went to China, along with gold dust, and birds nests, and it realized about twenty lacs of rupees. The Eastern trade is the only one which draws specie from China, and there are great benefits to be obtained by expanding this trade."

Without doubt the settlement would be a commercial success, said Scott, provided that the leader of the expedition was well chosen. "Choose a Chief cool, patient, active and penetrating, more a citizen of the world than an Englishman, with more of public spirit the better, one who has studied mankind on liberal principles . . ."[29] Without actually spelling out his name, here was his friend Francis Light. He spoke Siamese and Malay, he lived, when ashore, very largely as a Malay, in their comfortable clothes and eating their food, and he traded with acumen up and down the coast where he was respected and welcomed. This same respect by now he had won in Calcutta. While the old bitter comment of Madras gathered dust in its files, at Fort William it was decided that Scott was right and that here was the man it needed. On 2 March, 1786, Bengal decided "to accept the King of Queda's offer to the Company of the Harbour and Island of Pinang," and that "in consideration of the Board's favourable opinion of Captain Francis Light, his knowledge of the Malay language and the high esteem he stands with the King of Queda and other Malay chiefs, that he be vested with the charge and superintendence of the island of Pinang on the part of the Company until their pleasure be known or until further orders."[30] The usual small expedition was gathered together, the Company having had plenty of practice at this by now, the *Eliza* was

[27]S. S. (F) R. Vol. 1. Court to Bengal, undated.
[28]S. S. (F). R. Vol. 2. Light to Bengal, 15 February, 1786.
[29]S. S. (F). R. Vol. 1. Capt. James Scott to Bengal, 28 October, 1785.
[30]S. S. (F). R. Vol. 2. Bengal Public Consultations, 2 March, 1786.

provisioned, and a 400 tonner loaded with a few troops and some stores. In June, 1786, the two ships, together with Light's own craft, dropped unobtrusively down the Hooghly, bound for the coast of Kedah and the Island of Penang.

Penang lies some five miles off the mainland, shaped somewhat like a pear hanging from the north. Thickly wooded with hills rising quickly from the seaward side to peaks 2,400 feet high, indented by small bays where granite boulders shelter each end, and where graceful betelnut *(Pinang)* trees hang over sandy beaches, Penang is one of the loveliest islands in the Orient. It had been a useless possession of the Sultanate of Kedah for centuries. Lancaster had visited it in 1603, on his way to found a British base at Bantam.[31] He had buried some dead there, and though hundreds of years later, when Light landed, a few Malays emerged from the jungle to show that the island was not completely uninhabited, it does seem as if through the centuries Penang, effectively scoured at intervals by pirates in search of slaves, had remained very largely as Lancaster left it, the preserve merely of the dead.

New life now came to this dead island, brought from India by the British on their way to China. Although our gaze is focused now onto the island itself, and our narrative is concerned with its early administration, we should not forget the impulse that sent this expedition. Francis Light and his three small ships had a relevance not merely to the history of the Malay Peninsula. The settlement on Penang, as with the establishment of Singapore twenty-odd years later, must be seen also as part of the British Far Eastern story. Beyond Penang loomed China.

---

[31]W. Foster (ed): *The Voyages of Sir James Lancaster.* (for the Hakluyt Society. London, 1940). pp. 10-11. Penang was used also by the Portuguese as a rendezvous for their ships from Goa and Malacca. See Barretto de Resende's *Account of Malacca,* translated by G. Maxwell. *JSBRAS.* No. 60 (Dec. 1911). p. 6.

IV

THE EARLY ADMINISTRATION

Calcutta in 1786 was a magnificent place. Thirty years before, in 1756, it had been a miserable, obscure village, half-hidden in the jungle. A solitary British post in Bengal, it had clung to the flanks of a pitiful fort that quite failed to prevent a storming and an infamous Black Hole. A decade later however, with the victories of Clive to buttress it and British control over the lower Ganges immeasurably strengthened, Calcutta had become the heart of the Company's operations in India. In 1765 was begun a new fort, one of the finest outside Europe, far superior to anything in England and rivalling in strength and complexity the great bastions of Vauban. By its side, as the wealth of Bengal flowed in, there grew a great city.

Today Fort William still stands, enveloped by the teeming millions of what has become one of the largest urban conglomerations of people in this world. In the late eighteenth century the fort was a little way downstream from the "Black town," hovering over Esplanade Row, where large and stately homes, a few with the new fangled *punkah* cooling the upstairs rooms, stood by the water's edge. Further downstream, round a bend in the river, was Garden Reach, a broad stretch of the Hooghly, where even larger homes, even more stately, stood in their own luxuriant gardens. Here *nabobs* leisurely surveyed the lively river, through intermittent puffs at the *hookah,* and then journeyed to the new church, opened in 1786, in their barges and palanquins.

Although the ponderous three-tiered men-of-war came no further than Kedagree or Diamond Harbour, over forty miles downstream from Calcutta, smaller vessels, including most country traders, could maneuver up to Calcutta, to brush through the shouting mass of Indian water-borne traffic and to anchor near the fort. Here came the opium from up river, for sale in China, and here lay the protection, rarely invoked, of the still-maintained cannon of the Company. The three small vessels placed under the command of Francis Light were amongst the cluster of shipping anchored here, in May 1786, and it was amid this crowded scene, in a city of perhaps half a million people, busy superintending the bustling last minute preparations, that Light received, by flamboyantly dressed peon, the instructions of the Supreme Government.

Light had been looking forward to these instructions and advices with some eagerness. He was a country trader, competent at his task, well-versed in and sympathetic to the ways of Malaysia; but he had no experience of administration whatever, and as he was due to sail shortly and to govern a new outpost of the East India Company, he had hoped for some guidance, and had asked for some basic principles to adhere to. These were not forthcoming.

After noting "that the provisions, stores and detachment are all embarked, and that the *Eliza* and *Prince Henry* are ready to proceed to sea" (the *Speedwell,* Light's own ship, was ready also, but it went as an unofficial guest), the dispatch from Fort William began with a resumé of the offer by the Sultan of Kedah of Penang, and that "having taken into consideration the present situation of the Trade to the Eastward . . . we have resolved to accept this grant."[1]

It then proceeded, at great length, to give Light, appointed Superintendent of the Island, in entire command of all forces, his instructions. No doubt they were customary, and probably the clerk was following routine, but they were of little use and most were quite unnecessary. He was directed to weigh anchor, to sail to Kedah, there to deliver the Company's letter and presents, and then to occupy Penang. Once ashore, he was to survey the harbor, noting tidal strength and variations and prevalent winds and currents. He was to erect huts (but only those considered absolutely necessary), and to cultivate the soil. In clearing land, he was told to beware of common error, that of cutting down all the trees without regard to the convenience or pleasure of the inhabitants. He was to rear cattle, sheep, hogs and all kinds of poultry. He was to encourage trade by a mild but firm rule, and was warned to be always upon his guard; to avoid disputes, but to defend himself if attacked.

With all this most unnecessary advice over, Fort William then weakly requested that Light should "furnish us with a plan for the internal government and police of the island."[2] The Company, political masters of Bengal, with a host of officials and a mass of experience, was asking Light, the company trader, how best to govern! No clearer indication is needed that the Company regarded Penang in essence as an anchored country trader, not as a naval base or as a political objective but as a bazaar. Given this outlook, then the request is logical, just as Light, the trader, was the man to administer it.

While giving him the responsibility for this on one page, the next made extremely difficult his prospects of success. "As you cannot be empowered to punish Felonies, and have not officers sufficient to form General Courts Martial, all persons committing such crimes as cannot be tried but by either the Civil or Military Courts here, must be returned to Bengal with the necessary evidences. You are invested with authority sufficient to punish any lesser crimes or misdemeanours."[3] He was invested with a meagre and crippling authority, and even this power, that of a minor magistrate, was confined to

[1]S. S. (F). R. Vol. 2. Bengal to Light, 2 May, 1786.
[2]S. S. (F). R. Vol. 2. Bengal to Light, 2 May, 1786.
[3]S. S. (F). R. Vol. 2. Bengal to Light, 2 May, 1786.

inhabitants of Penang who were not British subjects. All offences involving a British subject, however trivial, as well as all murder cases and other serious crimes committed by anyone, had to be referred back to Bengal. When Light dropped downstream, one administrative hand was tied behind his back.

Without flurry or fault he proceeded about his task. He came down from Bengal slowly; it was not until June 29 that he anchored off Kedah River, where the *Speedwell* and the *Prince Henry* were waiting for him. He pulled upstream to Alor Star, handed over the presents and the Company letter, which made reply to the Sultan's terms of cession. With this accepted, he returned to the river mouth. He sailed then south for Penang, assisted by a flooding tide late in the afternoon of July 14th. Next day he reached Penang. Cautiously, for it does not appear as if he had ever been so near the shore before, Light anchored off a small island on the north side, in five fathoms.[4] Hoisting out the ship's boat for a closer inspection, he sent it to sound by the northeast tip of Penang, where it found two fathoms almost on the beach. Next day at noon, with a fair breeze (in July probably coming from the west) he went under sail once more, and ran round the tip into the calm strait between the island and the mainland. Immediately he anchored again, within a short musket shot of the land, in thirteen clear fathoms. The *Prince Henry* dropped close by, and the *Speedwell,* watched by all eyes, was ordered to run on southward until she reached reef or shallows. Half a mile from the other two she sounded eight fathoms, shoaling, and quickly anchored. The ships' boats were swung out and lowered, and their crews continued in the quiet afternoon, the sun warm on their backs as they established deep water close to the beach on the point, with flat land behind. This seemed the place.[5]

On July 17, 1786, Francis Light landed on Penang. We need waste no time in remembering the name he gave it, "Prince of Wales Island," for although the name lived a vicarious existence inside official files for perhaps fifty years, it never took life outside. Pinang it was, Penang it became, and has remained. "Georgetown," has survived, however, the name Light gave the settlement started that day by the marine detachment who started clearing "Point Penagger, a low sandpoint covered with wood"[6] to make room for their tents. Eclipsed rapidly by Singapore, Georgetown yet remained the second city of Malaya, and always has been the loveliest.

The business began of establishing the post. By July 18 enough space had been cleared of the dense tropical foliage to permit the erection of tents. The marines and lascars — East Indian native sailors — thereafter slept ashore. They were joined by the Dato of Quala Muda, a Malay chief from the mouth of the Muda River, who came with a fishing net and with hopes of settling. Next to his *prahu* on the beach that afternoon there slid another, from the Kedah River,

[4]In all probability this was Pulau Tikus.
[5]S. S. (F). R. Vol. 2. Diary of F. Light, June 29-July 16.
[6]Diary, July 17.

which probably had followed the fleet down. This brought the first of the thousands of Chinese who were to find greater prospects and more security under the Union Jack than up a Malay river. With this nameless pioneer came some Christians, Eurasians most likely, also armed with a fishing net. On the nineteenth, there emerged from the jungle some Malays, a small group who collected jungle produce at the foot of the central hills. With Chinese, Indians, Eurasians, Malays and Europeans, the polyglot appearance of modern Malaya began to take shape at once. On the Peninsula the old Malaya remained, for fifty, almost a hundred years, but in the new racial pattern is reflected, right from the beginning of the settlement the shape of a new Malaya.

Light, laboriously engaged in cutting down the dense stack of timber, asked the Malays early in August to assist him. He noted that "they cut down a few but I could not prevail upon them to cut any more." As he had commented that "the wood is so exceedingly hard that the tools double like a piece of lead,"[7] he probably was not particularly surprised.

By August 10 the cutting and clearing had been going on apace for over three weeks. The tents had proved useless against the heavy downpours and they had been replaced by huts, so that there was a recognizable cantonment. A small bazaar, supervised by a Noquedah Catchu, was in operation. Chinese and others were building on the point, food was coming across from Kedah, and the settlement was well established. That day there sailed in and anchored two stately East Indiamen, the first ever to call at Penang, the *Vansittart* and the *Valentine*, on their way to China for tea. They provided the opportunity for some necessary formalities.

The next day their captains, Richard Lewin and Thomas Wall respectively, landed, and, together with Francis Light and the entire community, assembled round the newly erected flag mast. The troops lined up, the Malays, Chinese and others crowded close, and at noon "all the gentlemen" wrote Light, meaning all of the thirteen Englishmen he could muster, "unitedly hoisted the Flag, taking possession of the Island in the name of His Britannic Majesty and for the use of the Honourable East India Company. The artillery and ships fired a royal salute, and the marines three volleys."[8]

The majority of those who had clung to the Union Jack were visitors. Light, his colleague and friend the commandant of the Marine detachment, Lieutenant James Gray, the captain of the Engineers, Elisha Trapaud, the captain of the Artillery, George Howell, and two merchants, John Beaton and George Smith, all lived ashore; the remainder were rowed back to their ships that evening, after the loyal celebrations were over. Captain Lewin and the *Vansittart* caught a favourable wind and sailed during the night, the *Valentine* soon after.[9]

[7]Diary, July 17—August 10.

[8]Diary. August 10-11, 1786.

[9]Elisha Trapaud, one of the participants in this ceremony has left us an impression of it, in a sketch in his book, *A Short Account of the Prince of Wales Island, or Pulo Pinang, in the East Indies, given to Captain Light by the King of Quedah.* (London, 1788).

Light must have begun building a fort soon after landing. It was the sensible thing to do, and all his actions indicate that he was a levelheaded sensible man. By early October he could write to Bengal describing the double row of *nubongs* erected, the ditch dug, and the bastions solid enough to hold six-pounders landed from the ship.[10] Diplomatically he named this fort after the new Governor General, who had gone to Calcutta after his arrival, and in true East India Company tradition the settlement took its name after the fort. Long after the timbered stockade had been replaced by stone walls, long after these walls had been abandoned as untenable and permitted to crumble and decay, Penang to the Company was Fort Cornwallis.

Cornwallis looked on his namesake with a slightly critical eye. "I will not go so far as to say that in the present embarrassed state of the company's finances I would have recommended the undertaking; before any advantage can be expected, expenditure to a large amount must be made which cannot be supplied without encroaching upon funds already appropriated to answer a variety of urgent demands. What in a more prosperous state of the Company's finances might have been highly advantageous, may from the reverse prove burthensome if not prejudicial. My objections," he concluded, "go rather to the time in which this measure has been resolved upon, than to the measure itself."[11]

Cornwallis maintained this attitude throughout his tour (1786-1793). No liberal expenditure assisted Light, nor his immediate successors, and they had to make do with very little indeed. More serious perhaps was the indifference shown towards this young offspring by Bengal in other matters, in particular in the administration of justice. The enforcement of law and order is the basis, just as in the eighteenth century and for most of the nineteenth, it was the bulk of the administrative responsibility of government. Government's primary duty, then as now, was to offer a minimum sense of security to those who lived within its jurisdiction. If it failed to do that, then its people would look elsewhere for that security, and the government would lose the support of the community. This never occurred on Penang, because despite the drawbacks to its administration its inhabitants felt more secure there than on the mainland. In the early period, however, this security came more from the actions of the civil servants on the spot than from the Company in London or India, for the Company consistently refused to take any action that would put the ad hoc administration of law and order into a legal framework. No Code of Laws reached Penang for over twenty years after its foundation. Until then the island had to struggle on with the rough and ready justice of its commandants, modified only slightly by some general instructions.

Among the first administrative steps taken by Light was the appointment of Capitans, headmen of the various communities, to keep the peace among them

[10]S. S. (F). R. Vol. 1. Penang to Bengal, 2 October, 1786.

[11]S. S. (F). R. Vol. 2. Bengal Public Consultations. Minute by Lord Cornwallis, 13 December, 1786.

by settling all internal disputes that did not involve a serious crime or an individual of another race. Light delegated his authority not long after he arrived and a population was assembling on the point. "I have appointed Checka, the most respectable member of the Chinese," he wrote in May, 1787, "to be their Captain, to settle their disputes and to superintend their conduct."[12] He added, rather resignedly one should imagine, "among the Mohommedans I have not been able to find one man fit to be entrusted with any authority."[13] As the population continued to increase, however, this difficulty disappeared. By 1792 Light had appointed Capitans to the three major groups in Penang, the Chinese, Indians (Tamils very largely), and Malays. There was an appeal from their court to the justice of the superintendent; in all cases it is obvious that these were not courts so much as arbitration centers, for there was no Code of Justice to administer. Nevertheless, they helped appreciably in keeping the peace.

Light had asked for some official regulations whereby he could be guided in the administration of law and order while he was loading stores in Calcutta, and he returned to the attack early in 1787. As the little settlement grew, his problem increased. "It is become necessary," he pointed out to an indifferent Bengal, "to have some regulations established for the peace and safety of individuals. Our inhabitants are composed of Chinese, Malays, Christians, Choolias, Siamese and Tannoes. The Siamese and Chinese are nearly of the same religion and manners, the Malays, Choolias and Tannoes are Mohommedans and governed by the Mosaic Law. A strict police for the punishment of such offences as disturb the public peace is sufficient, while each sect are governed by their own municipal laws.

"They have been told that murder is never pardoned; for the living I have found severe whipping to frighten the Malays better than putting to death; prohibiting gaming houses and suffering no arrack shops but those licensed and under proper regulations will in great measure take away the cause."[14]

In January 1788 he received an Assistant, Thomas Pigou. He brought with him on the *Speedwell* the Company's considered reply to Light's request for some legal regulations. They were blunt and largely useless. "The Governor General in Council does not consider himself at liberty to make any permanent Regulations for the Police of Prince of Wales Islands without express authority from Europe."

Bengal was well aware that it had no power to establish British courts. This was a prerogative guarded most carefully by the Crown. No subject of that Crown could take the initiative. It was poor planning however which had sent Light to Penang without securing the prior approval of London for the estab-

[12]V. Purcell: *The Chinese in Malaya* (London, 1944) p. 143, is, I feel, incorrect in claiming the first Kapitan China was appointed in 1792.

[13]S. S. (F). R. Vol. 2. Penang to Bengal, 7 May, 1787.

[14]S. S. (F). R. Vol. 2. Penang to Bengal, 7 May, 1787.

lishment of a British court and the administration of British justice. Weakly, Bengal agreed "that it be left to Mr. Light to preserve good order in the settlement as well as he can."[15] To the Company in Bengal and in London, Penang was a stable bazaar, a permanently anchored country ship. "It is our wish", Bengal wrote in 1788, "to make use of the island as much as possible in a commercial view only."[16] The commandant on that island then should have received the authority of a captain of a ship. To vest him with less was jeopardizing the whole concern.

Equally foolish was it to keep outside the administration of justice, and free of all legal restraints, the British subjects. This was the frontier, and the frontier attracts the lawless as well as the adventurous. For the safety and well being of all, the British subjects should have been brought within the stockade, and controlled by the commandant. As early as 1787 Light had written, "the riots the European seamen caused by striking and abusing and plundering the inhabitants made it necessary to establish a police,"[17] but strictly his only hold over British citizens was banishment, and with sailors off ships, or with useful members of the community involved in some misdemeanor, this penalty was quite inapplicable. Nevertheless with this he had to suffice; British citizens remained outside the law of Penang, what there was of it, for over twenty years.

This dangerous state of affairs became even more critical in 1793. In that year a seaman from an East Indiaman named Sudds, who was beaten so often by his captain that he seized a hammer and killed him, was arrested and tried in July by court martial, found guilty of murder and sent back to Bengal. There the evidence was examined and the Attorney General refused to bring trial, dismissing Sudds from a wrongful imprisonment. Wrongful, because the Royal Charter of Justice given to the Presidency of Bengal did not extend its jurisdiction—so the Attorney General maintained—to its dependencies, of which Penang was one. It had no authority whatever over crimes committed there. The Attorney General, after a professional criticism of the amateur procedure of courts martial in Penang, ruled that there were "no laws by which the well-intentioned and meant directions given to the Superintendent of Prince of Wales Island by Bengal could be supported as far as they related to the trial or punishment of murder or any other crime at that island" . . . He recommended the necessity of a Judiciary being legally established on the island.[18]

Light continued to administer justice, being guided by the 1793 instructions which read "for the purpose of rendering speedy justice you are to decide ultimately all cases that are brought before you, referring to the Board only in cases of unusual difficulty; and when there is an absolute necessity for doing

[15]S. S. (F). R. Vol. 2. Bengal to Penang, 25 January, 1788.
[16]S. S. (F). R. Vol. 2. Bengal to Penang, 15 February, 1788.
[17]S. S. (F). R. Vol. 2. Penang to Bengal, 7 October, 1787.
[18]S. S. (F). R. Vol. 3. Bengal Public Consultations. Attorney General to Governor General, 26 September, 1793.

so you are to send the offender to Bengal, transmitting at the same time a full statement of the case and of the evidence, together with your reason for declining to pass a decision."[19]

Apart from the unruly European riff-raff who rolled ashore from the trading vessels or who took up residence in Penang, another major cause of disorder for some time was the military force, the Sepoys, quartered in Fort Cornwallis. Their military functions were few, and they were employed very largely in the role of police. The policeman, symbol of European authority, representative of an alien power, has had a tremendous influence over the ignorant peasant or laborer, not merely in Malaya, not merely in this century. In the eighteenth century, when they represented a new, strange, incredibly remote and omnipotent European, the Sepoy was able to impose his authority over the Malays on Penang. Under the cloak of his position, and for a time without the knowledge of his officers, he was able to plunder and tyrannize the growing village.

The following appears to have been a common practice.

If for instance a Malay was carrying to market a basket of yams, coconuts, pumpkins, etc., one (Sepoy) by a shove would throw it from his head, which the other would pick up and be lost among the crowd while the Malay remained staring without his basket; or if he caught the runaway he would be surrounded and carried before the officer, when perhaps he would be lucky if he did not get flogged, because none understood the Malay's story, and the Sepoys were never at a loss.[20]

Captain Glass, the military commander, learned Malay and discovered the truth of these oppressions. He combatted Sepoy impositions with floggings and closer control. Determined as he was to move them back to India, the troops yet remained on the island year after year without relief, and gained a great hold. Glass died before an effective control of their corruption was established. Under his successor, Hamilton, the state of affairs grew worse.

Glass had looked at Penang through the eyes of Light, his superior, and the two had collaborated amicably in the best interests of the settlement. Hamilton, who succeeded Glass in February, 1794, regarded the entire population, by 1794 running to several thousand, as camp followers to his three companies of Sepoys. He soon clashed with Light, and the dispute illustrates the serious hold over the people that had been acquired by the long-resident troops.

Light had introduced a regulation that nobody was to board *prahus* or junks as they neared the Penang wharf or jetty. The vessels had to be passed by the police under the harbor master before they could be approached. He had introduced this in order to save the traders being coerced into selling their goods before seeing the state of the market. It was for the traders' benefit, to enable them to obtain a competitive price, and it had worked adequately, although the police were using their powers and their right to be the first on board to demand and obtain provisions and food from the incoming *prahus* for nothing.

[19]S. S. (F). R. Vol. 3. Bengal to Penang, 12 August, 1793.

[20]S. S. (F). R. Vol. 2. Memorandum on Administration, unsigned, dated, 1794.

In January, 1794, a sailor attempted to board one of these local craft approaching the jetty and was thrown off. He accused two men of having ill-treated him, and Light referred them to Hamilton for examination. Hamilton without further reference to Light conducted a court martial (of men not subject to his military authority) and sentenced three Malays to several hundred lashes. One of the Malays, a *Noqueda,* or ship's captain, had not been referred at all, but had been brought before Hamilton by his Sepoys. Before Light was informed of the proceedings the punishment had been executed.

This arrogant and severe treatment of three civilians by a soldier led to a protest from a deputation of inhabitants. It produced also a letter from the leading merchant, James Scott, demanding a regular civil government. Although the authorities in Calcutta were still loath to establish formal and regular courts until Penang had proved itself, an attempt was made to help Scott. The Penang establishment was increased by two more assistants, and to the senior, Philip Mannington, was assigned the magisterial work. The Penang jurisdiction, it was emphasized again, had no powers over British subjects, except that if a major crime was committed by one, he should be sent to Bengal for trial. If a non-British subject, however, committed murder or any other crime involving the capital punishment, the case was to be heard by the superintendent, who was to compose a court consisting of himself, the magistrate and one other.

The superintendent's position vis à vis the military also was defined again. The Governor General stated that the entire control of the Island was vested in the superintendent, and that no act of public authority could be exercised by anyone without his sanction. The dispatch made the point doubly clear by stating specifically that "the authority of the Commanding Officer of the Troops is restricted to the troops under his command",[21] and that all Sepoy crimes in which civilians were involved, or vice-versa, had to be heard by the magistrate.

These 1794 concessions, whereby Bengal after the departure of Cornwallis increased slightly both the authority and the staff of the superintendent, are signs that Penang by then was becoming recognized as a worthwhile outpost of Bengal. Unfortunately, however, this increased recognition came too late for Francis Light. A few months after the arrival of his new senior assistant, he was dead. According to his tombstone in Penang, he died on 21 October, 1794. According to the official dispatch of Philip Mannington, who succeeded him, he died four days later, on 25 October.[22]

Light had steered the settlement through eight successful years. His critics, still vocal today,[23] point to his failures in land regulation, to the large-scale allocation of townsites and jungle areas, that brought great troubles to his

[21]S. S. (F). R. Vol. 6. Bengal to Penang, 1 August, 1794.

[22]S. S. (F). R. Vol. 7. Penang to Bengal, 11 December, 1794.

[23]G. P. Dartford, *A Short History of Malaya.* (London, 1956). p. 86; Hall: p. 436.

successors.[24] This however, was a minor flaw when set alongside his achievements. Without the aid of the Royal Navy and lacking full authority, he maintained this settlement, peacefully, amid a lawless area. Under his sensible, tactful rule the most diverse of peoples lived amicably with one another. Chinese, Indians, Malays, Siamese, Burmese, Achinese, Eurasians and Europeans, sprung from different stock, worshipping different gods, with different laws and ways of living, all settled and developed. This was no mean achievement. We were to have riots in Singapore soon after it was founded, but while Light lived the race relations on Penang are a model to future generations, not least to our own. The credit for this must go, very largely, to this unassuming ship's captain.

Light had five children by his mistress, Martina Rosels. The eldest of these children, born in 1784, had been sent back in 1790 to Essex for his education. He became a dashing young engineer officer in the Peninsula War and served as an A.D.C. to Wellington himself. After Waterloo he went out to Australia with a new colonizing party, to survey and lay out a new town, Adelaide, that grew to become the capital of South Australia. His statue stands on a crest overlooking the city, and each year the city dignitaries honor 'Light's Day,' and applaud this son of an Englishman and, so it is firmly accepted, a Malay princess.

Young Light's sisters married well, but the family legacy was soon dissipated. Martina Rosels, their mother, had been followed to Penang from Junk Ceylon by a considerable number of relatives. The Roman Catholic inhabitants on the island in December, 1788, included seven other Rosels, Juanica, Andreza and Apolonica, females, and Juakim, Jeronima, Antoni and Thomas, males.[25] After a disastrous legal battle, they lived to see every inch of ground and the houses he left them either sold, in ruins or covered in jungle.[26] The family who remained on Penang slipped into oblivion, but the memory of Francis Light has been respected in Malaya ever since.

Mannington does not appear to have had the tact of Light. He and Hamilton became locked in petty arguments, until a successor was appointed, and Mannington's acting post was not confirmed. A military man, despite the 1794 regulations, was appointed. Major Forbes Ross McDonald took office on 14 May, 1795 and administered the island with the firm rule of a soldier. He made one attempt only to secure the cooperation of the civilians, in 1796, and

---

[24]As Mannington was quick to point out "Concerning your Order (August 1, 1794), to reserve ground in suitable positions for town buildings," he wrote to Bengal, "this is very difficult. At present the Company does not possess a spot of ground in the Town of a greater extent than 4 acres, and the situation of this is such that being at a considerable distance from the seaside, it must ever be attended with inconvenience and expense;...

"The Company have not a Go-Down of any kind; except for the military stores in the fort all else is lodged at present in the Customs House, which is attended with no small degree of confusion." S. S. (F). R. Vol. 6. Penang to Bengal, 25th February, 1795.

[25]S. S. (F). R. Vol. 2. List of Roman Catholic Inhabitants, December, 1788. (There were approximately 200 of them).

[26]For a comment on this, see J. Welch, *Military Reminiscences*. 2 Vols. (London, 1830). General Welch married Sarah Light and visited Penang in 1818.

discovered to his dismay that he had grasped a stinging nettle. He had formed a committee of merchants, to advise him on how best to promote the trade of the island. This committee took the opportunity, in the twenty one suggestions it made to him, to request the establishment of a Court of Judicature, and to ask that the Sepoys should no longer be employed in executing administrative orders. Obviously the power of the Sepoys still rankled, for the committee further suggested that the military guards and posts should be under proper military discipline, and supervised by their officers, and that they be not permitted to lend money, nor obtain redress by coercion. A glimpse of McDonald's character is given in the last paragraph from the committee, which stated that "we are sorry to observe that your government here is rapidly changing from the fostering hand of a kind father to the features of a severe master."[27]

The recommendations of the committee were not acted upon. The few dispatches of McDonald that have survived are all tremendous, running to scores of pages and including hundreds of long paragraphs. Almost entirely, they are devoted to attacks on the small group of European merchants on the Island. In particular they singled out time and again, James Scott, the midshipman companion of Light in 1761, his business associate on Junk Ceylon in the 1770's, and his colleague on Penang since 1787, who while Light administered had attended profitably to business. In the eyes of McDonald Scott and his associates suffered from being firstly civilians and secondly for not being members of the Company. He attempted to challenge their right to reside on Penang, and demanded of them their authority to remain. The tart replies this evoked produced some interesting biographical detail, but were otherwise negative of results. The Company in Bengal was well aware of its need for country traders, and they were permitted to remain. Not so McDonald; in 1799 he resigned, returning to Madras, and the administration of Penang entered a new stage, with abolition of the post of superintendent and the introduction of a lieutenant governorship.[28]

To understand this change in the status of Penang it is necessary to forget the internal scene and to consider the world outside. By 1800 Penang had proved its use to the Company in a number of ways. Militarily it had been found extremely useful to the vast designs of Whitehall. In 1795 Penang had provided an advance base for the capture of Malacca. In 1796 the Andaman settlement of convicts was closed and moved to Penang. In 1797 an expedition, sent to invade Manila, had used Penang as a rendezvous although it was then hurriedly recalled, and Manila was left in peace.

Penang was of interest not merely to the army and navy by 1800, but commercially too it was far more attractive than any previous outpost attempted by the Company to the eastward. It had acquired a population of thousands. (Estimates ranged considerably; Light in 1790 said 10,000, Kyd in 1794 said

---

[27] *Journal of the Indian Archipelago (Logan's Journal)* Vol. V. (1851). Penang to Bengal, July, 1796.

[28] At the same time there was created another post, Secretary to the Governor. W. Phillips was appointed to this.

20,000.) It grew or sold to ships going or coming from China a number of crops, such as padi, sugar, greens and indigo, as well as providing them with tin and straits produce; it provided a useful bazaar for the sale of opium and piece goods, while it was frequented by thousands of *prahus* and a goodly number of country ships and East Indiamen. It had become a considerable acquisition, to be held against French or Dutch aggression, and it was high time that its administration was placed on a sounder footing; so must have reasoned the Company.

In the initial instructions to its lieutenant governor, Sir George Leith, the Company told him that despite the history of the administration of justice on Penang from 1786 onwards and its refusal to accept responsibility for its administration, "it entertains no doubt of its being equally the right and the duty of the British government in India to provide for the administration of Justice to the native inhabitants of that Island, and that, having accepted that right and duty, Leith should frame regulations to implement that decision." He was instructed to incorporate in those regulations "the laws of the different peoples and tribes of which the inhabitants consist, tempered by such parts of the British Law as are of universal application, being founded on the principles of natural justice."[29]

Leith was saved from this task by the initiative of Lord Wellesley, the Governor-General. He appointed a trained lawyer, John Dickens, to the post of magistrate on Penang. It became the responsibility of Dickens, under Leith, "to define the constitution and powers of the Courts, the cases in which an appeal is to be allowed to you in the first instance, and in the last resort to the Governor-General in Council . . . they should also specify the fees."[30] Unfortunately Dickens and Leith clashed repeatedly over questions of responsibility. This was possibly an inevitable occurence when the executive and the judicial aspects of administration were not clearly separated, and where authority was ill-defined. Nevertheless it was a factor retarding the legal work stipulated by the supreme government. Years were to pass before the law came finally to Penang.

Leith attended to another branch of the administration of justice, the Capitans, and drew up a series of instructions for the better prosecution of their duties. These were printed on a form which was handed to the Capitan on appointment; in effect, it was his notice of appointment. "You are to keep good order among your people, to see that they behave quietly and peaceably in their inhabitations, as you will be protected and supported by Government in the duty of your office."[31] So ran the main clause. Others defined more closely

---

[29]*Logan's Journal*, (Journal of the Indian Archipelago), Vol. V. pp. 157-158. Instructions to Sir G. Leith, 15 March, 1800.

[30]Instructions to Sir G. Leith, 1800.

[31]Kyshe, *Cases Heard and Determined in Her Majesty's Supreme Court of the Straits Settlements, 1808-1844.* (Singapore, 1885) Vol. 1. pp. xxiii-xxiv.

his responsibilities. He was to hold a court twice a week where with two others he was to try all petty complaints and all religious or family disputes between people of his own race. In cases of debt, if over $10 in value, the right of appeal was allowed. Leith was careful to ensure that the two associates would be representative. He stipulated that each month the names of twelve good house-keepers were to be given to the magistrate, and that he would divide the dates of their attendance with the Capitan.

Apart from holding a court, the Capitan was to keep a register of all marriages, deaths and births amongst his people, for which purpose he was permitted a clerk. Further, he was to investigate any new arrivals, to inform the administration of them, and to tell if there was any disturbance, or unrest, or illness. It would seem as if these regulations helped the Capitans develop their role, for shortly after this Leith abolished "in consequence of the increase of business" the regulation which insisted they attend the magistrates' court to help explain the appeals, and said it was necessary only that their writers appear.[32] When Leith left Penang in 1804, he took with him, and subsequently published in his book,[33] the letters of good wishes written to him by Mahomet Sally, the Malay, Tikoo the Chinese, and Cader Meyden and Sandagur Bata Saib, the Indian Capitan.

Leith was succeeded by R. T. Farquhar, a Madras civil servant, who had been the administrator of the Moluccas after their capture, and had figured in the Balambangan debacle of 1803-1805 as well.[34] He administered Penang very briefly: from January, 1804, until September, 1805. Farquhar turned against the policy of Leith as regards the Capitans, and added his voice to the protests of his predecessors at the lack of a judiciary, and of a law code for it to administer. He found distasteful such other abnormalities as a gaol crowded with capital offenders, either waiting transport to Bengal, or serving sentences imposed by Bengal, unable to award the ultimate punishment through lack of evidence. He also criticized what he felt was the excessive authority of the Capitans. Despite his opposition however, the Capitans were to remain on the Southeast Asian scene as the very necessary link between government, and in particular the Chinese, for over a century longer.

This aspect of government however was minor compared to the administration of justice. Dickens, fresh from sophisticated Bengal, was horrified at all that was lacking on this frontier. He found the shortage of staff deplorable. There were none of the crowd of assistants he had taken for granted in Bengal. He found he was the sheriff, gaoler, coroner, bailiff and policeman in one. Perhaps most objectionable to this lawyer, there was "the total want of an efficient code of civil and criminal laws."[35]

[32]Kyshe: Vol. 1. pp. xxiii-xxiv.
[33]Leith: *A Short Account of Prince of Wales Island.* (London, 1804) pp. 65-69.
[34]See Chapter 9. p.
[35]*Logan's Journal,* Vol. V. pp. 191-92 Penang to Bengal, 1 October, 1801.

Finally, he was critical of his own position, at the subservience of the law to the administration. His judgements in fact were no more than opinions, requiring the approval of the lieutenant governor before they became official. When Leith went on leave in 1802, and the government secretary, Phillips, had the first of his innumerable acting governorships, he several times reversed the decision of Dickens. It must have been infuriating for a judge, a trained lawyer, to have to submit to this, a process that continued when Leith returned. Dickens obviously was steeped in the traditions of properly constituted courts and laws, and was deeply perturbed at the lack of a separately established judiciary. Leith was less conscious of the need for a clear division between judiciary and administration, had a curt and overbearing manner, and resented the constant efforts of Dickens to establish a judicial independence. The result was a flaming controversy.

At the same time Dickens, says Braddell, "by his stubborn conduct and untiring perseverance brought or hastened the East India Company into petitioning the King for a Charter of Justice for the settlement."[36] While the importance of his efforts may have been exaggerated by earlier writers, not least Braddell (himself a prominent lawyer) undoubtedly Dickens' appointment, and the resultant clashes with the executive, forced the Company to realize the unsatisfactory state of affairs. Both Leith and Dickens took a share in drafting the regulations for a code of justice, and their suggestions and comments on these regulations passed back and forth between Bengal, London and Penang like a ponderous and slow moving East Indiaman. In 1800 this exchange began with a bulky dispatch containing eight rather verbose regulations from Leith; by 1805 these had grown into a draft code of ten ill-arranged and even more verbose regulations, but by then Leith had gone and Dickens rapidly shrank them to four.

In 1805 far reaching administrative changes were made. They will be discussed again in the following chapter. Here we need note only that the island became a Presidency, equal though junior to the Presidencies of Bombay, Fort St. George and Fort William, and the lieutenant governor was replaced by a president. The review of the administrative position contained an urgent plea for the introduction of proper judicial regulations, and asked that the draft submitted by Dickens be finalized in view of the unacceptable conditions prevailing. These he then reviewed.

The only power we found on the island having the appearance of a regular administration of Justice was lodged in the office of the Judge and Magistrate, who decides, or rather gives his opinion on all suits, where the Parties, or at least the defendants, are not Europeans. This opinion becomes a sentence on being confirmed by the Lt. Governor, who also had the power of reversing or altering the same, if he thought proper . . .

Cases of Felony are tried by a Court (of Governor, Judge and another), who report to the Governor General. But cases are only brought when innocence is strongly as-

[36]R. Braddell. *Laws of the Straits Settlements, A Commentary*. (Singapore, 1915). p. 9.

sumed, as in no instance has the Governor General passed an order for execution of sentence, or even taken any notice thereof. So there remain in our jail twenty-one convicted murderers, likely never to be punished.

The more turbulent Europeans remain on the island free from all restraint, with the power of committing every act [of] injustice, and irregularity, towards his neighbour; having set at defiance all authority as not legally established on the Island.[37]

The president, as a temporary measure appointed a Mr. P. Kellner, a respectable German citizen, to be police magistrate and commissioner of a new Court of Requests, authorized to ajudicate in minor cases, and so relieve the pressure on Dickens. Kellner was appointed in March, 1806 and dismissed for corrupt practices in September, the appointment then going, as did nearly all appointments in the new Presidency, to a Scot, Mr. T. McQuoid.

While the new administration was facing this problem, the draft charter had reached London from Calcutta, and was being considered by the Company and the Crown. The consideration continued into, through, and beyond 1806, and it was not until 25 March, 1807, that the Royal Letters Patent, establishing a Court of Judicature at Prince of Wales Island, was issued. It was not until over a year later, 31 May 1808, that this charter of justice was published on Penang.[38]

This established a Court of Record, consisting of the President or Governor, and the first three councillors of the Factory, as four of the judges, and one other judge, called the recorder, who had to be a trained barrister. He was to have the casting vote, and no Act was to be done in his absence. No fees or salaries were to be paid the administrative staff for their legal duties, but the recorder was to be paid £3,000 per annum. The court had all the powers of a superior court in England such as the King's Bench, or the High Court of Chancery, although not, unfortunately, the powers of admiralty jurisdiction, that is, the right to try cases of piracy and other crimes committed on the high seas. It had full authority for all other criminal and civil cases. The charter of justice stipulated a right of appeal direct to the Crown, that is, to the Privy Council.[39]

This charter was brought to Penang by the first recorder, Sir Edmund Stanley. He landed on 28 May. The Letters Patent was proclaimed on 31 May, following a procession to the council chambers, where the governor and the other judges took their oaths, and where a royal salute was fired from nearby Fort Cornwallis. Sir Edmund Stanley then addressed the governor and the assembled gathering, stating that he was "pleased to introduce the inestimable blessings of British Law and British Judicature into a more remote part of the Eastern world than these great advantages ever yet had reached . . . it communicates to all His Majesty's Asiatic as well as British subjects the full enjoyment of personal security, personal liberty, and private property; and at the

[37]S. S. (F). R. Vol. 179. Penang to London, 12 November, 1805.

[38]S. S. (F). R. Vol. 179. Penang to London, 4 June, 1808.

[39]S. S. (F). R. Vol. 8. *Letters Patent, establishing the Court of Judicature at Prince of Wales Island in the East Indies.* 25 March, 1807.

same time it secures to all the native subjects the free exercise of their religion, indulges them in all their prejudices and pays the most scrupulous attentions to all their ancient customs, usages and habits. . ."[40]

It had taken twenty-two lawless years for this to happen. Although lawyers were not content, and occupied themselves happily in argument, in 1858, in 1871, and in 1872 in the Privy Council itself, as to whether the laws of England had ever reached Penang, it is clear; this code of justice brought the law of Great Britain to Malaya. It rules still today.

There is little more to add. In August 1809 the administration of justice was assisted by the selection of responsible European land owners in various districts to serve as high constables, that is to preserve the peace and to settle trifling disputes to the extent sanctioned by law and English custom. The court of judicature still felt over-worked, or possibly irritated at being called upon to decide trifling questions or disputes it considered too insignificant for it; for as the charter of justice contained no provisions for a police magistrate, able to deal summarily with these minor legal quarrels, the good work of Mr. McQuoid was unrecognized. In lengthy leisured phrases, embodied in one magnificent sentence, the President described the step taken to relieve the court of this unexpected work.

Considerable inconvenience having been felt on the first establishment of the Court of Judicature at this Presidency, from the want of legal powers vested in Mr. Cauntor whom your Honorable Court appointed Acting Magistrate, and there being no authority in His Majesty's Charter for the appointment of Magistrates or Justices of the Peace, we have on the suggestion of the Honorable the Recorder and under the authority of the Charter latterly sat in rotation at a public office in Georgetown as Justice of the Peace, Mr. Cauntor acting as Clerk to the Justices, and we trust that while the inconvenience felt from the informality hitherto existing in taking Informations, Examinations, and making commitments will be entirely done away, the local magistracy by this setting for that purpose as well as deciding petty disputes and breaches of the peace in a summary way, will at the same time afford considerable relief to the Court of Judicature, and by the establishment of an efficient police prevent the perpetration of the numerous crimes which we regret to say have so often been committed here.[41]

The long sentence takes us back to the leisured atmosphere of early Penang, isolated, with ample time for correspondence, for this is but paragraph 33 in a short 61-paragraph letter, and with ample time too, one cannot help thinking, for the little work there was, despite the pleading of the government. It was a tolerant island, in the light of the time and the place, and the Dutch, devotees of a stern, almost barbaric enforcement of rigid laws, were horrified at the humane treatment meted out.

I cannot commend the soft handling which the deportees and convicted wrong-doers receive under the English administration,

[40]*Prince of Wales Island Gazette.* Tuesday, 31 May, 1808.

[41]S. S. (F). R. Vol. 180. Penang to London, 10 August, 1809.

wrote one Java Dutchman, who continued,

to my great surprise I have found deportees admitted to the houses of the senior officials, discharging their duties alongside the ordinary household staff, and only to be distinguished from them by a small iron ring on the leg by which the deportee is recognizable.[42]

The Penang court was filled for the most part with south Indians, indulging in a national propensity for argument and litigation that, although deviated to a certain extent by the parliaments and trade unions of the twentieth century, still fill the courts of India and Malaya today. In 1811, a typical enough year, the estimated population of Penang was 25,000, of whom 10,000 were Malays, 7,000 Chinese and 6,000 Indians. The summons issued by the court in that same year numbered 8,800, of which 7,700 were in the Tamil language. A mere 400 went out in Malay, 300 in Chinese, and 400 in English. Over two-thirds of the cases involved Indians, who numbered less than a quarter of the population.[43]

Between them the court, the magistrate and the sheriffs, and high constables managed to administer justice to all, their main objection being to the "repeated inconvenience from the want of an Admiralty Jurisdiction to take cognizance of offences committed on the High Seas, and of Piratical depredations.[44] The settlement was forced to the expense and inconvenience of sending to Bengal or Madras captured pirates, and it often found that they returned free, although they were notoriously guilty men, through a deficiency in the papers or information sent back. It was a state similar to that existing on Penang itself, when murder was committed, before the charter of justice arrived; only in this case it was possible for the apprehended wrong-doers to be punished summarily without comment before dry land was reached. Nevertheless, although pirates invariably resisted when apprehended, and thus often were killed and never tried, sufficient of them were captured to make the lack of jurisdiction most inconvenient and dangerous, with vicious killers, sent to Bengal charged with murder and piracy, wandering the streets of Penang as free men. The position did not change until 1837, when Penang acquired admiralty jurisdiction; even then, it was not the increased power of the law so much that checked piracy as the superior force brought by the arrival of the steam boat. There were not, in fact, many piracy cases tried in the Straits Settlements courts, for the argument had been settled at sea.

[42]Colonel Nahuijs to De Kock, Governor, Netherlands India, 2 August, 1824. Journal, M.B.R.A.S. Vol. *XIX*. Pt. 11.

[43]S. S. (F). R. Vol. 8, Commissioners of the Court to the Secretary of Government, attached to Penang to Bengal, 11 September, 1811.

[44]S. S. (F). R. Vol. 181. Penang to London, 24 November, 1814.

V

THE PROBLEM OF A REVENUE

In the previous chapter attention was focused on the early attempts by the administrators of Penang to secure a code of laws and a proper judicial system, whereby the basis of their government and the bulk of their administrative work could be secured in law. A charter of justice came a few years after Penang had been elevated into a Presidency, and it is fitting that we should turn now to an examination of the ways by which the government attempted to secure a revenue, a task almost as basic as that of administering a law, for this Presidency is noted above all else for its chronic inability to make ends meet; from 1805 to 1826, and beyond, the greatest problem of the government of the Straits Settlements was financial. French privateers, Siamese forces in Kedah, Raffles in the south, all were minor vexations and problems to the Presidency compared to the worry constantly before it of how to find a revenue to pay for its existence. Unlike the last chapter, which chronicled a tardy success, this one must tell of disappointment and failure. The Presidency never did pay for itself, and as a result it vanished, to become merely a minor unit of a Straits Settlements Residency.

The problem of raising a revenue was in effect a problem general to all British settlements in the Orient. It had been made no easier by an early action of Francis Light. Light on his arrival had declared that the government would not tax imports and exports, which could move freely in or out of the harbor, or be transhipped, without a levy of any kind. This declaration of a "Free Port" made Penang unique in Southeast Asia, as it would seem that the rulers of every other river and port in that area, whether Asian or European, exacted taxes on goods passing in and out. The Dutch in particular have been criticized for their range of taxes, but these at least were known, and were adhered to, whereas, the levies of the indigenous rulers, from Bangkok to Bali, were capricious and crippling, and therefore far more detrimental to trade than those of Java.[1]

---

[1]The solitary exception to this general practice was the Bugis habit, both at Macassar, until it fell to the Dutch in 1667, and then at Rhio, of encouraging trade by nominal customs dues, consistently levied. Light may well have obtained his idea of a Free Port from the Bugis trading success; certainly there was no European example to inspire him. See B. H. Vlekke: *Nusantara.* (Harvard, 1945), pp. 112-114; B. Harrison, *Trade in the Straits of Malacca in 1785,* in *JMBRAS,* Vol. xxvi. Pt. 1. (July, 1953).

Admirable though the concept was, the "Free Port" declaration by Light denied the authorities one usual source of revenue. The Company gave Light eighteen months or so of grace, but then, faced with the costs of maintaining the settlement, it addressed him early in 1788 with a request that the island itself should begin to pay for its administration. "It appears from your information," Bengal wrote, "that many merchants are settling upon the island for commercial objects, and we are well disposed to encourage all attempts that have a tendency to promote them. But whilst these advantages are open to individuals we can see no reason why the Company should not participate in them." It went on to suggest two ways by which the Company could secure a revenue. "Firstly, to purchase on the Company's account such articles as are brought to the islands, and will furnish a productive remittance to China. Secondly, the imposition of such moderate duties in the exports and imports as may releave *(sic)* the Company, either in part or in whole from the expense of the Establishment without distressing the trade by too heavy burthens."[2]

Both these suggestions are typical. The Company constantly was watching the China market, and even Cornwallis, anxious though he was at the state of the Company's finances, was prepared to assist it in some way. The company was anxious also to avoid heavy losses in Penang, for while the country traders and merchants came to the island, and did not suffer, the Company did. Its basic problem was never faced. In seeking revenue by taxes, it is necessary to have an educated, responsible staff, adequately paid. This it never attempted to acquire. As a result Penang, as with Singapore later, was maintained at a loss by the Company for the benefit of its few employees and the private merchants trading to China and the eastward isles.

Light, however, suggested a number of revenue-raising proposals to the Company. These included, strangely enough, (after rents on houses and shops, and taxes on their sales), taxes ranging from 4 per cent to 6 per cent on imports. The levying of this duty would have demanded a considerable staff, and it was not acceptable to Bengal, which wrote practically in the same words as Light himself had addressed to it, "taxes on trade at present might be disadvantageous."[3]

His suggestion of a land tax was approved, so also a tax on arrack, Light being told to farm it. Farming in this context was a practice of licensing monopolies, for retail sales or for tax collection.

One other suggestion he made of great subsequent importance was accepted. This was that ships bound for England could exchange goods freely in the harbor without landing or depositing their goods ashore. This was to encourage, as Bengal brazenly said, the Canton trade; but it was not the Company trade it encouraged but that of the private traders, for it permitted the transhipment, at Penang by private traders, of tea they could not send direct to London. The

[2]S. S. (F). R. Vol. 1. Bengal to Penang, 25 January, 1788.
[3]S. S. (F). R. Vol. 1. Bengal to Penang, 25 August, 1788.

monopoly of shipping tea from Canton to Tilbury direct remained with the Company, but Penang's transhipment service permitted, legally, a shipment from Canton to Penang, and then Penang to Tilbury. There is thus a direct link between the founding of Penang, designed to assist the China trade, and the abolition of the Company's powerful monopoly of that China trade with London in 1833; and it was the officials of the Company in Bengal who acquiesced in the recommendation that helped considerably in the undermining of the trade already in progress in Canton.

Of all the unfamiliar aspects of government that Light endeavored to master, his worst failure was in that which he knew least — land administration. Treated in detail elsewhere,[4] here it need only be noted that his suggestion of securing a revenue from land and shop sales was doomed to failure from the beginning, as he was almost completely without staff. As this shortage of a trained civil service was the customary feature of virtually all the states of island Southeast Asia, it is not surprising that Light turned quickly to the mode of revenue collecting they all had adopted, a mode that was to continue until the present century, that of Revenue Farms.

The system of farming, that is of selling the right to retail opium, or to run a gambling hall for example, had been used extensively by indigenous rulers before the Portuguese first came, and continued long after. The British and the Moghuls used it in India.[5] Adam Smith mentions it in Europe.[6] Like the Capitan system, whereby locals governed themselves, it was a very useful administrative device indeed, aimed at producing the maximum revenue with the minimum of officials. The Dutch had developed it in Java during the eighteenth century to a degree envied by their less well-organized neighbors, and by reason of their power were able to make attractive and sell a wide variety of farms that included gambling, coining, opium, poll taxes, slaughter-house, bazaar, pork, fish, and betel-nut leaf.[7] The criterion of the tax was its productiveness and the facility of levying it; so very largely the farmers were Chinese, and the farms were monopolies in some form or other of the vices of the community, the most remunerative being those covering the vices (or the pleasures) of the Chinese themselves.

In 1787 Light had rejected an application by a Chinese for the right to run a gambling house, and by others to run opium houses. He felt that it was not the time, as people were only just arriving, to start farms. The attitude of both Light and Bengal soon changed. The arrack farm, already mentioned, was sold in 1789 for $250 per month, and other farms quickly followed. In 1791 the gambling house and opium farms were instituted, and functioned along with the arrack farm. They were added to in 1792 by another, on pork, a traditional

[4] As a paper in *JMBRAS*.

[5] R. C. Majumdar. *An Advanced History of India*. (London, 1948) pp. 554-565.

[6] A. Smith: *The Wealth of Nations*. (London, 1930) Vol. II. p. 386.

[7] For this, see V. Purcell: *The Chinese in South East Asia*. (Oxford, 1951) pp. 470-501; J. Moor: *Notice of the Indian Archipelago and Adjacent Countries*. (Singapore, 1837). p. 11.

Chinese delicacy. The total revenue that year was $11,500, of which over $10,000 came from the three big farms. In the year of Light's death, 1794, the growth of Penang was reflected by the increase in revenue. The arrack farm had slipped forever from its premier place. It yielded $6,600 in comparison to the $9,500 from gambling and the $5,500 from opium. The pork or hog farm yielded only $270, a shop tax produced $610, anchorage money brought in $700, and there was $116 from various small duties. The total was $23,300, of which nearly $22,000 came from the farms. This of course was nowhere sufficient to pay for the island, the expenditure that year being $150,000.[8]

Mannington, Light's successor as superintendent, perturbed at the discrepancy between revenue and disbursements, and less conscious than Light, (who had been associated as a non-active partner in trade with Scott throughout his tenure), that successful commerce was more important than a balanced budget, recommended at the beginning of his rule that the Company should secure a traditional monopoly, which it had farmed on Bencoolen, namely salt. This was unacceptable to Bengal, as was the long list of varied import duties that in a vast memorandun Mannington subsequently advanced, ranging from a one per cent duty on opium to a five per cent tax on all imported goods sold at public auctions. He would have imposed a revenue raising tax on imported tin, pepper, brimstone, opium, grain, all goods from China, all goods in foreign ships and all goods from India and the United Kingdom, as well as continuing the various farms. Such a massive variety of taxes would have been as unpractical as unwise, and fortunately for Penang the Supreme Government decided against them.

Mannington's exhaustive dispatch drained him of ideas, and rather naïvely he formed in 1796 a committee of merchants to advise him on how best he could tax them. While completely ignoring the purpose of their meeting, the merchants (Messrs. Scott, McIntyre, Lindsay, Hutton, Roebuck, Young, Brown, Sparran, Mackrell and Nason), proceeded to examine the whole of government. It always has been the danger in British Colonies, that unofficial bodies of Englishmen, constituted for purposes totally different, will proceed to discuss and criticize the government above them. The American Colonies had given an example of that, a few years previously, and Mannington, soldier and disciplinarian as he was, was furious at the twenty-one administrative criticisms they brought forward, in not one of which, so he maintained, was there a single constructive suggestion on how to raise a revenue.

Penang remained a free port, with its revenue coming very largely from its farms. Very quickly, however, the monopoly rights these gave to the farmers (particularly it would seem the sole right to retail opium), were circumvented by a Chinese smuggling ring on the Prai River, opposite Penang harbor, yet outside the jurisdiction of the East India Company. Here was situated an early

[8]S. S. (F). R. Vol. 1. Revenues of Prince of Wales Island, 1788-1794, Appendix A. Kyd. to Bengal, 2 August, 1795.

Secret Society;[9] and a successful opium-selling center, whose sales affected adversely the farmer's profits, and thus the revenue derived by the Company. Without doubt this loss to the revenue was one of the reasons why Prai was acquired from the Sultan of Kedah in 1800. The effect on the farm revenue was instantaneous. With the smugglers suppressed, or at least driven away, the opium farm was sold in 1801 for $15,840. The previous year it had fetched $5,000 less. Two new farms, begun that year, the tobacco and sirreh farm, and the attap farm, also helped swell the revenue, which rose from $53,000 to $74,000; even so, this was still $100,000 less than that year's expenditure of $174,000.

It was obvious that not by farms alone was Penang ever to become self-sufficient, and in the instructions issued to Sir George Leith in 1800 he was told that the expenses of the government were to be defrayed not merely by the revenue farms, but in addition by the imposition of duties on goods landed at Georgetown for local consumption only, and not for re-export; by the sale of marine stores, which were to be a Company monopoly; and thirdly by a duty on the produce of the island when exported.

These instructions embodied hopes that never eventuated. The sale of marine stores, on which so much was set, was expected to increase tremendously with the establishment of a naval base on the island. It seemed so imminent that Scott, guileful businessman, bought much of the land south of Georgetown where the base was planned, and named it Jamestown, while the government split the opium and other farms in two, a Georgetown and a Jamestown farm. But the scheme dragged on and was abandoned.[10] Similarly, the tax on agricultural exports also failed, as the peppers and other spices were not successful, and although an export tax is standard procedure for the under-developed tropical countries of the twentieth century, it quite failed to establish itself in the early nineteenth-century British possessions on the Malay Peninsula. It needed, for its profitable introduction, an export staple in great demand. To the regret of the administration it never had that until the advent of tin and rubber. Throughout the nineteenth century the British position in the Malay Peninsula was maintained and developed by a revenue derived very largely from the taxing of Chinese, supplemented for many years by large-scale payments from India.

Nevertheless, Leith in 1801 ended the brave free-trade experiment of Light, and imposed import and export duties. The tax on the produce of the island was abandoned in 1803, but a two per cent duty on re-exports was maintained. This farm went to a European, Scott and Co. being the successful tenderers,

---

[9]In commenting on the Chinese on Penang, Light wrote, (25 January, 1794), that "they are able to form parties and combinations in the most secret manner...", while Cauntor, Acting Superintendent, wrote (16 August, 1798), that "near 500 Chinese joined a Society under the strictest oaths of secrecy and fidelity to their captain, a servant of Mr. Roebuck." See also *Logan's Journal*. Vol. III, where in Low's *Account of the British Settlements in the Straits of Malacca* mention is made of the 1799 Chinese secret society at Batu Kawan on the Kedah coast.

[10]This is dealt with in Chapter 9.

presumably because there was no Chinese able to handle the shipping documents or to read in English. In 1805 this farm brought just on $20,000 to the revenue, the gambling farm was worth $25,500, the opium $25,000, and the arrack $21,000. The total revenue was $116,000, a considerable improvement from the $74,000 of 1801; but administrative expenditure, as ever, continued to climb above it. That year, (1805) it was $334,000.[11]

The efforts of the administration to support itself, however inadequate before, were doomed to failure by the decision made in London to constitute this little island as a Presidency, and to saddle it with all the necessary charges. The maintenance of this exalted position was a financial burden that it was quite unable to carry. Annually Bengal was called on to redress the balance, while the government of the island, expanded to farcical lengths by this administrative error in London, struggled to find more money.

The elevation of Penang in 1805 from a Residency, a minor outpost of Bengal, to a Presidency, dealing in most matters direct with London, (although junior to the Presidencies of Bombay, Fort St. George and Fort William, and under the Governor-General in Council) was largely, it would appear, a naval decision. It was one of the last public acts of Henry Dundas, the right hand man of Pitt, who in 1805, after being President of the Board of the East India Company for eighteen years, from 1793 until 1801, (and Chairman of the Secret India Committee since 1781) was also First Lord of the Admiralty.

Both Admiralty and Company might have benefited by the establishment of a naval base on Penang, had affairs shaped differently. The First Lord saw to it that the Dundas family was given the opportunity of participating in this benefit too. The first President was his nephew Philip Dundas, then and most fortunately in charge of the dockyard at Bombay. A large number of Scotsmen were moved into the Presidency as well, Dundas being not unmindful of the northern base upon which his political power rested. As Furber remarks, "the care which he bestowed on the selection of men for the highest position in the Government of India shows a sincere desire to curb and keep within bounds the widespread corruption in India."[12]

Even though "kept within bounds" meant for Penang, kept within Scotland, Philip Dundas was appointed also because of his dockyard experience, and one of the earliest paragraphs in the directive from the Company that sent him out referred him to "the orders from the First Lord of the Admiralty on the subject of establishing a naval base."[13] The instructions to Dundas from his uncle at the Admiralty were written on 5 April, 1805, and he replied to them from Penang, shortly after arriving, on 12 November. Between these two dates, seven months apart, the elder Dundas had resigned from the Admiralty (indeed but four days after his nephew received his instructions), to stand impeach-

[11] S. S. (F). R. Vol. C. 2. Penang to Bengal, 7 February, 1816. Appendix: Revenue and Expenditure, 1805-1815.
[12] H. Furber: Henry Dundas, First Viscount Melville, 1742-1811. (O.U.P. 1931); p. 167.
[13] S. S. (F). R. Vol. 179. President to Court of Directors, 12 November, 1805.

ment and to retire entirely from public affairs. Of far greater importance, on 21 October, just three weeks before Dundas wrote from Penang, eager to employ his large administrative service and to build his naval base, the battle of Trafalgar was fought, the maritime strength of the enemies of Britain was shattered, and the need for such a base largely vanished.

Unfortunately the Penang civil service remained. What could its members do? A little over ten years before there had been Francis Light and perhaps two assistants. With the Presidency, there landed at Georgetown on 19 September, 1805, a president, three councillors, a secretary and his assistant (Thomas Raffles), a collector of customs, an accountant and an auditor with an assistant, a warehouse-keeper, a paymaster, three surgeons, a chaplain, a master attendant, a school-master, ten writers, and a supernumerary staff of over sixty. Comprehensive though this list may appear to be, that was not the end of government, for Lieutenant-Governor Leith had set up, for the more efficient administration of Georgetown itself, a committee of assessors, composed of the principal European and Asian merchants of the town, with the responsibility of levying rates and of assisting in the municipal government. It was this primitive town council, the predecessor to the mayor and the councillors of the present, that superintended the bazaars, the streets, and the drainage etc., and, with a government subsidy, watched over the young town, bounded by Light Street, Beach Street, Chuliah Street and Pitt Street, muddy tracks passing by attap huts that today exist as broad roads in the modern city. Yet despite all this officialdom, it was quite unable to raise the revenue necessary for its existence.

The court of directors could not understand this, nor could it accept the practice of obtaining a revenue from opium. It happily, indeed eagerly, encouraged the export of opium by traders from India and its sale in Canton. The court had permitted since 1798 the export by the Company itself of 250 annual chests of opium to Penang, the profits of their sale being assigned to help defray the expenses of administration. By some quirk of conscience, however, it could not accept an opium farm, the customary form of taxation in the Dutch and indigenous states of Southeast Asia. "At present," the court wrote severely in 1805, "the principal sources of revenue arise from the Farms of Opium, Arrack, Gaming, Tobacco and Bettleleaf, and a duty on the exportation of goods and merchandise. We consider opium a vice; endeavour to suppress it."[14] It went on to recommend the introduction of import duties, to be undertaken by the Company's officials themselves, and not farmed.

Penang took sometime to swallow this rather severe pill. It pointed out to London that an import levy had been tried before, that in 1801 and 1802 a duty had been charged on tin, pepper and betel nut coming in to the settlement, but that it had been abandoned as unsatisfactory. The major criticism had been that the farmer could tax merely those *prahus* that he wished to tax

[14]S. S. (F). R. Vol. 179. London to Penang, 18 April, 1805.

and could admit and ignore those craft affiliated to his own business. The tax had been bitterly resented and was most inefficient, and it had been for this reason that a general export tax had been established, farmed in 1805 for $19,800. The government represented to London that the cost of collection might consume the greater part of this, and decided to take advantage of the time provided by the existing leases, which did not expire until 30 April, 1806, "to weigh maturely the policy of literally obeying your present instructions."[15]

The mature judgement of Penang was apparently that it would be wise to do what London said, for by March 1806, not only had a wide range of import taxes been imposed, but also, the Company, as instructed, had abolished the farm and was taking steps to collect these taxes itself.

The farmer's duties were taken over by Mr. W. Phillips, the faithful ever healthy Company servant who first came to Penang as secretary to Leith in 1800. He had nine years of undistinguished base administration in the Company's army to his credit, as fort-adjutant to the military auditor-general's department at Fort William. He was to stay on and on in Penang, always acting for deceased or absent governors, but never confirmed in his post. His local knowledge constantly was acclaimed by newcomers who served briefly and died; but he was an Englishman, and in this Scottish enclave he never reached the top. It was typical that he was appointed to this thankless task, in addition to his hopeless undertaking as collector of land revenue.

Penang, however, was far from being an enthusiastic supporter of London's idea that revenue farms might well be abolished. In 1806 a tobacco farm and a salt farm were begun. Great hopes were held for the latter, a traditional mode of taxation. It was impossible however for the farmer to control the retailing of these commodities, both tobacco and salt being sailed into Penang in innumerable *prahus,* and both farms were abolished by 1808. By 1813 the government informed London that direct revenue management had been affected to the greatest possible extent, without going into details. Such details would have revealed that the farm system, apart from the export tax, was still in full operation. It had in fact been increased by the revival of the pork farm, the formation of a *toddy* and *bhang* farm (toddy and bhang being intoxicating beverages consumed by Indians) and — significant pointer to the uphill task of Phillips — an import duty farm.

The farming system had been judged by the men on the spot as the most effective way of securing a revenue, and it came back into favor as these men became fewer and fewer. With expenditure constantly exceeding the revenue, and the idea of the naval base obviously pigeonholed by the Admiralty, the Court of Directors in 1809 sent the first of the many dispatches to Penang instructing it "to adopt immediate measures for the reduction of the public expenditure in every branch of the service."[16] In the first instance, a councillor

[15]S. S. (F). R. Vol. B. 1. Penang to London, 12 November, 1805.

[16]S. S. (F). R. Vol. 180. London to Penang, 21 April, 1809.

was removed, leaving a governor with but two senior advisors. Some $3,000 per year was pruned from the Civil Department, $5,000 from the Judicial Department, and $1,000 from the Marine Department. Penang had been "deeply impressed with the indispensible necessity of a general reduction,"[17] and for a moment the savings in staff, and the complete abandonment of the naval dock, arsenal and other public works, satisfied London, but not for long.

In 1811 the British conquered Java, and the lifting of the restrictive practices of the Dutch encouraged many small traders to sail there, rather than northwards to Penang. The removal of the French-Dutch naval menace encouraged the East Indiamen sailing to Canton to avoid the Straits of Malacca and the call at Penang and to sail directly with better winds to the Sunda Straits and a quick entry to the South China Sea. Both these effects of the conquest of Java affected adversely the trade of Penang, while the revenue, which of course was linked closely to the island's trade, also was affected by London's decision to abolish the gambling farm, one of the greatest single units in the farm system. It was opposed also to the opium farm, but it gave Penang discretionary powers to abolish or retain it. Although the island hurriedly and in detail gave reasons why both should be retained, the gambling farm had to go, and although gambling was not eliminated, it was no longer controlled in any way after 1811, nor did the government derive any revenue from it. The result was clear. Revenue from the farms in 1811 was $150,000; it dropped to $85,000 the following year.

Bannerman, the governor, decided that this negative policy of pruning Penang was not sufficient. In 1816, the year the Dutch returned to Java and European ports were open again with the defeat of Napoleon, Penang's trade amounted to almost a million pounds sterling. Bannerman felt that Company participation in this trade, together with increased taxes on the commercial community, might close the gap between expenditure and revenue.

Bannerman pushed the Company at Penang into becoming an active trader in tin, the only time in its Southeast Asian existence when the Company emulated its seventeenth-century commercial role. This Company trade with the Malay States is dealt with elsewhere.[18] In addition to this however, Bannerman argued fiercely with London over the necessity to reintroduce the gambling farm. He fought a successful battle against its attempts to abolish the opium farm, and he endeavored to impose on Penang a variety of new taxes.

In some of Bannerman's suggestions, a stamp tax, for example, and a carriage licence, and a house registration, he was merely ahead of his time. Much of what he suggested was impracticable not merely through his shortage of staff, a score or so of administrators of all grades in a settlement that by 1816 had grown to 55,000, but because official contact with the multi-racial population of Penang was of necessity very slight, particularly with the Chinese. A

[17]S. S. (F). R. Vol. 180. Penang to London, 1 February, 1810.
[18]See Chapter 8.

committee was formed, led by Phillips, to study his suggestions. They were never introduced.

In 1819 a new settlement on Singapore was established. British trade in Southeast Asia, thus provided with another stable bazaar, developed considerably. It would appear as if this had a stimulating effect on Penang's trade, for it increased from a value of £900,000 to over one million in 1819, and to £1,200,000 by 1824. Yet during the same period the Company's revenue declined from $190,000 to $130,000. It is figures such as these that have led previous writers to infer that the foundation of Singapore had an adverse effect on the Penang settlement, whereas the revenue, of considerably less importance to the island as a whole than the trade which sustained it, declined largely through local factors.

Over half of this revenue came from the revenue farms. In 1819 they brought in $93,000, the import and export taxes brought in $92,000, and the total revenue (which included a few minor items), reached $190,000. But from 1820 onwards the farmers of the various farms reached an agreement with each other not to bid for what had become family properties. The Chinese farmers, clannish, secretive, particularly in business matters, lived lives and arranged their affairs with an administration almost completely ignorant of their activities. They provided their own peons or agents to see that their farming monopoly was maintained and relied hardly at all on the few police who existed on Penang. The police, perhaps the sole link between the administration and the Chinese farmers, were South Indians. As their numbers had been very considerably reduced after 1816, and as they consisted of men who had come to seek their own fortunes, they were grossly inefficient, collaborating to their own advantage with the farmer.

Fullerton, who assumed command in 1824, discovered that Georgetown had only twenty-four watchmen and twelve peons to police it; the rest of the island had merely twenty-four peons to keep order. The military detachment, usually from Madras, was also employed in police duties, but it too was of poor calibre, and it seems fortunate that Penang on the whole was a law-abiding place.

Fullerton also was perturbed at the lack of control exercised by the administration over the immigration of Chinese. He discovered that there was no check over their entry whatever. By the 1820's the *sinkheh,* the migrant from South China, had been discovered by Chinese merchants as a staple article of export, and every year they were sending down lumbering junks, crammed with this cargo. Some were unloaded in Singapore, others came up to Penang, there to be sold for twelve-months' labor at prices ranging from two to fifteen dollars. There was no official scrutiny of this flood.

Despite this lack of control and the paucity of his administration, Fullerton was able to satisfy himself as to the reasons why the revenue from the farms was declining when the population and trade were increasing. "The Opium and Arrack Farmers hold shares in each others Farm, and most if not all our

Monied Chinese capable of being competitors for farms are shareholders in them," he wrote.[19] The Chinese, instead of competing against one another for the monopoly of opium retailing, or of arrack selling, a competition that would have forced up the price to be paid to the government, agreed among themselves to permit one *towkay* or business man to tender low, while accepting a share in the subsequent increased profits.

A similar scheme to thwart the interests of the administration had been attempted in newly founded Singapore. Here Crawfurd, the Resident, had defeated the scheme by breaking the single monopoly into a number of small units, licences being auctioned to the highest. The more licences there were to sell opium, for example, the less chance there was of any possibility of combination. This had proved very successful, and Fullerton introduced the idea into Penang. In 1826 twelve licences were put up for auction, but each received such a low bid that the licences were called in and the administration reverted to the old single farm. The scheme had failed. Only subsequently was it discovered that the farmer himself had introduced his own system of licences, by sub-renting or sub-farming sections of his monopoly. A large number of retail shops had licences from the farmer with which they were perfectly content, and they had seen no reason to change.

One other local reason for the decline in revenue from the farms was the increase in smuggling by the Chinese, caused primarily by an intense rivalry between two south Chinese groups, the Hokkiens (who had migrated from Fukien, and who may have been the pioneer Chinese in Penang),[20] and the Cantonese. These two groups fought one another for control of the opium and arrack farms. The farms were in the possession of a group of Hokkien merchants, who controlled also the Kedah farms. In 1824, the Cantonese group managed to secure the arrack farm, and the rival parties attempted to destroy each other, not by open bidding when the farms were due for auction, but by secret and intensive smuggling, to break the farmer's profits. Both sides, naturally, appealed to the government for aid against the smuggling activities of their rivals, and their clamor led to the appointment in 1827 of a committee to enquire into the whole position of revenue raising and farming.[21]

This committee brought into the open the existence of the powerful Hysan secret society, led by Low Ah Chong, a Cantonese who had secured the arrack farm in 1824. This society controlled the minor Cantonese clubs, some eight in number, formed among the three thousand Cantonese on the island. In addition the society had strong links in Ligor and Perak. The Hokkien merchants gave evidence freely, endeavoring to implicate Low Ah Chong in the 1821 invasion of Kedah by Ligor, and the Rajah of Ligor's threat to invade Penang

[19]S. S. (F). R. Vol. A15. Penang to London. 3 September, 1825; encl. T. Cauntor to Governor, *Observations on the Opium Arrack, Toddy, and Bang and Seree Farms.*

[20]Purcell. *The Chinese in Southeast Asia.* p. 7. Wynne: *Triad and Tabut* p. 89 maintains that the Cantonese were.

[21]S. S. (F). R. Vol. A. 28. Penang to London, 25 October, 1826. *Report of the Committee of Revenue Farms.* 1826.

in 1824.[22] There was no need for them to refer to the smuggling, of which the police superintendent himself wrote, "The rival spirit of competition which exists between the Macao (Cantonese) and Chinchew (Hokkien) Classes will always be the cause of more or less illicit dealings in spirits and opium. Large quantities are now almost nightly brought across from Batu Kawan in the opposite shore. And the open nature of the Town, Harbour, and Adjacent shores will always be favorable to such proceedings."[23] With the staff at his disposal however, there was little he could do.

Although the Cantonese appear to have been the more numerous, and their secret society well organized, this struggle, which extended into Perak in 1828, ended in a Hokkien victory. Both the arrack and opium farms were secured by their leaders in 1829,—those that still survived that is, for secret society murders had eliminated several of the most prominent,—and although peace descended on Penang, the government derived little other benefit. In 1817 each of the farms had been let for $2,800 per month. By 1830 the opium farms had dropped to $2,100, while the arrack farm was a mere $1,400. Someone was doing well, but it was not the government.

The administration during these years had conserved or restricted its activities in most fields, but it had been called upon to establish officers, in a manner quite befitting its Presidency status, in its subsidiary territories. In 1821 a district magistrate was stationed permanently in Province Wellesley, following the flood of Malays that poured in after the Siamese invasion of Kedah. In 1830 he was provided with a minute police force all his own and a separate opium and arrack farm was instituted. Chinese began the cultivation of sugar, and the province became something more than a mangrove jungle with a scattering of Malay *kampongs* squatting on the *permatangs,* which were ridges of ancient beach raised a few feet above the swamp.

Penang also was called upon to supply an administrator to Malacca, captured from the Dutch in 1795 and brought into the Prince of Wales Island Residency in 1803. Briefly Penang had the remote and useless Balambangan Island within its charge, and participated in the abandonment of the naval base there in 1805. The Moluccas, annexed during the Napoleonic Wars, called for a Penang civil servant, and for a few years, following the successful war against Ava in 1826, Penang supplied a government officer for the administration of the ceded Tennasserim Province. Against this drain on its depleted staff, it acquired the civil servants from Bencoolen when that outpost was ceded to Holland by the Anglo-Dutch Treaty of 1824, but it never had enough staff to administer a direct revenue system itself (and would not have for a hundred years), even though the staff it possessed cost more to maintain than Penang alone could afford.

[22]S. S. (F). R. Vol. A. 18. Penang to London, 9 June, 1825. *The Statement of Che Soong, Che Toah, Beng and Keat, the Head Chinese Merchants in Georgetown, at the Recorders Chamber, 9 June 1825.*

[23]S. S. (F). R. Vol. A. 66. Penang Consultations. Report of Superintendent of Police, 27 June, 1829.

The administration lacked a bureaucracy, a trained and educated subordinate staff. It had been largely an appreciation of this that had induced Governor Petrie to support the suggestion in 1815 of the Rev. Robert Hutchings, newly appointed chaplain to the island, that a free school should be established for "the training of a race of intelligent and honest servants for the Government."[24] Petrie appointed a committee to consider the project, an appeal for funds raised $6,000, the government promised a small monthly subsidy, and the first school of Malaya, other than schools for Muslim religious teaching, opened with twenty-six boys in a rented house in Love Lane on 21 October, 1816. Its one and only teacher, Mr. Cox, the government printer, was able in 1817 to secure a government grant of some unoccupied land near where the Anglican Church was being built. Both school and church rose up that year, both to struggle for funds from a heartless Court, both nevertheless to survive and flourish to this very day.

The Penang Free School as it came to be called, offered its lessons in English, taught reading, writing and arithmetic, all highly commendable courses for a prospective civil servant. The government kept a close eye on it. The examinations were conducted by the resident councillor, and the affairs of the school and its property remained the responsibility of the administration until 1866. By 1830 over one hundred boys were being educated there, and a thin trickle of graduates was moving into government offices.

Another trickle was moving, by the 1830's, from another educational institution, this one founded by the Roman Catholics. There had been a community of Roman Catholics on Penang since 1786, when a French padre named Garnault had moved across from Kedah with his flock. Light had given him "a spot in the woods about 400 yards from the fort"[25] for his church, while subsequent migrations of Eurasians from P'huket (Junk Ceylon) had added to the faith. In 1824 Father Boucho arrived to take charge of the mission and church. He found Roman Catholic boys being educated at the Free School, and took immediate steps to form an English school under his supervision. This opened in January, 1826, and received a small annual government grant after periodic inspections. For his exertions, Father Boucho was created a Bishop in 1846, while his small school, transferred to more spacious grounds, in 1857 became St. Xavier's Institution, the name by which it is known to this day.

These sources of supply were hopelessly inadequate to fill government personnel needs. No attempt at abolishing the farm system was made. The 1827 committee recommended the continuance of the system, despite its low yield, as the only possible way by which the administration could secure a sufficient revenue. Down south Singapore was leaping ahead, and after anxious discussions, Penang in 1827 suspended a few of its duties, notably those on the re-

[24]S. S. (F). R. Vol. 181. Penang to London, 8 July, 1816.
[25]S. S. (F). R. Vol. 2. Penang to Bengal, 12 September, 1786.

export of goods from the east, in the hope of attracting or maintaining the trade from the islands which by that date was converging on Singapore. In 1826 Fullerton in his search for revenue re-imposed the duties. There was an immediate outcry from the merchants, and he was unable to hold his position. The growth of free-port Singapore and the recommendations of London combined to change Fullerton's attitude. In November, 1826, Penang abolished all its import and export taxes, and the administration was thus forced back to its revenue farms as almost the sole source of revenue.

In the previous year, 1825, the Court of Directors had taken the logical steps (once Singapore's retention and Malacca's cession were assured by the Anglo-Dutch Treaty of 1824), of instructing Fullerton to take superior authority over Singapore and Malacca, and of creating a Straits Settlements Presidency effective from August 1, 1826. At the same time the number of civil servants under the President again was reduced, from fifteen to nine in Penang, and nine others elsewhere: three at Singapore, two at Malacca, and four supernumeraries. Also at this time, the total value of the trade of Penang stood at £1,100,000; Singapore with amazing growth had a trade valued at £2,600,000; while Malacca contributed its mote of £300,000; all in all £4,000,000. Yet it was impossible with the means at hand to secure a revenue from this, and in India, immensely more wealthy, the Company faced the same difficulty. It wrote from Calcutta of a tremendous deficit of two Crores (20 million rupees) and went on to say that "the attention of every one connected with the administration of this branch of affairs must be directed to the means of retrenching expenditure and increasing Income . . . we beg to express a hope that no means will be omitted of reducing the Expenditure of the Settlements under your control, so as to diminish the drain they occasion upon the resources of India."[26]

The hope was not fulfilled, and the warning not heeded. Early in 1829 the governor-general himself, Lord Bentinck, arrived at Penang. He was fully aware of the fact that the Company's position in the China trade was being undermined, and that it was maintaining the Straits Settlements for the benefit of the nation. Financially he was more interested in India than in the Chinese, Indian, Malay and European traders who were flocking to these ports, and his decision to reduce the costs of an administration which benefited India scarcely at all was sound.

His views, previously communicated to London, were paraphrased and returned to Penang. "When it was determined many years since to constitute Prince of Wales Island a separate Presidency it was in contemplation not only to form that Island into a Marine Station for the rendezvous, refitting and supply of His Majesty's Squadrons in the Eastern Seas, but also to make it a Naval Arsenal for the building of ships for the Royal Navy. These objects may now be considered as abandoned, and with regard to Political or Commer-

[26]S. S. (F). R. Vol. A. 32. Bengal to Penang, 12 July, 1827.

cial benefits resulting either to Great Britain or to India from the tenure by us of Prince of Wales Island, Singapore and Malacca, We consider that these benefits may be effectively secured by an administration of the Settlements upon a very reduced scale. . .[27]

Upon a very reduced scale indeed. The Presidency was abolished, and the three settlements were constituted on 1 May, 1830 as a single Residency, a unit under the Presidency of Fort William. Fullerton suggested that Malacca be made the headquarters, but Penang was retained until 1832, when the capital was moved to Singapore, which had long outstripped it. The administration was cut to the bone. Under a Resident there were Resident Councillors (entitled assistant residents until 1832), at the three settlements, in Singapore two other officers, in Penang and Malacca one other, and an additional assistant for Province Wellesley; in all, nine officers who were called on to administer all the British territory east of India.

[27]S. S. (F). R. Vol. C. 6. London to Penang, 7 April, 1829.

VI

PENANG AND KEDAH

During the conversations between Monckton and the Sultan of Kedah in 1772, and between Francis Light and the new ruler, son of the Sultan, in 1786, the reason constantly advanced by Kedah for a British establishment near by was the threat to the safety of the state by the Bugis-dominated Sultanate of Selangor. Siam to the north was mentioned once only, not in 1786, but in 1772, by the Sultan of Kedah, after Monckton had declared that as he could not act contrary to instructions he could not move aggressively against Selangor, and so would return to Calcutta. The Sultan agreed that there was no point in Monckton's remaining, and said that anyway, as Siam had forbidden any European to settle in his — the Sultan's — territory, it would be best if Monckton sailed. It was said, one feels, as an afterthought. It does not ring true. Possibly by referring to Siamese authority, and pretending that he was bound to it, the Sultan of Kedah may have been endeavoring to save Monckton's face. Had Monckton been more skillful as a negotiator, it is doubtful if Siam would ever have been mentioned.

Certainly Siam was not referred to in the subsequent discussions involving Light. In 1786 the Sultan of Kedah was content with far less than his father had asked for in 1772. Then the Sultan had insisted upon an attack on the Selangorese who had driven him in flight to Perlis. By 1786 the son was back in Alor Star, and he offered to cede Penang to the Company on six conditions. These were, first, that the Company would guard the seas, and whatever enemy came to attack Kedah would be an enemy of the Company's as well, and the expense of repulsing him would be borne by the Company. Second, that no vessel bound for any Kedah port would be stopped or hindered by the Company. Third, that the Company would pay the Sultan $30,000 per annum in respect of the former profit from his monopoly of tin, opium and rattans at the mouths of the rivers nearest to Penang, the Muda, the Prai, and the Krian. Fourth, that the Sultan not be held responsible for the debts of any of his relatives if they should borrow from the Company. Fifth, that any enemy of the Sultan of Kedah was an enemy of the Company's, and the Company would not protect the enemy. And finally, that should any enemy attack by land, the Company would supply assistance. This last clause possibly may refer to

Siam, but apart from that, there is no sign that it was feared at all. In the early months of 1786, the danger to Kedah came from Ava (whose latest southward lunge had been blunted at P'huket only that January), and in particular from Selangor; not, it would appear, from Siam. It seems incorrect to state then, as several historians have done,[1] that Penang was ceded to the British because Kedah feared Siam. That came later.

These conditions of course were the maximum bargaining points put forward by an impoverished and petty ruler. He could not possibly have hoped to secure all this for his virtually uninhabited and (to him) quite useless island. Nor did he. To his first condition, the Company replied that it would always keep an armed vessel stationed to guard the island coast of Penang. The second condition was accepted, vessels being permitted to trade with Kedah or with Penang of their own free will. The request for $30,000 was avoided, and the Sultan merely was informed that he would not be a sufferer from an English settlement on Penang. The fourth condition was accepted, as was the fifth; but the sixth, whereby the Sultan asked for assistance to repel his enemies on land, was referred (and the Sultan was so informed), to London.

The Sultan of Kedah had made clear that it was not necessary for there to be fulfillment or even acceptance of all these conditions before a settlement could take place. He granted permission in his letter to the Company to erect its flag and to send people to take possession prior to and independent of the statement of conditions, and on the same day as a letter was drafted to Kedah, it was resolved by Calcutta that a detachment be made ready and that Light lead the expedition. This was an untidy beginning, a new settlement being pushed out by acting officials between the departure of one governor-general (Hastings, who had left in 1785), and the arrival of the next (Cornwallis, who came in 1786), and with the terms of occupation not completed with Kedah. From the outset, the nature of this beginning bedevilled Light and his successors, and the establishment and maintenance of amicable relations with Kedah became their chief political problem, particularly as Kedah grew to resent the growth of the island, and as by August 1786, it had become aware, suddenly and disturbingly, of the new Siam.

"I must proceed to give your Honourable Board an account of the great change which has happened," wrote Light in September, and he then describes the new Siam that counterattacked successfully after the 1785-86 invasion by Ava. "The brother to the King (of Siam) came to Ligor with a small army and had no sooner put to death the 2,000 Burmers left there than he resolved to call to account all the neighbouring states who had not given the Siamese aid. He sent for the chiefs of Pattangi (Patani) and the Kings of Tringano and Queda." But all sent gifts and excuses, and kept away.[2]

[1] D. G. E. Hall, p. 434. F. Swettenham, *British Malaya* (London, 1955) pp. 39-41; R. Winstedt, *Malaya and its History*, (London, 1946) pp. 53, 54. C. D. Cowan. *Nineteenth Century Malaya. The Origins of British Political Control* (London, 1961). p. 10.

[2] S. S. (F). R. Vol. 2. Light to Bengal, 12 September, 1786. (see also Light's Diary, 30 June, 1786, in same volume).

Well might Kedah keep clear, and feel suddenly alarmed. Light explains its position:

It does not appear either by writing or by tradition that Quedah was ever governed by Siamese laws or customs. There would have been some remaining had there been any affinity between them. The people of Quedah are Mahomedans; their letter arabic and their language Java; their Kings originate from Minacabo in Sumatra. But as Quedah was very near Ligore, a Kingdom of Siam, they sent every three years a gold and silver tree as a token of homage to Ligore. This was done to preserve a good correspondence, for at this period the Siamese were very rich and numerous, but no warriors, and a considerable trade was carried on between Ligore and Quedah.

After the destruction of Siam, the King of Ava demanded the token of homage from Quedah, and received the gold and silver tree. When Pea Tack drove away the Burmese and built a new city in Siam the King of Quedah sent the tree to Siam; and has kept peace with both, paying homage sometimes to one and sometimes to the other and often to both. Last year, impressed by the might of the Burmese, and expecting that Siam would be destroyed again, he sent arms and ammunition to Ava. This the Siamese have discovered, and are angry. The Siamese general is exterpating Pattangi; all the men, and women and children are bound and trampled upon by elephants, and the King of Quedah might sacrifice Penang, if it would appease Siam, and save him.[3]

The panic created by the successful movement south of Siam persisted until December, on both sides of the Malay Peninsula. "I have received repeated solicitations from the King of Quedah to come and consult with him respecting the Siamese," said Light, and "the King of Tringano has written for Captain Glass to come and assist him, as he too expected a Siamese invasion."[4] Light had heard in October, however, that the Siamese had retired from Ligor, and the scare slowly subsided.

Early in the new year, Light received the considered reply of the Company to the deferred condition, wherein the Sultan of Kedah asked for armed assistance to protect him from his interior foes. It was an answer in keeping with the 1784 India Act, and the eighteenth-century outlook that still considered territorial possessions secondary to commercial profits. The Company had no desire to intervene in the Malay Peninsula, it had no rights or interests there to defend, nor could it discover any justification for the pledging of British capital and lives. The January dispatch read:

The King of Quedah, although entitled to a pecuniary consideration for his grant of the island, which we have no objection to you discharging by instalments, must not expect that our government will enter into or become a party in his disputes with other Malay Princes, nor could our protection be effectively afforded him without involving us in disputes with the Burmers and Siamese, the latter of whom are at present the most powerful, while the former might do great injury to the English trade at Pegu.

We think it most prudent to refuse assistance to either party; indeed the security of the island should be your sole object, and to this all your military operations must be confined. We therefore direct that refraining from assisting either party you endeavour to

[3]S. S. (F). R. Vol. 2. Light to Sir John Macpherson. 12 September, 1786.

[4]S. S. (F). R. Vol. 2. Light to Bengal, 25 November, 1786.

acquire the respect and secure the goodwill of all as far as possible. This we conceive may be easily obtained by a proper and guarded conduct.[5]

This conception of the Company, that Light could win friends and influence people by promising them nothing, soon was shown to be false. The British decision, that it did not intend to guard the passes leading to Ligor and Siam, and that Kedah must defend its frontiers itself, could not have been unexpected; nevertheless it was unwelcome. So too was the lack of a financial settlement. In August of the previous year (1786) the Laxsamana, the Sultan's second great officer of state, had asked if the Company intended to pay $30,000 per annum, and if not, how much? The King himself had intimated that possibly he might be interested in less, but six months later, no payment whatever had been promised or made, while Bengal officialdom confused the issue, and the Sultan became restive. As the Siamese soldiery vanished, the Sultan felt free to turn on his erstwhile friends, and to extract what profit he could from the settlement he had been so anxious that they establish.

Beginning in May 1787, the Sultan of Kedah managed — sometimes for weeks at a time — to stop the export of rice and other provisions to Penang from the Kedah rivers. Light urged on Bengal the need to arrive at an amicable settlement with the Sultan, and in 1788, he was authorized to conclude an agreement not exceeding $10,000 per annum, for seven to ten years. He was warned not to enter into "any acts or promise which may be construed into any obligation to defend the King of Quedah," and was advised (Cornwallis now being on the scene), that the governor-general was "against any measures that may involve the Company in military operations against any of the Eastern princes."[6] To assist him in his haggling, Cornwallis sent him, as gifts to the Sultan, a pair of pistols, another of blunderbusses, a spying and a looking glass, and a few other trinkets. They availed Light nothing.

Light began negotiations with the Sultan, whom he describes as "a weak man too fond of money, very lax in the execution of the laws, not so much from a principle of clemency as timidity. His income consists in monopolising all the trade and the produce of the mines. He receives likewise a great deal in presents, and fines every person who has any demand to make or suit to prefer who first presents a sum of money which he thinks inadequate to the demand. If the King approves the demand he signs the paper and his suit is obtained, unless another person comes with a greater sum."[7]

The negotiations failed. The Sultan and his officers declined the offer of Light to pay $10,000 for eight years. Light, experienced man in these waters, had estimated that the Sultan's friendship was worth $10,000 and had so advised the Company. The Sultan and his advisers, however, were apparently

[5]S. S. (F). R. Vol. 2. Bengal to Light, 22 January, 1787.

[6]S. S. (F). R. Vol. 2. Bengal to Light, 25 June, 1788.

[7]S. S. (F). R. Vol. 2. Light to Macpherson, 12 September, 1786.

so convinced of their greater worth that when Light made a subsequent offer, of $4,000 per annum for as long as the Company remained in possession of the island, they contemptuously ignored it and no answer was made.

Who were these advisers? Light mentions five of them.

The Bendahara is the first officer. He has charge of all the King's vassals, has a large portion of land and a certain number of Riotts [villagers] to maintain his state. He is the general of the army in time of war. He is of an ancient family and although he is of a weak understanding and very indeterminate in his actions, yet the King does not remove him. *The Laxamana* is the Admiral, and the King's brother-in-law. He governs all the islands, and the *Qualla,* river mouth and has charge of the coast. He has a great number of dependents, and is more powerful than the *Bendahara,* as he has more resolution and is more steady in his attachments. Tuanka China is an old fox. He has little to do with the government, but being rich, and having married a daughter of the old King, he bears a considerable sway in their Becharas or Council. *Datoo Sree Raja*[8] (formerly named Jammaul and a common cooly) is now the King's merchant. He is a deep, cunning and villainous Chooliah. By working upon the King's pusillanimity and raising jealousies he reduced the power of the great men and engrossed the whole of the administration.... He built a small brick port and shut him (the sultan) up as in a cage. No one durst presume to get audience without his knowledge.... By monopolising every species of commerce and oppressing the people he found means to supply the King's necessities without his having the trouble to enquire how it came.

Light goes on to mention various acts of tyranny and piracy committed by the Dato, which made him so hated that "he eagerly listened to the proposal I made for giving this island to the English, in hopes to secure a retreat for himself." He may have been villainous then, but Light was not revolted by it; he took men as they came. Finally there was Tungku Jea. "Toonkoo Jea is nearly related to the King as to be an object of jealousy. He is wise enough to keep himself free from suspicion by professing a particular regard for the King and avoiding all kinds of official greatness. He is a man of some honour and integrity and very grateful. He advise me to strengthen myself as far as I can and trust to none of them."[9]

Of these six advisers, power rested, it would seem, with the Dato and the *Laxsamana.* Both were affected by the settlement on Penang, to a certain extent adversely. Although the purchases of food by Georgetown brought some new wealth to the rivers, the ships and *prahus* stopped coming to Kedah, and commerce and trade deserted it for the safety and shelter of Penang. By 1788 no doubt this already was apparent, for those with authority in Kedah looked on the island with disfavor, and following the collapse in the financial discussions, the two steadily moved apart.

Dislike and jealousy often are expressed in rather violent ways. During 1789 the Sultan endeavored to secure other European support. He wrote to the French at Pondicherry and to the Dutch at Batavia and Malacca. He was

[8]The modern spelling would be *Dato Sri Rajah.*
[9]S. S. (F). R. Vol. 2. Light to Sir John Macpherson, 12 Sept., 1786.

disappointed here, for although the Dutch sent a cruiser to Kedah, two more
anchored in Penang harbor and saw for themselves the British position, and
thus no offer of support was made. The Sultan then turned to less respectable
allies "the Langoons, . . . the same nation that attacked and plundered
Balambangan."[10]

This is not quite accurate, as Balambangan was overrun largely by Suluks,
gentlemen from the Sulu Archipelago, while the Lanuns hail from the southern
Philippines. But the two are very similar, and, with the Balingini from the
same area are often broadly classed as Moros. The Lanuns excelled at piracy.
While this regional activity was practised by nearly all of Southeast Asia in a
local and intermittent way, the Lanuns brought to piracy an organization and
intensity that made them feared throughout the entire area.

From their bases on Mindanao, the Lanuns each year sent out large fleets
on organized cruises. The fleets were divided into squadrons, the squadrons
into units, and each *prahu* was a disciplined fighting force. They ranged widely,
utilizing the monsoons, circumnavigating Borneo, ravaging the Java Sea, and
venturing wherever trading posts or centers of population offered prospects of
loot or slaves. With the development of Rhio by the Bugis, this became a
favorite haunt of Lanun pirates, and they cruised off both coasts of the Malay
peninsula as well. They were attracted northwards up the Straits of Malacca to
the newly formed Penang, as bees are to sources of honey, and from 1788
onwards, as their long powerful *prahus* ghosted over the shallow mud flats and
disappeared behind the mangrove of the Kedah rivers that faced the bustling
port, the presence of Lanun pirates was apprehensively recorded in the official
dispatches.

In 1790 the regular yearly Lanun visit took on a more formidable appearance.
Skirmishing with the Dutch off Malacca and then at the small fort at Perak,
and raiding the Malay coastline as they came, a substantial Lanun fleet moved
that year up the Straits of Malacca. In October they had been raiding Perak;
in November they were south of Penang; eight slaves had been seized on the
mainland opposite, and the apprehensive Indian merchants had loaded a considerable amount of their stores back on to vessels returning to India. Light,
hearing that the Lanun fleet was lurking at Pulo Kra, a small island some
eight miles south of Penang, sent there his entire naval force—three small
cruisers and two long boats. It was quite ineffective.

The Lanuns were found at dawn on November 29, eighteen long *prahus*
armed with guns, and drawn up in line. In the rear were grouped some thirty
smaller *prahus,* containing in all over one thousand men. The three Penang
cruisers could reach no closer than 600 yards from the *prahus* as they were
anchored over shallows, close to shore, and it was useless to attempt firing as
they were well out of range. Lack of wind made it difficult for the frigates to

[10]S. S. (F). R. Vol. 2. Light to Bengal, 22 December, 1790.

move. On seeing their difficulty, the Lanuns sent a flag of truce over to the becalmed frigates, saying they were friendly traders, and wished merely to pass through the harbor to visit their friends in Kedah, rather than sail round outside the island; a much longer journey. They were told by Captain Lorrain, the squadron commander, to depart at once; and a breeze springing up from the land they did depart, moving up the coast over the shallows to Kedah.

Early in December, shortly after this alarming incident, Light heard from a reliable source that the Sultan of Kedah had thrown in his lot with the Lanuns. This made the situation serious in the extreme, and events now moved towards a climax. Light had reprimanded Lorrain for his weakness, and he now sent all his cruisers to the north to attack them. They came up with the Lanuns off the Kedah river and endeavored to attack.

The short range of Penang guns and the shallowness of the water resulted in little impression being made, and the Lanuns entered the rivers to prepare with the Sultan for an attack on Penang.

In Calcutta this development was taken seriously. It was decided to reinforce Penang with two companies of native infantry and to dispatch to Light ten eighteen-pound guns for the defence of the port. At the same time Cornwallis sent news to his brother, the commander-in-chief of the East Indies station, then sheltering out the winter in the Andamans, of the alarming situation east of him. One of the Company's own fleet, a small unit of the Bombay Marine, armed with six-pounders, also was ordered to proceed to Penang.

There was need for anxiety, as Penang was very weakly defended indeed, only slightly better than Balambangan had been fifteen years before. Under Light's charge were merely two weak companies of Sepoys, commanded by Captain Glass. For the defence of Georgetown and the harbor, these two companies under the direction of their officers, Lieutenants Fireworkers Rabau and Murray, had built a small wooden fort at the northern point of the island. In 1786, when the fort was first built, it had brushed aside the jungle in a highly successful way. But these wooden forts do not last long in a climate where over one hundred inches of rain falls each year, where the sun blazes down every day, and where high humidity attacks every form of construction. Tropical growth is rapid; so too is tropical destruction, and in the same letter of October, 1790 in which Light first refers to the movement north of a large condottieri of *prahus,* he said the fort was rotted, that whole faces were falling down, that bastions were crumbling, with guns salted and useless, and that Glass was shrinking the square into a triangle. By the time the Lanuns were sighted, the fort was almost useless.

In February, Cornwallis and his squadron arrived. In March, Penang learned that the Sultan of Kedah had appointed the Tungku Muda, his brother-in-law, his new son-in-law, Rading Mahomed, and the Laxsamana to command his forces, authorizing the three either to negotiate or to attack, as they thought proper. With Cornwallis in port, they chose to negotiate. Light decided to accommodate them, for as he told Bengal, the principal merchants from the Malabar coast had fled back there, a number of Georgetown inhabitants likewise had fled, the stock of cattle on the island had been consumed, and no more was forthcoming from Kedah. The traders from Sumatra (those that still ventured in), were surprised that nothing had been done, and all felt that when Commodore Cornwallis sailed the attack would come.

Captain Scott, therefore, was sent to Kedah with terms. He met the Laxsamana at Qualla Muda, the mouth of a river winding through its delta of swamp and jungle to the sea—a place where man has lived on raised ridges of beach since prehistoric times; and there they agreed that all hostilities should cease and that Kedah would send the Lanuns away. Scott promised an immediate payment of $10,000 and guaranteed that the old suggestion, of an annual $10,000 payment, would be referred at once to India. Light, reporting this, urged on Calcutta an immediate reply. It came too late.

Scott had secured a slackening of the tension, and Cornwallis took off his fleet for Madras. It sailed on 15 March. On the nineteenth, the Lanuns quitted their north Kedah rivers and came down to Prai, the Kedah river immediately opposite defenseless Georgetown. The next day they were joined by the Kedah force, over ninety Malay prahus sailing past the fort in the clear light of noon, and by the twenty-second, stockades and forts on Prai Point were clearly visible, less than three miles away. By the twenty-third the merchant ships had all quitted the harbor except one gallant East Indiaman, the stately *Bombay Castle*. The trading *prahus* had hurried away as fast as they could, and the water between Penang and the mainland, usually dotted with all types of vessels, anchored or coming and going, was empty. The two protagonists stood face to face, and it seemed impossible that Penang would not be overwhelmed and Georgetown looted of all it contained. But Light struck first.

Light's description, in matter-of-fact terms, of the attack on Prai almost hides from us the level of the achievement. Glass embarked his men, concentrating the whole force in this one thrust, in the early morning darkness of 12 April. Here was to be executed a combined operation upon an enemy shore. Strong currents and tides lay between him and Prai, and the three companies of Sepoys had to cross in darkness to land at one particular spot. If they were discovered at sea, in unwieldy ships' boats, or if they landed in the morass of mangrove and not on Prai Point, or if the naval support force failed to cooperate, they would be in an untenable position. Yet all went well.

They embarked, they crossed, they landed at the right spot, all unobserved. They then formed up and "surprised at dawn of day the fort upon the point, dispersing with little loss the large force that had been collected for its defence; then proceeding to the second, where the enemy made some show of resistance. But the Sepoys having mounted the ramparts, we soon put them to flight. Both these forts were immediately burnt." Then came the navy.

"The gunboats advanced to the attack of the fleet of prahus, amounting at least to 200, under the command of Lt. Rabau at day light, and for a considerable space of time bore heavy fire upon the whole fleet. At length the vessels which were retarded through lack of wind were towed in, and the enemy's fire silenced by noon. . . ."[11]

Many of the *prahus* had fled up the winding Prai River, to hide from Rabau, who followed five miles until the ebb became too powerful, in mangrove-concealed sidewaters. The *prahus* re-appeared on the fourteenth, two days later, in great numbers. They were attacked again, Rabau having mounted an eighteen-pounder on a large shallow punt, and this time considerable loss was inflicted, and they were flushed from their hole. They fled south, and with the loss of four men (three Sepoys and one Company slave), some 10,000 Malays and Lanuns, with 250 armed *prahus*, had been dispersed.

Light, having disposed of the military threat, turned at once towards a political settlement. Bengal had written, giving him authority to institute an annual payment of $10,000, and to include the arrears due the Sultan since 1786.

The Sultan's emissaries came to Penang in April 1791, and demanded again that, in any treaty between the two, the old condition that the Company should give assistance if attacked by land must be included. Light came back with a counterproposal that at once killed the issue. "As this had long been a subject of importunity from the Raja, and appeared the only obstacle which prevented a settlement with the Company before, I represented that the Company would of course demand an equivalent, that the districts of Qualla Mooda, Prai and Crean, including a space of 600 square miles and being contiguous to Penang, would hardly compensate. His Vakeels[12] said they had no authority for this. I said I had none for their suggestion. No further demands for protection were made, and an agreement was concluded" on May 1.[13]

This was a nine-point treaty. Two clauses only were important. The cession money was fixed at $6,000 per annum. This was $4,000 less than that offered before the April attack, but the Sultan, having failed ignominiously, could expect no more, and in all probability was surprised to receive as much. The second clause explains why. Provisions for Penang were to sail from Kedah without let or hindrance. Penang depended on Kedah for its sustenance, indeed it still does, and the queues of trucks that wait today at the ferry where the pirates' fort once stood are merely the twentieth-century equivalent of the *prahus, sampans,* and *tongkangs* that once again, with the signing of the 1791 treaty, pushed out from the rivers of Kedah and crossed to the market at Georgetown. Seven minor clauses stipulated that both parties would exchange

[11]S. S. (F). R. Vol. 4. Light to Bengal, 19 April, 1791.
[12]Ambassadors, or Representatives.
[13]S. S. (F). R. Vol. 4. Light to Bengal, 30 May, 1791.

and return runaway slaves, debtors, forgers, and murderers, while neither would shelter criminals, and Kedah would not permit any Europeans, other than those from Great Britain, to settle on its territory. On this basis the two states settled down.

Penang had one great attraction for the Chinese middlemen, the Malay padi planters, and the Indian cattle herders of Kedah. It paid in Spanish dollars for that which it acquired. Yet between producer and consumer was an uncertain link, and this supply of dollars remained precarious. So too did the safety of Penang harbor, as long as the coastline opposite remained uncontrolled. In 1796 among the recommendations to the government from a committee of Georgetown merchants (formed by MacDonald, Light's successor), was the suggestion "that a portion of the opposite coast be obtained from Quedah so as to secure the sovereignty of the port."[14] Their reason for acquisition was to prevent merchants from depositing their goods on the other side of the harbor, near Prai, and so avoiding the Penang taxes on imports and exports.

Arthur Wesley, later Sir Arthur Wellesley, and still later Duke of Wellington, who paused in Penang in 1797, may have been thinking of this same difficulty in tax collecting when he recommended that Georgetown again become a free port; surprisingly, in his long memorandum sent to India Wesley made no reference whatever to the imperfect and inadequate defense that was afforded the port, by the retention of what was, in effect, only one arm of its harbor. Prai, with its constant lurking bands of pirates, Pulo Kra, a little south, with its *prahus* drawn deep under mangrove, waiting for the breeze to drop or darkness to fall, and slavers so audacious that ship's boats plying to the jetty were cut out and kidnapped; all this received no mention in the dispatch of a brilliant soldier who for once was unappreciative of the defensive problem.

It was the problem of pirates as much as the need for food that induced the Supreme Government to instruct Leith, the new Lieutenant Governor in 1800, to obtain if possible a tract of land on the coast opposite the port. Leith attended to this at once. On arrival at Penang a young officer, Cauntor, was dispatched to Kedah charged with the acquisition of such a tract of territory. He found the Sultan at Perlis, and quickly discovered that power rested with the Sultan's confidential servant, Inche (Mr) Ibrahim. Ibrahim thought that the matter could be arranged; the Sultan was not averse to luring the British on to the mainland and the coastal strip by Prai was nothing but marsh and mangrove. An opposition arose from various ministers, who felt that their rights in this matter were in danger of being neglected, and Cauntor was in something of a dilemma, seeking for compromise amid a welter of procrastination and subterfuge. Subtly it was conveyed to him that a present or two might weaken or even withdraw the opposition, and this was proved correct.

[14]*Logan's Journal.* Vol. V. (1851). p. 99. Penang to Bengal, July, 10, 1796.

By promising $2,000 to the Sultan's ministers and harem, every obstacle was removed, and the coast opposite Penang was ceded to the Company.

For an annual payment of $4,000, the Sultan ceded a strip three miles deep, from the Muda River in the north to the Krian twenty miles south. It was taken possession of formally on 7 July 1800, and named Province Wellesley, after the governor-general in India, elder brother to Wellington. It was largely uninhabited as coastlines in the Malay Peninsula always were, through fear of slavers and pirates, and although it reduced the piratical menace, it was far too thin and marshy for any food production. For this, Penang, as before, relied on Kedah, and it was not until the 1840's that sugar and padi replaced the elephants, crocodiles, and tigers that previously claimed nearly all of the Province as their own.

For a decade or more, in this narrow field, all went well. Elsewhere developments of some significance occurred. Kedah was so placed, by the flank of the Southeast Asia mainland, that it was involved to a varying degree in any quarrel between its two northern neighbors, Ava and Bangkok. Between 1786, when the British acquired Penang, and 1800, when Kedah ceded Province Wellesley, neither of the two powers had worried it particularly, and it had been left to a considerable extent alone. Then conditions began to change.

Ava, although somewhat weaker than in its great eighteenth-century days, was still extremely aggressive. In 1809 it raided P'huket again, capturing the island in August; the fleet moved south towards Kedah, but was defeated at sea, and retired. A larger force came south in October 1809, capturing the Siamese ports on the Kra Peninsula and finally devastating P'huket after a four-week siege. Siamese gestures induced them to retreat, but yet again they returned, 1811-1812; Siamese force this time, which included *prahus* from Kedah, was too threatening, and they returned to Ava. Never again has Burma attempted to invade the Malay Peninsula since that date.

Siam watched these aggressive moves with slackening apprehension. It was becoming each year a more powerful state, recovering from utter defeat by its traditional enemy in 1767.[15] From early in the nineteenth century, it addressed itself to the task of checking Ava, utilizing in the process those of its former client kingdoms over which it could re-establish control. Thus, willy nilly, Kedah was dragged into the affairs of the great, with Penang bobbing awkwardly and rather ineffectively behind.

With Bangkok visibly growing, Kedah resorted, as a matter of course, to the diplomatic behavior that had secured for it *de facto* independence in the past. Siam had been content with the triennial *bunga 'mas,* and the occasional levy of food or fighting men for some pillaging to the north. Neither through Ligor nor directly had it attempted more than this nominal control; so Kedah sent a fleet to help stop the Burmese in 1811, and regularly the *bunga 'mas* went over-

[15]For a detailed description of Siam at this time, see W. F. Vella, *Siam Under Rama III, 1824-1851.* (N. Y. 1957). This study makes frequent use of Siamese source material.

land. But this time to no avail, for Siam was moving into its greatest expansionist period, and in its attempts to establish direct and effective control in all areas from whence nominal tribute previously had sufficed, Kedah was to be one of the most unfortunate of victims.

Even if history and character had not dictated it, Kedah's suppliant attitude was forced on it by its weak, divided, and isolated state. In 1799 Sultan Abdullah had died, and after the usual family intrigue (for no satisfactory trouble-free method of political inheritance was ever evolved by the Malays, and the death of a ruler from A.D. 1400 to 1900 was invariably followed by dispute and dissension), the throne was seized by Sultan Heaudin. The fact that he was residing at Perlis, when Cauntor visited him in 1800, and not at the capital, Alor Star, is indicative that the struggle for power had not ended. In 1804 Heaudin weakly obeyed a Siamese order that he abdicate. His nephew, Sultan Ahmad, who had been to Bangkok and who had been invested with a Siamese title there, was installed in his place.

Although this pleased Siam, the eight brothers of Ahmad continued the intrigue, and the country was divided and disturbed. As a natural consequence, Penang was adversely affected. The disputes for power constantly interrupted the supply of food from the Kedah rivers, and despite the instructions given to the new government in 1805, when Penang became a Presidency, that "you are on no account to aim at an extension of territory or take any part in political affairs,"[16] it was suggested to the Supreme Government in India that either Ahmad should be given such powerful support that the opposition to him would collapse, or alternatively that the Company should purchase from him a large addition to Province Wellesley, both north up the coast to the Merbok River and inland to the central mountain ranges. In addition, Penang urged on India the need to open friendly relations with Siam direct.

All this counsel was rejected. The arguments were repeated in 1808, but India maintained its policy. It was not interested in acquiring more territory, particularly when Penang, which was proving a financial liability, was in no way threatened.

There were no considerations whatever, political or commercial, that could be advanced as valid reasons why Britain should participate in the affairs of the peninsula. Penang had managed to exist for over twenty years without the necessity of annexing Kedah, and its trade with the state would scarcely have increased appreciably if this was undertaken, while politically it would be most unwise to acquire a large primitive territory where the costs of administration could not be recovered. Anything short of annexation would merely embroil the Company in local disputes of never-ending character. The Company was not interested in spreading British peace and order to little known areas, but merely in profitable trade. Wisely, the Sultan was left to face the realities alone.

[16]S. S. (F). R. Vol. 9. Bengal to Penang, 18 April, 1805.

He faced them alone, for he was disliked by his neighbors to the south as much as by his erstwhile overlords to the north. Despite a common tongue and a general community of interest, the states of the Malay Peninsula were as hopelessly divided as the Greek states before Macedonia. Yet Siamese intentions were becoming clearer each year as its "policy of maximising and expanding control in the Malay Peninsula"[17] was implemented. In 1818, Kedah not only acquiesced in this policy but actively assisted its development and so lost all hope of Malay assistance.

The pressure on Kedah to participate as a lackey for Siam had been exerted since 1813. Bangkok ordered Kedah, in August of that year, to invade Perak and to insist on the dispatch to Siam of the *bunga 'mas*. Kedah was evasive, and with good reason. Perak was an old, established Malay state. Its sultans, although at that moment weak, were of ancient lineage, and the structure of the state reflected clearly, as it did a hundred years later, its Indian or Indianized origin. Its rivers gave access to old, established and well-known tin deposits; more tin came from Perak than elsewhere on the Malay Peninsula, and it had been this asset that had attracted Portuguese and Dutch interest (there had been a fort at the river mouth, and a whole series of sixteenth-, seventeenth- and eighteenth-century treaties between them), and both Achinese and Bugis conquest. The *bunga 'mas* had gone across to the queens of Acheh in the seventeenth century, but it had never gone to Ayuthia, and this ancient country saw no reason why it should go now to Bangkok.

The consequence was war; Kedah on Siamese orders invading Perak in 1817, a fleet under the Laxsamana entering the mouth of the Perak river, and an army under the Bendahara moving overland, behind Province Wellesley, advancing down from the headwaters. It was a slow affair, with resistance finally collapsing in September 1818.

Kedah by its invasion of Perak had isolated itself. For the moment it was completely without allies, and in an untenable position; it began searching for support. It searched in the wrong place: Burma. Ava was still a very formidable power, and being the traditional enemy of Siam it seemed the logical state in which to look for friends. Unfortunately for Kedah, Burma was becoming increasingly involved with Britain in India and although it still savaged Siam occasionally it was looking more to the west than the east. In 1785 Bodawpaya, the ruler, had conquered Arakan, thus establishing a common boundary, soon to become a line of friction, with the Company in East Bengal. The friction increased during the next thirty years, as Bodawpaya regarded Britain's indifferent control of the border with provocative contempt. Tenuous diplomatic relations, established by Symes in 1795, finally snapped in 1812. Henceforth, there was no link between the two. With the death of Bodawpaya in 1819, this contempt was translated by his successor into a forward policy

[17]W. F. Vella. p. 63.

in Arakan and Assam to its north, with the conquest of Bengal itself as the over-riding objective. Thus, at a time when Kedah looked to it for support, Burma had turned its back on Siam and was content to leave the jungle paths between them untrod, while it moved its forces and concentrated its attention to the west, preparing for an invasion of India. Kedah was ignored.

But not by Siam, which in a swift campaign in November 1821, rapidly overran the state. Little resistance was offered to the Siamese and Ligorian *prahus* as they swept up the rivers. Scores of Malays were bound and trampled to death by elephants, while thousands (including the Sultan) fled south to Province Wellesley. They were pursued by the Siamese, who, on meeting a company of Sepoys, hurriedly withdrew. The Sultan took refuge on Penang.

Penang had watched the conquest of Kedah with horror. It did not, however, interfere. Anderson, the tin agent of the Penang government, for this gives three reasons.

He held that the force available on the island was insufficient for a vigorous war of intervention, and that it could not maintain a hold on Kedah once Siamese re-inforcements began to arrive. But he did not stress this point. Of more validity was his second reason, that Penang had learned the imprudence of acting without the consent of the Supreme Government. Since the time of Light, the policy of non-intervention had been stressed and insisted on. Finally, it would have been folly to arouse the enmity of Siam (although all the peninsula now saw the intent of its Malayan ambitions), at a moment when a mission from India was in Bangkok. This perhaps was the major reason for a neutral attitude. It was hoped that this mission would produce trade concessions for the Company, and a favorable treatment for Kedah. Penang (basically anti-Siamese) recorded then the horror and the anguish of this invasion[18] and watched as Kedah was extinguished; but in view of the larger issues, particularly the fear of jeopardizing the mission from India, Penang maintained its neutral attitude. This mission was one of several, and to their consideration we must now turn.

[18]An account, very pro-Malay, can be found in Anderson: Logan's Journal VIII. (1854) pp. 135-139. This account is printed also in T. J. Newbold: *Political and Statistical Account of the British Settlements in the Straits of Malacca*. (London, 1839). Vol. II. pp. 8-16.

VII

THE BRITISH, SIAM AND KEDAH

The suggestion that an official mission should visit Siam appears to have been put forward by Penang originally in 1814 and then, with more weight, by Governor Bannerman in June, 1818. The Kedah forces were invading Perak, while Siamese pretensions of sovereignty were disturbing nearly the whole peninsula and posing a threat to the trade between it and Penang. Bannerman stressed these local points, but drew attention also to issues that more directly concerned the Company: the opportunity of advancing the trade of India to the eastward, of forestalling other traders, particularly the Americans, and of augmenting British influence. While waiting for a reply, Bannerman sent some gifts to the King of Siam, fishing for friendship.

Siam for the last century had abandoned its earlier tolerance of Europeans, and had turned a contemptuous and hostile back upon them. Early European adventurers had not prepared the way, as they had in India and Java, for the establishment of trading "factories," and for the growth in the eighteenth century of European control. Rather we must look to Japan for an example, as by the early nineteenth century Siam was a country almost as mysterious and as unknown as was Zapangu. No European lived there, Europeans rarely traded there; and yet, by various ways, through conversations with Chinese traders, by contact with the merchants previously on Junk Ceylon, and by the contacts through Kedah and Kelantan, Penang in particular was well aware of the possibilities of the state, and contemplated the opportunities with some enthusiasm.

Bannerman's gifts received a surprisingly warm welcome, and the King of Siam's minister wrote to Penang inviting trade. "In the last year the Sheikh Mohamed, Nakhoda of a Surat ship brought a letter and a few presents from your Honor the Governor of Penang. If your Honor is willing to send ships to trade here I shall be most happy to receive them. His Majesty the Emperor has ordered me to send this letter to your Honor and to say that he thankfully receives the letter and presents and has sent your Honor a Pecul of Ivory and a Bhar of Tin as a sign of his friendship, and that if your Honor likes to send ships to trade either at Siam or Ligor you are welcome; that Musquets will be good for merchandize as well as anything else, except Opium which is prohibited."[1]

[1]S. S. (F). R. Vol. F. 1. Siam to Penang, January, 1819.

The reply to the gifts, the offer to trade, and the suggestion that muskets would be welcome are all signs that Siam perhaps was becoming aware of Britain vis-à-vis Burma. But the Supreme Government in Bengal, harrassed as it was with Burmese chaos on its Arakan border, apparently had not regarded Siam as a possible ally in checking the predatory power that lay between the two, for its reply to Bannerman's suggestion was to rebuff the whole idea. It objected to sending a mission to "a haughty and arrogant court, at the hazard of the loss of reputation attending a failure, and at the risk also of exciting the jealousy and alarm of the Burmese."[2] Bengal's missions to Ava and to Cochin China had been insulted and ignored, and no doubt this experience had provided a lesson. Bengal saw no possibility of the local problems cited by Bannerman, such as the Malay trade with Penang, and the Kedah invasion of Perak, being solved by a mission, and it did not think for a moment that the inconsiderable trade from India could be increased or protected in any way by negotiations at Bangkok.

This rebuff did not deter Penang. It continued to press for some direct contact with Bangkok. In January, 1819, in July, 1819 and in July, 1820 Penang returned to the attack, and by this time affairs had changed so, both in Malaya, with the establishment of Singapore in 1819 and the growth of Eastern trade as a result, and in India, with the increasing threat to Bengal from Burma, that the Company had become more appreciative of the possibilities, although not less mindful of the pitfalls, of a mission to Siam. Accordingly, in November, 1820, Penang obtained the sanction it had sought for more than two years.

It was a very grudging sanction it had acquired, it was no full-scale Ambassador from the King of England such as the one by whom the Company had attempted to open intercourse with China in 1793, nor was it the powerful display that had gone up the Irrawaddy to Ava, a few years later. All that the Company would permit, in the first instance, was the support of a private trader engaged in the country trade, one John Morgan. He was recommended to the Governor General by the powerful John Palmer of Calcutta, the most prominent perhaps of those merchants who looked eastward for their profits. The Supreme Government considered it inadvisable to send a public deputation and contemplated any opening of relations in a very cautious and guarded way. It considered that a private agent would not arouse the suspicions of Burma or of Siam, while in any case the expense would be inconsiderable. So Morgan sailed.

The results of this mission to Siam were comparable to the spirit in which it was dispatched. It did not achieve anything, yet it did not lose anything either. It cost the Company a mere $5,000 in expenses incurred by Morgan in Bangkok. He came out of it well. He managed to sell his shipload of opium, which was strictly forbidden, and he had an audience with the King, who ap-

[2] S. S. (F). R. Vol. 182A. Bengal to Penang, 26 November, 1818.

parently was satisfied in discovering that Bengal disliked Ava as heartily as he did. But as he appears not to have discussed the Malayan troubles, and as he recommended to India that it would be foolish to conclude any trade agreement unless a British representative was left in Bangkok to fight the frauds that would be practised, which at that time was unthinkable, the mission did not advance the interests of Penang or of India much at all.[3] Nevertheless, with the line of behavior once begun, and with no reason for any alteration to be made, it was decided to follow up this private beginning with an official mission, and in that same year the Governor General selected Dr. John Crawfurd as his envoy. The Crawfurd Mission marks the second stage in these Siamese-Kedah-India relations.

Crawfurd (later to become the second Resident of Singapore, 1823-1826, and then the first Resident at Ava in 1826, and to establish himself by his learned writings as a recognized authority on Malayan affairs), sailed from Calcutta with instructions from India that reveal clearly the role played by Penang in this affair. Bengal addressed him thus: "the need of cultivating a more intimate connection with Siam has been repeatedly brought to the notice of the Supreme Government by the Government of Penang, and towards the end of last year a proposition from that Government to depute an Agent to Siam received the sanction of his Lordship in Council.[4] That sanction has, however, only been partially acted on, and the design may now be conveniently superseded by the Mission which his Excellency in Council has resolved to commit to your charge."[5]

Crawfurd was charged with several responsibilities. His major task was to secure an improvement in the conditions then hindering British trade. In Penang he was asked to secure the return of the Sultan and the withdrawal of the Siamese from Kedah.

The book that evolved from the journey[6] gives a fascinating picture of one small portion of the Far East before it was overlaid with European veneer, when everything to the westerner was still strange and mysterious and largely unknown. He describes Bangkok.

Numerous temples of Buddha, with tall spires attached to them, frequently glittering with gilding, were conspicuous among the mean huts and hovels of the natives, throughout which were interspersed a profusion of palms, ordinary fruit-trees and the sacred fig. On each side of the river there was a row of floating habitations, resting on rafts of bamboos, moored to the shore. These appeared the neatest and best description of dwellings; they were occupied by good Chinese shops. Close to these aquatic habitations

[3]O. Frankfurter: *The Unofficial Mission of John Morgan*. Journal, Siam Society, Vol. xi pt. 1. (1914). See also S. S. (F). R. Vol. A15. Penang to Bengal, 27 December, 1821.

[4]A reference apparently to John Morgan's mission.

[5]Instructions to John Crawfurd. 29 September, 1821. Printed as Appendix B in J. Crawfurd: *Journal of an Embassy from the Governor-General of India to the Courts of Siam and Cochin China*. 2 Vols. (London, 1830). Vol. II p. 443.

[6]Apart from the two volumes of Crawfurd, cited above, the journey produced another book, by the surgeon naturalist who accompanied him. G. Finlayson: *The Mission to Siam and Hue, 1821-1822*, (London, 1826).

were anchored the largest description of native vessels, among which were many junks of great size, just arrived from China. The face of the river presented a busy scene ... we were not aware that there are few or no roads at Bang-kok, and that the river and canals form the common highways...[7]

This is still a description of Bangkok today; not so that of the courtiers, for example the Foreign Minister, who gave Crawfurd an interview. "His person was without ornaments, and indeed, it may be said, nearly without dress; for he wore nothing saving a piece of crimson silk, which was wrapped round his loins."[8] He describes much more of interest interspersed with such comments as "I had another long conference last night with the Prah-Klang, the results of which, I am sorry to say, were far from satisfactory,"[9] for although he met the King, and although he and his gifts were welcomed, long discussions over his objectives were fruitless. After months of switching and changing he secured a commercial undertaking in June, 1822 which merely stated that British ships would be welcome to visit Bangkok to trade, and that "as soon as they are anchored, the Superintendent of Customs shall afford all assistance in buying and selling with the merchants of Siam, and the duties and charges shall not be more than heretofore, nor afterwards be raised," ominous words which meant that all the difficulties that had hindered trade, such as the uncontrolled and crippling taxes and arbitrary levies, would continue as before. And the affairs of Kedah were equally as insoluble.

He had arrived in Siam on March 22. It was not until late May, after two months of innumerable commercial conferences, that he turned to Malayan affairs. "At this conference," he wrote on May 21, "The Siamese negotiators stated that they knew nothing more of this matter than that the Rajah of Quedah, a tributary of Siam, had abandoned his own country and fled to a foreign one for protection. They said that instead of seeking an asylum at Prince of Wales Island, he should have come to the capital and represented his grievances to the King, and, they added, if he would still come, ample justice would be done to him." It was obvious that they were not prepared to compromise on this issue. Their pride had been wounded and they were very irritated by the Sultan's action in fleeing to Penang.

Crawfurd continued that:

The point of getting possession of the person of the Rajah of Quedah seemed one upon which the Siamese court were fully bent, and in which they believed their honour or character implicated. The restoration of this prince being of considerable moment to us, I proposed, as an easy means of settling the quarrel between him and the Rajah of Ligor, the sending of a Siamese commissioner, superior in rank to both parties, to the spot, to enquire into and adjust the affair. This proposition, which the Siamese imagined would have brought their authority within the influence of our power, owing to the neighbourhood of the Quedah territories to ours, was without hesitation rejected ...

[7]Crawfurd. Vol. 1. p. 121.
[8]Crawfurd. Vol. 1. p. 121.
[9]Crawfurd. Vol. 1. p. 251.

The language which I was compelled to use at this interview was such as a Siamese Minister could not have been much accustomed to listen to, and such, of course, as must have been offensive to his pride. The reception given by our Government to the King of Quedah, and our refusal to deliver him up, wounded the vanity of the Siamese; and there can be no doubt that this had throughout a prejudicial influence upon the main objectives of the mission, although these, indeed, might not have been attainable without such obstacle.[10]

Crawfurd's main object was to improve trade facilities, and there is evidence to suggest that he was embarrassed in his other role as representative of Penang and champion of the Sultan. He secured a tacit acceptance by the Siamese of the British occupation of Penang, "the right of the Malay prince to alienate a portion of his fief, being once admitted by the Siamese Court, and a total silence of 36 years, must be looked upon as a valid and substantial admission of it"[11] so he wrote, and he made sure that they realised that the $10,000 cession money would go not to the conquerors of Kedah, but as before to the Sultan; but the other matters on which he was charged by Penang he forbore to press.

Although this was unfortunate, Crawfurd did not regard it as a catastrophe. He accepted the Siamese right to Kedah, and he felt that the occupation of Kedah by Siam might even be advantageous to Penang and to the British in India generally. The Siamese would be brought into close contact with the British, and so he hoped would be rendered more dependent upon the friendship and good offices of Penang, and would become confident in the fair dealings of the British, and this in turn would tend towards an opening of their country to British traders.

While Crawfurd negotiated with the Siamese at Bangkok, and gathered a fund of friendly experience from Laotian chiefs, Buddhist monks, French priests, American traders and Javanese peasants passing by, Penang attempted to establish relations with the Siamese in Kedah. Phillips, the acting-governor, sent the military secretary, Captain Henry Burney, to Alor Star in March 1822. Burney, who had learned Siamese and Malay, was to have a distinguished career, to lead a mission to Siam and to succeed Crawfurd at Ava; but his efforts in Kedah both in March and in May, were fruitless. He could secure no information regarding Siamese intentions and he could not secure the release of the Sultan's relatives. The "moderate and temporising policy,"[12] as Phillips put it, was no more successful than the diplomacy of Crawfurd.

Meanwhile the Sultan was becoming restive. He was receiving $400 a month from the government, but nothing else, and his presence and the hopes it bred in the hearts of Malays across the water was encouraging just that lawlessness and unrest that Penang abhorred. Penang wanted food from Kedah, not fighting, and it firmly resisted all requests by the Sultan for aid.

[10]Crawfurd: Vol. 1. p. 242-252, 255.

[11]S. S. (F). R. Vol. 87. Crawfurd to Bengal, 12 July, 1822.

[12]S.S.(F).R. Vol. B.6. Penang to London, 15 November, 1822.

His attempts to secure support from the Rajah of Tavoy, in the north, were repulsed, and no assistance whatsoever was rendered to an abortive move by his younger brothers to drive out the Siamese. In dejection, the Sultan decided to leave, but waited with hopes not fully extinguished until Crawfurd returned.

Crawfurd arrived in Penang on December 5, 1822, and immediately, so he wrote:

...paid a visit to the Raja of Queda, accompanied by the Secretary, Mr. Cracroft. This chief was an old acquaintance. I had paid him a visit at Queda in 1810. At that time he was a young man of little more than 30, of goodly appearance and extremely fair for a Malay. He was now very much changed indeed, and although only 42 or 43, had the appearance of 60.

His manners, like those of all Malays of rank, and generally indeed, like those of the whole race, were soft, pleasing and unassuming. I had the mortification of being the channel of communicating to him the result of my unsuccessful efforts at Siam in his behalf. He received my statement with composure, and said that with the assistance of his friends, the Princes of Perak, Selangor and Siak, he would make an effort to recover his country; which after laying it waste, and driving the population into exile, the Siamese themselves had now in a great measure abandoned.[13]

The Sultan's public declaration did his cause harm. Penang had accepted the attitude of Crawfurd, that Siam's control of Kedah might be put to good effect, and it regarded the Sultan as a nuisance. Every effort was made, Penang virtually made obeisance to convince Siam of its good intentions, while more and more the Sultan, his usefulness expended, was treated as an enemy. Early in 1823 the Sultan requested permission to leave. It was refused, and Phillips warned him that should he leave Penang neither he nor his family could seek refuge there again, the protection of the Company would be withdrawn, and his annual payment would be stopped immediately. For the moment it was increased to $500 per month, which once received he used to finance his eldest son, Tunku Abdullah, in another wild and unsuccessful attempt in April, 1823 to regain Kedah.

The Sultan turned again to Burma, and applied secretly to Ava for assistance against its traditional enemies the Siamese. Ava was poised in Arakan and Assam; its southern subsidiary, Tavoy, came with letters and presents to the Sultan, too openly, for this was observed by Phillips, who informed Ligor of the Sultan's new friends.[14] He disclosed this development, so he claimed, in hopes that Ligorian fear of Burma would lead to the reinstallation of the Sultan. After several conferences with representatives sent by Ligor, he drew up the terms of an agreement which would have had the Sultan back in Alor Star. These stipulated an annual payment of $2,000 to Siam from Kedah, in lieu of the *'bunga 'mas,* the withdrawal of Siam from Kedah and the release of the members of the royal family imprisoned in Kedah. It is doubtful if this surpris-

[13]Crawfurd: Vol. 1. p. 459.

[14]*The Burney Papers.* 5 Vols. (Bangkok, 1910-1914), Vol. II, pt. 2,

ing act of initiative on the part of Ligor (undertaken perhaps in the hope of gaining time), would have been accepted by Siam, and in any case, at this moment, the Supreme Government, faced with the naked and ignorant aggression of Burma across its frontiers into India, declared war, and launched a sea-borne invasion of the Irrawaddy.[15] Rangoon was captured on 10 May, 1824, without a shot being fired; and although the British were then bogged down until the following year, Ligorian fears of Ava vanished. The draft agreement was never ratified, and the Sultan remained on Penang.

The Supreme Government, anxious to attack Ava from all quarters, used Penang as its contact with Siam. In July, 1824 the Penang government, complying with instructions, sent Lieutenant James Low on a mission to the Rajah of Ligor. Low, in his army surveys of Province Wellesley and his less official excursions in south Kedah, just north of the Muda river, the boundary of the Province, was the first to record the remnants of the ancient Indianized settlement there.[16] In 1826 Low was to give service to Malaya of another kind, as the narrative will show, but on this mission he failed completely. His object was to persuade the Rajah to send to Rangoon every available boat to move up the Irrawaddy to Ava, the British troops confined in Rangoon through lack of transport. Low failed to contact the elusive Rajah, although he searched tediously in Ligor from May to August 1824, and he concluded that the Rajah was frightened to meet him, did not want to help him, and in any case had no independent power; and could not have sent a single boat even had he wished to. He returned in disgust to Penang, and the British in Rangoon were neither hindered nor assisted by either Ligor or Penang.

Despite the lack of success that attended Low's mission to Ligor, the British forces attacking south Burma still searched for that will o' the wisp, Siamese cooperation, and with some desperation; for they were held up at Rangoon, and the campaign was stagnating. In September, 1824, news came to Penang of the imminent occupation by the British of Tavoy, Mergui, and Tenasserim, the Burmese states on the Kra Peninsula. This news was brought by Lt. Colonel E. W. Snow, the deputy adjutant general of the Madras Division of the forces. He came to Penang specifically to obtain the cooperation of the Siamese. He met with no enthusiasm in Georgetown, which contented itself with furnishing him with letters of introduction to the Siamese chiefs nearest the Burmese boundary, asking them to aid the British troops by supplying provisions and transport cattle. Needless to say, they never did.

In August, 1824 a new governor arrived at Penang, Robert Fullerton. Professor L. A. Mills, who over thirty years ago pioneered research into the Straits Factory Records, and whose *British Malaya, 1824-1867*[17] is a valuable

[15]D. G. E. Hall: *Burma*. (London, 1956). pp. 102-105.

[16]In the *Journal of the Asiatic Society of Bengal*. Vol. 17 (1848).

[17]L. A. Mills, "British Malaya, 1824-1867." *JMBRAS*. Vol. III, pt. II. (1925). Reprinted as Vol. XXXIII. Pr 3. (1960).

contribution to Malayan history, describes the new vigorous anti-Siamese outlook that came with him. "Hitherto," he wrote, "the Governors of the Penang Presidency had acquiesced in the Siamese claims to overlordship in Malaya. The bare official records of the proceedings of a Council are not an ideal source for evidence of character; but Governor Fullerton was a man of such strong personality that it stands out clearly even in the dry accounts of the meetings of his Council. He was able, energetic and determined, and in foreign policy his guiding principle was to protect British interests in the Malay States wherever possible. Moreover, when the orders of the Supreme Government ran counter to his plans, he was in the habit of interpreting them in a somewhat liberal manner, so that in the end he often got his own way."[18]

This estimate of Fullerton has been substantiated by later studies. It is from his arrival that the Siamese move south was regarded as a threat to the Malayan Peninsula, and steps were taken to check it. It was checked by such men as Fullerton and Low, officials with an independent Malayan outlook, who acted well in advance of, even at times in opposition to, instructions from the Supreme Government. The East India Company and later the British Government looked at Siam from India. Until the beginning of this century it was considered by the British more important to cultivate friendly relations with Siam, and to help maintain its internal stability, particularly as France began expanding east of it, in Indo-China, than to force a crisis by disputing its occupation of the northern Malay States. Siam was regarded not as a menace but as a buffer. This policy was accepted by the Court of Directors in London, and later supported naturally by the Secretary of State for India. This point of view, from the time of Fullerton on, found few friends in the Straits Settlements, whose anti-Siamese attitude was frowned on by Company and (later) by the Colonial Office (a minor department in any case, compared to India and the Foreign Office), until the time of Joseph Chamberlain. Even then the conflict of attitudes was not fully resolved, and a compromise between the outlook of India and that of Malaya has led to the retention within Siamese control during the twentieth century of Malay-Muslim minorities. But that was decided in 1909, when at last Kelantan, Trengganu, Perlis, and Kedah escaped from Siam; in 1824, when Fullerton arrived, the Siamese move to the south was in full flood, and his aim of necessity was to stop the flood, to check the move. Time later, perhaps, to reverse the flow.

Fullerton's first efforts were devoted to an investigation of the powers of Ligor, the peninsula state that played the role of Siam on the peninsula stage. Captain Burney was sent there to endeavor to arrange a meeting with the Rajah, and to ascertain his exact status, whether he was independent, semi-independent, or dependent. He sailed from Penang in January 1825, but he too failed to obtain a personal interview. The Rajah wrote to Fullerton apologizing for not meeting Burney, but as he gave no valid excuse for evading him,

[18]L. A. Mills: p. 137.

Fullerton decided that the whole object was futile, and withdrew him, convinced that Ligor was a puppet state whose Rajah avoided European negotiators under instructions from Siam.

Burney was withdrawn for another reason, not merely because Fullerton considered his mission a waste of time, but because he had received information from A. D. Maingy, superintendent of Province Wellesley, that the Siamese southward move was about to be resumed. Kedah had been digested, now it was the turn of Perak and Selangor. As Fullerton minuted on Maingy's terse note, it would appear "to be nearly the final step to the complete subjection of the Malay Peninsula."[19]

Fullerton acted with prompt resolution. He demanded of Ligor the reason why so many *prahus* were fitted out and waiting in the Trang, Kedah, Lingau, Situal, and Perlis Rivers. Maingy was sent north to the rivers, to inform the Rajah and his chiefs that the fleet would not be allowed to pass Penang, and a small collection of Company vessels, all that Fullerton possessed, kept a vigilant watch. They reported the movement south into the Kedah River of over 200 *prahus,* together with the Rajah of Ligor and some four thousand men. This most unapproachable gentleman—the Rajah—was contacted at last by Maingy, who managed, in the course of a long evasive interview to extract from him the statement that the King of Siam had ordered him to punish the people of Selangor. Fullerton's determined attitude, the patrolling squadron off-shore, together with the warning that an invasion of Selangor and Perak, where Britain had inherited treaty obligations from the Dutch, might involve not merely Penang but the Company and Siam, kept the Ligor fleet on the beach. It never shoved off, and Selangor was saved.

It was saved by a bluff. Fullerton had been told months before that the Supreme Government did not consider that Penang should attempt to protect the southern Malay States, and that it "entertained the strongest doubts of the practicability of inducing the arrogant and haughty Court of Siam to waive its pretensions."[20] The Company did not consider it wise to question the demands of Siam; and yet Fullerton not merely questioned but denied and thwarted them.

Wisely Fullerton sent to India an emissary who shared his views—Captain Burney. Burney agreed with Fullerton that not merely British interests in the Malay states, but the interests of the Malay states themselves were best served by maintaining or securing their independence from Siam. He represented to the Supreme Government the utility of Fullerton's actions, and advanced his case for the need to re-open negotiations with Bangkok. The southern dependencies of Siam possessed powers too limited for any conference of worth, and if the outstanding questions were to be settled without war, an agreement was necessary. Fullerton's actions and Burney's arguments were accepted, and Burney was named the leader of a mission to Siam.

[19]S. S. (F). R. Vol. 99. Superintendent of Point Wellesley to Secretary, Penang, 15 February, 1825.
[20]S. S. (F). R. Vol. A. 20 Penang to Bengal, 7 April, 1825.

The mission of Crawfurd in 1822 had been dispatched largely for commercial reasons inspired by India. Burney went to argue the case for the British
in Malaya. The Supreme Government by 1825 had lost interest in Siam as a
possible ally against Burma, for the successful war was nearly over, and the
Government's original idea of ceding the south Burmese states along the
Tenasserim coast to Siam in return for such support against Burma had been
replaced by an awareness of the strategic importance of these states and a
determination to retain them. The Supreme Government also had lost interest
in Siam as a possible trade emporium. The treatment meted out to Crawfurd
and his inability to secure a commercial treaty, indeed made the government
hesitate before it again humiliated itself needlessly. But whereas the Supreme
Government in 1825 was less interested in Bangkok than before, both Penang
and the new bustling Singapore, with its tentacles of trade reaching up the east
coast of the peninsula, pressed their problems for attention. So Burney sailed.

As with Crawfurd who by this time was Resident at Singapore, his first
landfall was Penang. Here Fullerton pressed him into service. The *prahus* of
Ligor still were assembled in Kedah, where they continued to threaten Selangor and the half-throttled Sultan of Perak. The Sultan had managed, with the
not-altogether-appreciated help of Selangor, to throw off the hold of Kedah in
1822, after Kedah itself had been over-run by Ligor, but then he had been
forced to acquiesce in the permanent residence at the river mouth of a Selangor
chief, who taxed all and sundry. Ligor had managed to infiltrate a number of its
men overland into Perak. Could these be reinforced, Perak would succumb,
and Selangor probably would fall also.

The Rajah of Ligor, who had hesitated in Kedah for six months, obviously
was apprehensive of Fullerton. In addition, the Supreme Government was not
so acquiescent, not so completely pro-Siamese as in 1821 when the Rajah had
overrun Kedah. Burney was welcomed then, when he appeared in the Kedah
River in July, 1825, and the Rajah accepted his offer to settle by negotiation
with him, his dispute with Selangor.

The result of these negotiations was a "Preliminary Agreement" as Fullerton termed it. The Rajah of Ligor agreed to vacate the Kedah River within
twenty days and to sail his fleet back north. Further, he agreed to withdraw
his men from Perak, and to abstain from attacking either Perak or Selangor. In
return, Burney pledged that the Penang government would obtain from
Selangor a compensation of $2,000 for having attacked some Ligor *prahus*
off Perak in 1822, and would secure the withdrawal from the mouth of the
Perak River of the Selangor chief, Rajah Hussein, the Sultan of Selangor's
nephew, whom the Sultan had placed there in 1822, after the Kedah-Ligor
forces had been driven out.

This last clause indicated that Ligor was still interested in Perak, and
wished to remove a troublesome barrier to the free access of the Perak River.
Apart from that clause, however, the agreement denoted a partial withdrawal

by Ligor, and the first check to Siam's southward move. Burney and Fullerton hoped for more. There were other clauses, which needed the ratification of Siam. These stipulated the restoration of the Sultan of Kedah, the release of his relatives, and the return to Ligor of the occupation force, with Burney pledging, on behalf of Kedah, the triennial dispatch of the *bunga 'mas* and an annual payment of $4,000, through Ligor to Bangkok. Had these clauses been accepted, without doubt the tide would have turned. Even though that did not eventuate, the agreement paved the way for political negotiation with the Siamese.

Fullerton was delighted. "It has brought us to some understanding with that chief," he wrote, "our relations with whome have since ejectment of the King of Quedah, been in a very uncertain and unsettled state."[21] In India the Supreme Government agreed. Here was a political treaty negotiated and signed in defiance of the traditional, oft repeated, and emphasized policy of abstention from peninsula engagements, yet Penang was informed that the provisions of the agreement were unobjectionable, and in full accordance with the views and interests of the Company.

Fullerton turned immediately to fulfilling his part of the agreement. As soon as he heard from Maingy that the Rajah of Ligor had dispersed his *prahus* from the Kedah River, he sent south to Selangor, John Anderson, the Malay translator to the Government and a firm supporter, with Low, Maingy, and Burney, of the governor's policy. Anderson's task was to induce the Sultan, Ibrahim, a fine old leader, to accept the clauses pertaining to Selangor. In the rejoicing and relief that followed the relaxation of the Ligor pressure, Anderson was welcome, and his mission was a complete success. The nephew, Rajah Hussein, was withdrawn from his toll post on the Perak River, and a clear-cut line, the Bernam River, fixed for the first time the boundary between the two states. Selangor promised not to interfere in the affairs of Perak again and relinquished all claims to suzerainty. Tolerable peace fell over the western rivers of the peninsula as Maingy sailed north to administer Tavoy and Mergui for Penang, and Burney sailed on to Siam.

The objects set before Burney by Fullerton, and accepted by the Supreme Government as fit topics for discussion, were four. They were the restoration of the Sultan of Kedah; the withdrawal of the Siamese infiltrating into Perak, and the ending of its claim to suzerainty there; the prevention of further southward conquests by inducing the Siamese to define the limits of their interests in the peninsula; and the establishment of a freer intercourse and trade from Penang up the west coast rivers and overland routes to the interior and the east coast.

In contrast to these detailed and specific objects, the Company in India charged Burney in the most general of terms. "Your Mission to Siam must be,

[21]S. S. (F). R. Vol. A. 22. Penang to Bengal, 3 August, 1825.

in the first instance, entirely of a complimentary and conciliatory character. You will appear at Bangkok to offer the congratulations of the Right Honourable the Governor General on the accession of the new King, to assure His Majesty of the friendly disposition of the British Government, and its desire to cultivate a good understanding with the State of Siam, and to afford the fullest explanation on every point connected with the Burmah war."[22]

Bengal did not expect sensational results from this mission. It had decided before the mission sailed from Calcutta, that it was not prepared to cede its newly acquired Tenasserim Provinces, which it had considered previously might be exchanged for reinstatement of the Kedah Sultan. Burney was thus denied one of the few bargaining counters upon which he and Fullerton had depended. Burney's visit to the Rajah of Ligor in January of that year (1825) had shown him that the eldest son of the Rajah, who had led the 1821 invasion of Kedah and who had killed the Laxsamana at the Kedah river-mouth, was installed at Alor Star with 500 men. Here he was collecting for his father the monopoly payments on padi, timber, and tin exports from all the rivers south of Setul (the pocket state north of Perlis), while other sons were scavenging the birdsnest and other revenues. The Rajah's family and its supporters as robber barons had acquired a vested interest in Kedah. They were better off there than in their own country, and unless the Company could offer them fresh fields, which India was not prepared to do, mere argument was unlikely to move them. Burney's hands then were tied before he left; yet he himself admitted that to cede Mergui and Tavoy would be to surrender them to pillage and destruction. As neither he nor even India, as far as is ascertainable,[23] received any instructions or communications on the subject from London, there remained "no other instruments than those of conciliation and address."[24] Not much in all truth to use against the Siamese.

The mission sailed from Penang on 25 September 1825, calling at Malacca and stopping briefly for discussions with Crawfurd at Singapore. Then, unlike Crawfurd three years previously, who sailed as directly as possible to Bangkok, Burney went up the coast of the Malay Peninsula, past the Pahang River, to pause at Trengganu. Burney, charged with establishing that the Siamese had something less than full sovereignty over the River, was anxious to ascertain at first hand the position there; but this procedure of making enquiries, without so much as "by your leave," in the ill-defined borderlands, combined with other suspicions to create consternation throughout Siam. At Trengganu there was apprehensively anchored the King of Siam's ship, which traded regularly with Singapore, but which had ventured no further south on news from some Malays (based on nothing more substantial than the arrival of a small contin-

[22]S. S. (F). R. Vol. A. 18. Bengal to Penang, 13 May, 1825. The "new King" was Rama III, 1824-1851.

[23]Burney refers to "the difficulty and embarrassment" that faced India "in the absence of all communication of the sentiments of the Home Authorities" regarding Siam and the Malay Peninsula. Report Mission p. 28.

[24]Report of Mission, p. 32.

gent of troops in Singapore and the coastwise crawl of Burney) that a British expedition was advancing north to capture Bangkok.

The same rumour had run to Ligor and to the capital of the Empire. Burney reassured the commander of the King's vessel, who continued south to Singapore; but when the mission arrived at Ligor (which stretched from east to west across the peninsula), he found the Rajah, who had become his friend and whom he had persuaded to accompany him to Bangkok, alarmed both for the life of his youngest son, who was ill, and for the safety of his state, which he feared was about to be attacked. Burney visited the sick child and then pulled out, although asked by the Sultan to wait with him until the son was better. The northeast monsoon, which hits the eastern side of the peninsula with some severity (although not approaching the savagery that smashes at Madras), had begun, and Burney was off a dangerous lee shore. He left with the Rajah the mission doctor, Sub-Assistant Surgeon Harris, of the Penang establishment. Harris was instructed to cure the boy, and then come with the Rajah overland to Bangkok.

Long before Burney sailed he had calmed the apprehensions of his host that he intended to invade Ligor. Then as now, South Siam was a poverty-stricken place, envied for its meager wealth by no one. In many respects Burney's description is still valid today.

The tin mines are much neglected and said to be exhausted. We have been shown some old brick foundations alleged to be the site of the Dutch Factory. There appears to be no direct trade with China, Cochin China or other Foreign port. What little trade there is, is with Siam and it is entirely engrossed by the Chief. There is not a single brick dwelling house in the town, but a great many temples and pyramids of that material, and most of them in ruins.[25]

The Chief's house is of plank with a tiled roof: it is situated within the fort, which consists of an old high wall in a most dilapidated condition, and without a gun mounted in any part within or upon it. Indeed, I have seen scarcely a musket here, and presume that the Chief has sent the whole of his Military means to Kedah. The number of women also far exceeds the number of men.[26]

Although Ligor was reassured that Burney and his little brig meant no harm, the absurd rumor that he was an invading force had preceded him, and it be-devilled all his attempts at negotiation. Burney reached the mouth of Bangkok's river on 28 November, to find confusion and alarm on all sides. He was detained there a week, and only after constant demonstrations and assertions of his peaceful intent was he permitted to sail upstream to Bangkok, where hurried and ineffectual attempts at defence had been made.

Shortly after Burney's arrival, the mission were granted an interview with Rama III, being escorted to the Palace past rows of Siamese soldiers "seated on their Hams,"[27] and with all the Siamese attendants, from the door of the

[25]The jungle covered ruins of South Siam remain today the major unexcavated archaeological attraction on the mainland of Southeast Asia.

[26]S. S. (F). R. Vol. 108. Burney to Penang, 8 November, 1825.

[27]S. S. (F). R. Vol. 108. Burney to Penang, 22 December, 1825.

Hall of Audience, moving beside them on knees and fore-arms. The King accepted the reasons for their presence (and their gifts) with composure, and Burney regarded him as a moderating element during the more than six months they parleyed in Siam. But throughout this time he had to fight against the suspicion generated by ignorant, fearful yet arrogant leaders.

The wildest and most improbable tales respecting the hostile intentions of the British Government continued to be brought to Bangkok by Burmese, Chinese and above all by Malays, who reported that immediately after the conquest of Ava the British Army was to move against Siam, and that the British Government had resolved upon expelling the Siamese from Quedah and taking possession of that territory, and of every other state in the Malay Peninsula. . .

The first measure also which we had occasion to propose at Bangkok brought down upon us the hostility of almost all the Ministers and subordinate officers of the Court. Viewing the inhuman treatment which the Burmese captives from the Coast of Tenasserim experienced from their Siamese masters, we were urged to make great exertions to effect the immediate release and return of these poor creatures. But they had been allotted as slaves and gratuitous labourers among the different Ministers and officers, whose personal interests were strongly opposed to the measure of restoring them. . .[28]

This question of securing the release of the Burmese prisoners, humanitarian though it was, was pursued at such length by Captain Burney, and resisted by the Siamese so fiercely, that the main objects of the mission might have been jeopardized. He argued their case from December until early February, winning his point—the release of the prisoners, upon news of the complete surrender of Ava and the end of the Anglo-Burmese war in February, 1826. But even the special and most unusual clause in the treaty signed by Ava with the British, the Treaty of Yandabo, which read (clause 10), "That the good and faithful ally of the British, the King of Siam, should, to the fullest extent, be included in this treaty," did not lessen the suspicion held by the Siamese of British intentions. It merely made them aware, as never before, of the victorious might now gathered just outside their frontiers, for other clauses of the same treaty transferred to the Company the Burmese provinces of Arakan, Assam, Manipur and Tenasserim. Fearful though it became, suspicious though it remained, the court was determined not to yield or to concede on any point that affected its pride or prestige. It was Ava all over again.

On the last day of January, the Rajah of Ligor and the mission doctor arrived at last in Bangkok, and Burney turned towards a discussion of the Malay Peninsula. Five states were involved, each varying in actual dependence on Siam, all claimed by Siam as part of its empire. Kedah was completely engulfed, Perak but partly, and Selangor scarcely at all; while on the east coast Kelantan (which sent the *bunga 'mas),* and Trengganu also were moving into

[28]Report. p. 39.

the Siamese field of influence. The extreme position of Fullerton was that all must be wrenched away; Siam clung to the lot. Burney, after five months of memoranda and submissions, assisted to a certain extent, when his own interests were not involved, by the Rajah of Ligor, achieved a compromise that was so vaguely worded that either power, depending who was the stronger, could interpret it as it saw fit.

He was quite unable to budge Siam over Kedah. The Rajah of Ligor, the court, the emperor, all were united. Burney asked that the Sultan be restored, his relatives and followers be released, and that the Siamese troops be evacuated. In return he promised that the *bunga 'mas* would be sent, together with $4,000 annually. And he assured the court that Penang would never attack Kedah. All this was unacceptable. Ligor was obtaining $30,000 annually from Kedah as it was, and over a thousand Malays were slaves in Bangkok. It obviously was not to Siam's advantage to terminate the occupation, and nothing that Burney said changed its attitude. Kedah remained under the control of Ligor. Burney did secure some stability in the food arrangements, the Rajah of Ligor proposing in June that no duties would be levied on the export to Penang of cattle or poultry, but that as long as the Sultan of Kedah stayed in Penang, a tax on grain would be imposed; should he leave, it would be dropped. This Burney accepted.

Burney broke the unanimous face of the court on several occasions, and made several friends. He was able to speak in Siamese, and to understand and to a certain extent appreciate their outlook. He achieved a notable success with Selangor and Perak, where he induced the moderates to admit that the former had never sent the *bunga 'mas,* and that Selangor's 1825 treaty arrangements with Penang, if enforced, would alleviate the necessity of Ligor punishing it; and that the Sultan of Perak, who had never sent the *bunga 'mas* before Kedah compelled him to in 1818, could govern his country as he saw fit, sending the *bunga 'mas* at his pleasure. Burney appreciated the Siamese fear of a loss of face if this appeared too obviously in the treaty as a retreat from an untenable position, and so acquiesced in a somewhat vague wording. He was attacked by Fullerton for this, but Burney had gained his point and maintained their sympathy.

On the east coast too, after long months of evening discussions, Burney persuaded Siam to retreat, and to state that provided Trengganu and Kelantan continued sending the *bunga 'mas* it would interfere in their states no more than at that moment, and would not interrupt their trade with Singapore. Here again face had been saved. Burney had realized the impossibility, and indeed the impolity, of forcing the Siamese by written treaty to abandon their pretensions; but by inducing them to accept an agreement, in this and in other respects deliberately worded so loosely that various interpretations could be made of it, he drew a broad line across the peninsula, achieving far more than Crawfurd had done, and far more than Fullerton appreciated.

The Burney Treaty was signed on 20 June, 1826. There were fourteen clauses, of varying importance. Burney obtained trifling trade concessions, as was expected. Nevertheless, it took six clauses to state them. Clause 5 stated that trade between the English and the Siamese was permitted, 6 said that merchants had to pay the duties in force, 7 said merchants could or could not take up residence ashore, at the government's desire, 8 offered assistance if a merchantman was injured, 9 stipulated that English merchants must secure governmental approval before trading in remote areas, and 10 said there was unrestricted trade between Penang and Kedah. All this more or less recapitulated the accepted facts.

The Malay Peninsula was considered in three clauses (apart from Clause 10). In Clause 12 both Siam and England agreed not to obstruct or interfere with the commerce of Trengganu or Kelantan. In Clause 13, Siam's possession of Kedah was accepted, and Siam's intentions to tax padi exports to Penang unless the Sultan moved elsewhere, was noted. Perak's right to govern itself as it saw fit was recognized in Clause 14. Other clauses dealt with correspondence, runaway subjects, threats of war and the peaceful settlement of boundary problems.[29]

The mission left Bangkok on 18 July after a friendly farewell audience with the King, reached Singapore on 25 August, and arrived at Penang on 9 September. Here Fullerton saw the treaty, and took an instant dislike to it, while his disappointment at its partial success blinded him to the fact that Burney had performed an exceptional task. He was less than fair in his criticisms. The arrangements with the east coast states, he said, amounted to an admission of the actual dependence of Trengganu and Kelantan on Siam, the denial of which was one of the main reasons why Burney had been sent to Bangkok. Was he correct?

The relevant clause, (Clause 12), reads as follows: "Siam shall not go and obstruct or interrupt Commerce in the States of Tringano and Calantan. English merchants and subjects shall have trade and intercourse in future, with the same facility and freedom as they have heretofore had, and the English shall not go and molest, attack or disturb those States upon any pretense whatever." It is not necessary to agree with Fullerton that this is an admission of vassalage on the part of the Malay States. The wording is such that there is valid room for other interpretations. Burney was attacked also for surrendering Kedah, and for accepting in the treaty "a stipulation amounting to nothing short of the entire abandonment of the King," and he was told by Penang "that in all matters connected to the Malay Peninsula, the Mission must be considered in some degree to have failed."[30]

This was a dream world. To Anderson, Low, and Fullerton, the Siamese were what the Dutch were to Raffles — hostile, ambitious objects that must be

[29]For this see Maxwell and Gibson: *Treaties and Engagements affecting the Malay Peninsula.*
[30]S. S. (F). R. Vol 135. Fullerton to Bengal, 5 October, 1826.

hated and blocked. Burney was opposed to the Siamese as far as their pretensions south were concerned, but they were people to him, and he did not hate
them in toto and unreasoningly. He would have made a very poor negotiator
if he had. Many were his friends, nationalists as we would call them now, and
he saw the validity of many of their arguments. Their hold over Kedah, for
example, was unquestioned, and Burney had no means by which he could
have shifted them. Yet if he had accomplished nothing there, he had cause to
be moderately pleased with his negotiations concerning Selangor, Perak, Kelantan, and Trengganu, where he had saved Siamese face yet effected a British
gain. Fullerton maintained his hostility, but in India the Supreme Government
applauded Burney and welcomed his treaty as placing the political as well as
the commercial relations of the British Government with Siam on an improved
footing.[31] As time was to show, India's judgement was correct; Burney had
done well.

Fullerton fulminated, but he quickly appreciated the opportunity the treaty
gave him of stopping Ligor, which had continued to regard Perak, from which
it had been excluded by Burney's Provisional Agreement of 1825, as a possible
place to plunder. In defiance of that agreement Ligor had continued to slip in
small contingents of men. They were not resisted, and their pressure on the
court of the weak Sultan was most unhealthy. Penang had protested to the
Rajah of Ligor, but remonstrances were useless, and when Burney returned,
Fullerton decided to send a mission to Perak to tell the Sultan of the Burney
Treaty, and in particular of its implications to him.

Captain Low, the leader of the mission, was instructed by Fullerton to tell
the Sultan that "he is an independent sovereign, to rule his Kingdom without
any interference of Siam or Selangor."[32] This was reading into the Treaty with
a vengeance. In addition, Fullerton said firmly, Low was to make it quite clear
to the Sultan that he did not have to send the *bunga 'mas*, unless he wanted to,
and that he could rely on the assistance of the British Government in expelling
any Siamese who entered Perak.

Low, accompanied by a detachment of troops and two Bombay marine
cruisers, crossed to Perak from Penang in October 1826.[33] The cruisers were
forced to anchor ten miles upstream, but Low continued with his force in boats,
pulling for two days, until the capital was reached. Here Low discovered that
the Sultan had been almost the slave of the Siamese. The troops from Ligor
that had infiltrated into Perak had usurped much of the Sultan's power, had
won over many of his leading chiefs, including the Raja Muda, or heir apparent,
who had sworn allegiance to Siam, and had placed the Sultan in personal danger. The Siamese, however, had lost all by fleeing before Low reached the

[31]S. S. (F). R. Vol. 138. Bengal to Burney, 23 February, 1827.

[32]S. S. (F). R. Vol. 130. Governor Fullerton to Captain Low, 15 September, 1826.

[33]The story of the Mission, here summarized, is told in detail in J. Low: *Retrospect of British Policy from the period of the first Establishment of Penang, 17 July, 1786-1839. Burney*, Vol. v. Pt. 1. pp. 147-152, 156-158.

capital, and the Sultan, a weak man, was overcome at his deliverance.

With Low driving him, the Sultan acted swiftly. A proclamation was issued forbidding any intrigue with Ligor or with Siam. The Chiefs of Perak were summoned to a conference, also attended by Low, the captains of the cruisers and the military contingent. Here the Raja Muda had his claim to the succession formally annulled, as having committed treason. A new list of ministers and officers was read out. No resistance was made, for Low had acted so promptly and the Siamese had fled so precipitously that there was no time for the pro-Siamese leaders to collect their men. The gathering dispersed without incident.

Low went further. He had assured the Sultan that he need send no *bunga 'mas* to Siam and that he—Low—had been instrumental in placing him upon an independent throne. On October 26, Low signed a treaty with the Sultan, in complete defiance of the traditional policy of non-entanglement and far in excess of the instructions given by Fullerton. Again it was a case of the man directly concerned, the driving force on the perimeter, acting rather than referring, and as a consequence, pulling a reluctant headquarters after him.

The Sultan of Perak had pointed out, logically enough, that if Fullerton's assurance of British support meant anything at all, then it would be better on paper. A written guarantee would give far greater reassurance than a verbal promise. Low, charged with ejecting the Siamese and with making the Sultan secure, agreed. The Sultan thankfully stipulated that he would hold no intercourse of any kind with Siam or its vassals, nor would he send the *bunga 'mas* nor receive embassies or ambassadors from Ligor or Siam. If at any time he was troubled by these states, then he would call for the assistance of the East India Company. And Low promised faithfully that if he called, Penang would come.

This 1826 treaty was never ratified, and the Supreme Government condemned it. Fullerton was censured, and the Governor General in a long dispatch defending Siamese interests in the peninsula, including Perak, rejected all Fullerton's hostility to Ligor and Siam as without foundation. Fullerton, however, had achieved a *fait accompli,* and although he received the Governor General's dispatch with regret and concern, it did not shake him in his convictions. The Burney Mission, he wrote in his defence, had failed to restore the Sultan of Kedah. The next state south was Perak, and unless that was saved, the Siamese would go there, perhaps install the Raja Muda as their puppet, and then move on to Selangor. He was convinced that this southward move was detrimental to the best interests of the British in the Malay Peninsula, and he had taken it as the responsibility of Penang to stop it. By Low's action in Perak this had been accomplished.

Fullerton carried his case. The Supreme Council acquiesced in what had been done. Low's treaty, never ratified, became accepted, and when the Sultan of Perak subsequently appealed to Penang for aid, in 1844 and 1853, the terms of the treaty were accepted as binding. In 1874, when the policy of installing British officers as Residents in the Malay States was inaugurated in Perak, it was Low's treaty that was cited as the authority.[34]

Little recognized though it was, little known as it is today, this treaty of Low with Perak, following the Burney Mission and accompanied as it was by a show of military force, had a more practical effect, particularly on the west-coast states of the Malay Peninsula, than the better-known treaty signed two years previously, the Anglo-Dutch Treaty of 1824. The latter had been an agreement between two European powers to a very large extent recognizing what already was in fact. It tidied up the European map of Southeast Asia, but in no significant way did it alter the internal position of the Malay Peninsula. By 1824, the Dutch clung merely to a minute and moulding Malacca, with a few unobserved and out-of-date treaties with the Malay states. The Dutch decision to withdraw from the Peninsula was scarcely noticed, and the confirmation it gave to the British settlements did not affect their position to any extent whatever. Low's treaty, however, had momentous results. The long creep south of Siam down the west coast, which might easily have overrun the entire peninsula, was checked decisively, and on the east coast, too, there was a long, considered pause. Siam came no further. Of all the misfortunes that might conceivably have blighted the peninsula in the nineteenth century, Siamese domination would have been the worst, as it was, in the 1820's, the most possible. It is difficult not to think then, that this 1826 treaty marked an event more momentous, both to the internal development of the Malay Peninsula and to the British position in Malaya, than the decision of Holland and Great Britain in 1824 to confine themselves to the respective fields of interests they had already secured. Both treaties gave a clear indication of how far and in what strength Britain had moved east since 1786.

Fullerton had checked Siam, but he had not restored the Sultan of Kedah, and he had to endure another sixteen years in the wilderness. In Article 13 of the Burney treaty the promise was made by the Company that it would not assist the Sultan to recover his territory, and it would not permit him to reside in Penang or in any Malay States. The Sultan refused to accept the implications, and could not be induced to leave Penang. In 1830, he escaped to Province Wellesley, and his forces invaded (or attempted to liberate) Kedah the following year. They failed, and he was forcibly deported to Malacca. In 1836 he escaped to Perak, but again was brought back, and after the failures of 1838 and 1841, when his followers attempted to secure Kedah, the old Sultan finally succumbed. His son pledged loyalty to Siam, Britain brought pressure at last to bear, and the son was re-instated.[35] Every three years the *bunga 'mas* went overland to Bangkok, the last one arriving in 1909, in time to be dispatched as a coronation gift to King George V. Presumably then, the last gold flowers of Kedah now repose in Windsor Castle.

[34]L. A. Mills. p. 159.
[35]L. A. Mills: pp. 161-163.

VIII

TRADE

The instructions given to Light before sailing were divided very broadly into those which regarded the new settlement as a refreshment stop for ships bound for China and those which regarded Penang as a trading center; and apparently not so much a trading center for the East India Company as for the country ships. The two branches of British Far Eastern trade, as detailed research has shown,[1] were inextricably linked together, and on the country trade the Company's tea purchases heavily depended. Penang was established then largely to assist, in the first instance the country traders, yet the action of the Company may not have been so altruistic as it would appear; for many a cargo on a country ship was the speculation of a Company official. By helping the country trade, not merely was the amorphous and indefinite "Company" assisted, but more particularly, numerous Company officers as well. John Palmer, eminent Calcutta merchant, was not the associate of governors-general merely because of his engaging presence, nor did James Scott remain the friend of Francis Light merely because they had once been shipmates. The Company lost over Penang, in that it paid an annual deficit; but, as in India, somehow official and trader alike amassed fortunes.

Light set sail well aware of why Penang was founded. The conduct of the Dutch, he was told, had made the settlement essential, for by their capture of Rhio (in 1784) it had proved impossible for any country ship to trade with the *prahus* and junks from the Moluccas, Borneo, Celebes, Siam, Philippines and elsewhere. Contact had to be re-established. Light was told to govern mildly, and to keep the island free from impositions and restrictions. He was to communicate news of establishment to all the Malay princes, and was to advise India on how best the Dutch at Malacca could be prevented from stopping the *prahus* coming north. "Dutch jealousy will be a great obstacle," he was told, "be ever watchful of their designs, and be always upon your guard."[2]

This fear, it would seem, was largely unnecessary. The Dutch Company had secured Rhio, where it established a Resident, but it had no more secured its trade than a stick in the center secures an ant heap. De Bruijn, governor of

---

[1] In particular by Pritchard, Furber, Parkinson, Greenberg and Bassett.
[2] S. S. (F). R. Vol. 1. Bengal to Light, 2 May, 1786.

Malacca in 1785, described that trade,[3] the 20,000 annual pikuls of tin, the China goods "in the junks which came in great numbers," the Bengal opium, the Coromandel piece goods, and the Sumatran pepper, but he was quite unable to divert it to Malacca, or to sustain it in Rhio; some part of it came up to Penang, while the rest dispersed elsewhere. Light used against the Dutch a trading weapon they could not counter: a Free Port. "We desire you will refrain from levying any kind of duties or tax on goods landed or vessels importing at Prince of Wales Island, and it is our wish to make the Port free to all nations."[4] This policy of free trade, enunciated by Bengal when already in practice by Light, pulled the *prahus* to Penang more effectively than a dozen commercial treaties, and while the Dutch continued to pin their faith on control and regulation, nothing they could do could rival the great trading attraction of the new port up north.

It is possible to perceive a pattern in this trade almost from the very beginning, a pattern that has remained constant to this very day. In the first comprehensive list of ships compiled by Light, from December 1786 through to May, 1787, out of a total of 42 that called at Penang, 17 came from Pegu, Mergui, Acheh, Malacca or eastwards, 6 from southern India, 11 from Bengal, 7 from Canton and Macao, and 1 from America.[5] Another list, dispatched early in December, 1790, of the previous six months, gives a total of 104 ships that called at Penang. In May, a representative month, the 16 traders came from Pegu, Acheh, Selangor, Malacca, Batavia, south India, Bengal, Canton and Cochin China. In October, again, the pattern is similar, with 17 ships from Pegu, Rangoon, Acheh, Kedah, Borneo, Trengganu, Bengal and China.[6]

This pattern perhaps can best be visualized if Penang is imagined as the center of a circle, a ring encompassing its neighbors. Its rim would touch the ports of Burma, would swing down the Kra and Malay Peninsula, would then curve away from the northern Malay states to cross to east Sumatra and circle back to Burma through the ports of South India. This was and this remains, the main trading area of Penang. Penetrating that circle, striking at Penang as arrows strike at a target, were the ships from Bengal to the northwest, from China to the northeast, and, some time later, the vessels direct from London. In addition, there came annually arrows indeed heading for a target, and one never knew whether their point was sharp for plunder or blunted for peaceful trade—the Bugis fleet from Rhio and the Celebes.

Penang was founded to assist the China trade. Cornwallis, the governor-general, after studying the papers concerned with the settlement, had seen this clearly. "From all that I have learned I apprehend that we are not to look upon

[3]P. G. De Bruijn: *Trade in the Straits of Malacca in 1785*. (Translated from the Dutch by Professor B. Harrison). *JMBRAS*. Vol. XXVI. Pt. 1. (July, 1953). pp. 56-62.

[4]S. S. (F). R. Vol. 2. Bengal to Penang, 22 January, 1787.

[5]S. S. (F). R. Vol. 2. Penang to Bengal, 13 June, 1787.

[6]S. S. (F). R. Vol. 4. Penang to Bengal, 6 December, 1790.

it as a source from which much specie can be drawn," he minuted in December, 1786. Rather he saw by the foundation of Penang the "eastern trade becoming more extensively than at present a mart for the barter of opium and the productions of Bengal for tin and pepper to be applied as funds on the Chinese market for the purchase of tea, instead of the ruinous export of specie from this country."[7]

It is not possible to ascertain to what extent that purpose was realized. That it was not fulfilled is clear; by the 1820's Britain's trade with China had need for neither pepper nor tin, and so no need for Penang, and in the period before, between 1786 and 1826 or so, the figures of trade with China are so scanty that conclusions scarcely can be drawn. One, however, which becomes increasingly clear, is that even if Penang had the tin and pepper it did not have the ships, whether junks or square-rigged vessels, to take them to their eastern market. China bought opium because opium was delivered to its doorstep; it did not buy from Penang because no similar service existed.[8] But even if in this respect Penang possibly disappointed its parents in Calcutta and London, nevertheless it established itself as the useful, growing center of its own trading area; and this we shall now examine.

Acheh in particular, and northeast Sumatra in general, reacted quickly to the establishment of Penang. The prevailing winds were ideal for them to sail across the straits and to return, and pepper, their chief commodity, was such that the journey was rarely in vain. As early as August, 1786, Light was recording "five large Achin prows with pepper and bettle-nut are in harbour,"[9] while two months later he wrote "there are a large number of Achin prows here, and more are daily expected." Their arrival was expected with some apprehension, for as Light said, "as these people have lately succeeded in plundering Tapanooly (an outpost of Bencoolen, the factory in Sumatra), it is not unlikely that they will make some attempt here."[10]

Even though no such attempt was made, trading with northern Sumatra had its dangers, for a few months later, in January, 1789, a vessel of James Scott was captured by its mutinous crew while off Pedir, and the European officers were killed. At Pedir, the ship was secured by the Sumatrans, who refused to return it to Scott. Light narrates the interesting sequel, which shows how quickly Penang had become indispensable. "The people of the country, being afraid to come here until satisfaction was made, and finding themselves distressed by not being able to dispose of the articles they were used to sell at this Port, have since prevailed upon the great men to come to a determination, who accordingly have prepared to send the vessel over and have written for people

---

[7]S. S. (F). R. Vol. 2. Bengal Public Consultations. Minute by Governor General, 13 December, 1786.

[8]For comments on this, see J. Cowan: *Early Penang and the Rise of Singapore*. JMBRAS, Vol. XXIII. Pt. 2. March, 1950. pp. 6, 14-15.

[9]S. S. (F). R. Vol. 2. Bengal Public Consultations, 13 December, 1786. Appendix 1. Ships arrived, July 15-September 30.

[10]S. S. (F). R. Vol. 2. Penang to Bengal, 5 October, 1786.

to take charge of her. At the same time they requested a promise that I would
not in future call them to account for this transaction; in which particular I
have satisfied them."[11]

Risk or no risk, the trade with northern Sumatra went on, and although the
conditions in Acheh grew steadily worse, just as steadily trade rose. The Sultan
of Acheh with whom Desvoeux had dealings, in 1772, had died in 1781. His
successor, a little over ten years later, "plundered on all sides by the people of
no character whom he has employed to reduce his subjects to obedience, is at
this time reduced to a state of great distress and poverty, and remains confined
within the town of Achin, a circuit of two or three miles only."[12] Confined
though the Sultan was, the trade was not. It continued, and although no inter-
vening figures are available, in 1802, some 29,468 pikuls of pepper reached
Penang in exchange for opium and piece goods, with some iron, and in 1805 it
was recorded that "a very considerable trade is carried on."[13] In that year
(1805), "the low state of the king's finances, impoverished by a fruitless
struggle to enforce, by means of an expensive marine establishment, his right
to an exclusive trade, had induced him to make proposals for mutual accommodation, to the English government of Pulo Pinang."[14] This offer ushered in
a new and rather frustrating stage in Penang's relations with Acheh.

The new Presidency that took over the island in 1805 had come out charged
with the erection on Penang of a naval base. London realized however that
this would not shut the Bay to tne French, for Acheh was available as a rival
port. De Suffren in 1782 and Sercey in 1796 had utilized it as a sheltered
rendezvous and sally port, close to the British shipping routes, and London
feared a more permanent French base might be made there. Penang was informed that its projected dock yard and base "will not deprive our European
enemy of the means of infesting with his ships the Bay of Bengal, because
there is still an inviting port open to him in Acheen on west coast of Sumatra."
Therefore it was very desirable that Britain "should occupy the port."[15]

This was far easier said than done, particularly as no naval encouragement
seems to have been forthcoming. Acheh was in a tumultuous state. Its young
Sultan, Jauhar al-Alam, had ascended the throne in 1802. While a minor he
had served some time on board HMS *Nonsuch* (the British and French ships
all had a number of Malays and other Asians among the crew; the custom was
by no means uncommon),[16] and when he became Sultan "he gave disgust to
his subjects by assuming the dress and customs of Europeans, drinking strong

[11]S. S. (F). R. Vol. 2. Penang to Bengal, 4 February, 1789.
[12]S. S. (F). R. Vol. 5. Penang to Bengal, 26 September, 1792.
[13]S. S. (F). R. Vol. 179. London to Penang, 12 November, 1805.
[14]W. Marsden: *A History of Sumatra*. (London, 1811). p. 463.
[15]S. S. (F). R. Vol. 179. London to Penang, 18 April, 1805.
[16]Parkinson: *War in the Eastern Seas*. p. 343.

liquors to intoxication, eating pork in public, and neglecting every ceremony of the Mahomedan religion."[17]

This led to a rebellion instigated by the Sultan's mother and uncle, and this in turn led to his offer to Farquhar at Penang, early in 1805, of a place for a Company fort and settlement, provided that the Company help him retake his own fort; for by then he was nearly destitute, and quite without authority. Dundas reviewed all this, and advised London that "although a very considerable trade is carried on, we are of opinion that to establish and to maintain a permanent post there would require a very considerable body of Europeans as well as native troops in force sufficient to overawe if necessary a populous and turbulent city, and to cope with such an equipment as the French Islands may be able to send against it."[18]

Conditions in Acheh began slowly to improve, but Penang continued to regard the suggestions from London that a Resident be established as quite incompatible with the facts. The natural turbulence of the chiefs of Acheh was best regarded from a distance, and although in 1806 Jauhar Alam, who was regaining power, suggested a treaty giving Penang a monopoly of all Acheh's pepper, Dundas considered that the state was still too unstable for any commercial advantage to be gained from it; "it is safer to have the pepper purchased here," he wrote.[19] If Penang would not move however, India would, and in 1810 it dispatched a mission to Acheh.

Penang, more realistic than London, had not worried unduly about the possibility of Acheh becoming French, and had been quite content to receive the pepper prahus, for in the disturbed conditions of Acheh, the leading chiefs had found it extremely profitable to trade without paying the Sultan the traditional and prescribed customs duties, and naturally enough, there were merchants on Penang who themselves participated in the profits from illicit trading, and who were quite prepared to support the rebellious chiefs. The pepper imported into Penang in 1809 was valued at $115,592, and although four years later Jauhar Alam was still struggling for power, the pepper trade had risen. Petrie, the governor, wrote that "Achin at present labours under a state of tumult and disorder. Foreigners are regarded with jealousy and dislike, particularly if they are foreigners who are admitted to the Council of the King. This has produced a state of rebellion, the King has lost possession of the capital and is reduced to the coast and the government of Tulasamoy."[20] Despite this, or perhaps because of it, pepper imports at Penang had risen by 1814 to $134,420.

India and London had been less interested in the pepper trade than in French pretensions and the possible attitude of Acheh towards the planned invasion of Java. The mission in 1810, sent by Lord Minto, had endeavored to ascertain

[17]J. Anderson: *Acheen* (London, 1840). p. 29.
[18]S. S. (F). R. Vol. 179. Penang to London, 12 November, 1805.
[19]S. S. (F). R. Vol. 179. Penang to London, 20 March, 1806.
[20]S. S. (F). R. Vol. 180. Penang to London, 30 June, 1813.

the exact position of the state regarding these questions, but Major Campbell had been unable to meet the Sultan, even though he bore a hundred muskets as a present; nevertheless he reported favorably on his character. The muskets went back the following year in charge of Mr. Lawrence, sent by Penang, which at the same time had sold a cargo of arms to the rebel provinces. This ensured that Acheh's attitude, whatever it might be, was quite ineffectual. Minto's armada received no interference from Sumatra.

One of the Penang merchants who benefited economically from Acheh's indifferent political state of affairs was a certain Syed Husain. His grandfather, an Arab trader, had married a daughter of the last of the famous female rulers who ruled at Acheh from 1641 to about 1700. He was thus descended from a member of the ruling family, and until 1809 he had been permitted to trade at Acheh without paying the usual customs dues. In that year the privilege was withdrawn. Extremely wealthy and influential not merely in Penang but, through his agencies, with Bengal as well, and with John Palmer in particular, he became the bitter opponent of Jauhar, and assisted in rendering the Sultan's position most insecure, while making quite sure, through a lucrative trade with the great chiefs, that he suffered no serious loss of profits.[21]

In 1814 Bengal, again taking the initiative in the face of the reluctance of Penang, sent another mission, headed by Captain Canning, and he too, either through folly or ignorance having called first at the rebels' ports and held communication with the chiefs before sailing to Acheh, was unable to meet the Sultan. The reason of his visit was the seizure by the Sultan of a Coromandel ship; but as it had stopped at a rebel port, without a licence, and traded there in clear defiance of the well-known and long-standing Achinese regulations that permitted foreign ships only at the port of Acheh itself, it is doubtful whether even a personal interview would have produced much satisfaction for Bengal; or so Penang concluded.

In 1815 the Achinese rebellion had reached the stage where the chiefs were no longer content merely to challenge the Sultan. In that year an invitation was extended to Syed Husain either to accept the throne or to send one of his sons instead. Penang officially warned the Syed that he was fishing in troubled waters, a rather unnecessary warning, but made no effort to stop him when he sailed, ostensibly to visit the tombs of his ancestors, his five ships equipped for the pilgrimage with large cargoes of cannon, muskets, pistols, pikes, swords, ammunition and some commercial goods. Upon arrival in Pedir the son of the Syed was duly proclaimed sultan, and Jauhar fled to Penang, where "in view of his aggressive acts . . . we abstained from any official recognition of him. He remains at anchor."[22]

Jauhar did not remain at anchor for long, but once upon the sea, even though

[21]For this, see T. Braddell, *On the History of Acheen.* Logan's Journal, Vol. 5. (1851), C. Gibson-Hill, *JMBRAS.* Vol. XXIX. Pt. 1. pp. 11-13.

[22]S. S. (F). R. Vol. 181. Penang to London, 13 December, 1815. Anderson: *Achin.* pp. 54-68, et. seq.

barred from much of Acheh, he so harrassed the trade between that state and Penang during 1816 and 1817, that although he achieved only partial and occasional successes in his political aims the trade was completely dislocated. Exports to Acheh in 1817 dropped to $84,568, less than a fifth of the 1810 $461,117. Bannerman, who assumed office in November 1817, decided that in view of the widely conflicting rumors and the lack of reliable information, a mission must visit Acheh to discover the situation, and to bring about a restoration of trade. Captain Coombs, who had drawn up a detailed but incorrect narrative of Achinese events from 1797, was dispatched early in the new year. He had decided that the Syed's son was the rightful ruler, and nothing in his visit convinced him that he was wrong. He recommended that a treaty be concluded with him.

Meanwhile, however, the energetic and thrusting Raffles had arrived at Bencoolen (in March, 1818), and the Dutch had returned (the Napoleonic Wars having ended), to the East. A Dutch frigate had visited Acheh with gifts and promises of arms and other assistance to Jauhar Alam. Raffles reacted vigorously at this suggestion of an extension of Dutch power, and sailed at once for Calcutta. His main object of course was to impress upon the government there the need for a base south of Penang to safeguard British trade, and this led to Singapore; but he also took the opportunity to urge a treaty with Jauhar, whom he regarded as the rightful ruler. Calcutta compromised. Both Bannerman and Coombs, champions of rivals, were appointed Commissioners to Acheh, and instructed to support whoever they decided was the logical contender for the throne. Raffles was given the casting vote.

There were some delays, Singapore had to be founded, but Coombs and Raffles duly arrived, and after an intense argument, while their ship, the *Indiana,* lay off Acheh for seven weeks and while 1,000 pages of foolscap passed between them, Raffles exerted his senior status, and a commercial treaty was signed on 22 April, 1819, with Jauhar Alam. It was a nine-clause agreement, of which the main points were that the Company would do all it could to bring about the removal from Acheh of the Syed's son, and to keep out his family's influence, while the Sultan would accept a British agent, and would exclude the subjects of all other European countries, and Americans, from the state. Penang, given the task of implementing this (Raffles at Bencoolen being ignored), brought pressure to bear on Syed Husain and his son, culminating in the dispatch, early in 1820, of HMS *Dauntless,* to remove the son; but he fled to India, and suddenly, inexplicably, the turmoil on Acheh collapsed, and Jauhar Alam reigned until his death in 1824 over a peaceful state.[23]

In 1824, the year of Jauhar Alam's death, Britain and Holland signed the Anglo-Dutch Treaty, by which Britain undertook neither to enter into any

[23]*Anderson,* pp. 146-158.

treaty with, nor establish any Resident or settlement on, the island of Sumatra, and so of necessity the 1819 commercial agreement lapsed. The treaty could not break a trade route, however, and the Acheh trade with Penang continued to increase. A thousand devout Muslims crossed each year to Penang, bound on pilgrimage to Mecca. Beside them in the Chinese junks or heavy Achinese prahus were bags of pepper, coffee, betelnut, camphor, gold dust, rattans, and large quantities of rice.[24] The trade that returned from Penang, the piece goods, opium, ironware, sticklac (for dyeing), paper and a variety of other goods, which had dropped to $154,801 in the rebellion year of 1814 had risen, ten years later, to $445,053. The imports from Acheh were of the same value; a trade in the aggregate of nearly a million dollars, which was steadily increasing. Despite the century and a third that has elapsed, and has seen Acheh's reluctant and savage submission to the Dutch, this broad tradestream could not be twisted, and today the connections between the two are stronger than ever; slightly illegal, and somewhat raffish and shady, as of 130 years ago, but of tremendous importance to them both.

So too is the trade between Penang and the northern Malay States, for it has remained the natural port of supply for them, and as their standard of living has risen so Penang has benefited, and risen too. When Penang was founded in 1786, and for long after, these Malay states, and not merely the northern states, had a very long way to rise indeed, as a brief description will show.

Kedah was a flat plain crossed by slow rivers, from the banks of which the padi planters were laying low the jungle. Wrote a visitor, "The bank of the river for a distance of 20 or 30 paces is left uncultivated. I landed, and making my way through the thick bambus, stood on the side of a magnificent plain which I can only compare to one of the wide plains of Bengal, for there is nothing like it in the rest of the peninsula. The whole is an immense paddy field, broken at great intervals by clumps and belts of trees, . . . in some places ploughs were at work drawn by buffaloes and oxen, and in others the women were already planting out the young paddy." Impressive though the Kedah plain had become, its capital, Alor Star, even by the 1840's, was still merely a grubby little village. "I walked through a long narrow muddy lane, with dirty and slovenly attap shops on each side, in several of which cloths were piled up, while most exhibited only the usual Malay commodities."[25]

South of Kedah was Perak, virtually nothing but a river amid a magnificent jungle, a tortuous river accessible only to small craft, winding down from the central mountain range for a hundred miles or more. "On the banks of this river," wrote Crawfurd in 1856, "are situated the bulk of the inhabitants, consisting of Malays and a few Chinese. . . . The whole country is in fact a vast

[24]*Anderson.* pp. 228-230, gives specimen cargoes of an Achinese prahu and a Chinese junk, to and from Acheh and Penang.

[25]*Logan's Journal.* Vol. V. (1851). J. R. Logan; Diary, September, 1850.

jungle, in which are scattered a very few villages."[26] He gave its population at 20,000. Captain Glass, writing in 1787, estimated 30,000, whom he described as "in general very ignorant, their revenues so small and their residence so far inland that little is to be feared by their animosity and less to be hoped for from their friendship,"[27] . . . Although this state had acquired some importance through its tin, to the extent of a Dutch fort at its river's mouth, the ruler was so poor that when Captain Forrest went upstream to the Sultan's kampong in 1783, all that could be given him, in return for his ceremonial gifts of rich Bengal cloths, was a collection of jungle fruit.[28]

South again was Selangor, a minor river which had been virtually uninhabited, unlike ancient Perak, until the eighteenth century. Bugis migration had produced a state of some thousands, led at the time when Penang was founded and until his death in 1826, by a doughty warrior, Ibrahim. With his brother, Raja Hadji of Rhio, Ibrahim had fallen on Malacca in 1783, but his near-victory had been averted by van Braam, his river had been devastated, and when Captain Glass visited it in 1787, "the population does not, I am creditably informed, exceed 1,000 or 1,500 people."[29] By 1839 the population had risen to 12,000. "They are extremely illiterate, and in a state of great physical and moral depression. Piracy, slavery, and the slave-debtor system prevail among them to a great extent."[30] There was tin here too, worked by small groups of Chinese, members of the Triad Society, and controlled, most ineffectually, by the Dutch.

The Dutch were based until 1795 at Malacca. Its glory had long since departed. Its earlier entrepôt trade had left it largely for Rhio. Although it acquired some part of the tin of Perak and Selangor, and remained the rendezvous of South Sumatran traders, so that in 1790, Penang could write "at present there are no merchants in Penang possessed of an extensive capital equal to those at Malacca, who have collectively a million of dollars to go to market with,"[31] yet Malacca had really never seen the beginning of better things. Penang in 1786 and Singapore in 1819 with their greater liberality and freedom from restrictions took away northern and southern trading connections, so that by the 1820's its trade was negligible.

South of Malacca was the wilderness of Johore, which stretched across the base of the peninsula. It was almost empty. It boasted of one river, the Johore, which flowed not eastwards or westwards, as did the other peninsula rivers, but south, to empty into the Johore Straits, opposite Singapore. Scattered in remote Kampongs up that river, or crouching in obscure coastal corners, were some 25,000 people, Malays and *orang laut,* primitive proto-Malays

[26]J. Crawfurd: *A Descriptive Dictionary of the Indian Islands and Adjacent Countries.* (London, 1856). p. 336.

[27]S. S. (F). R. Vol. 2. Captain Glass to Bengal, 29 April, 1787.

[28]Forrest, Voyage from Calcutta to the Mergui Archipelago, etc.

[29]S. S. (F). R. Vol. 2. Captain Glass to Bengal, 29 April, 1787.

[30]*Newbold.* Vol. II. pp. 27-33.

[31]S. S. (F). R. Vol. 1. *Historical Retrospect of Pinang.* (An anonymous article, undated, but probably circa 1790).

who lived still in their boats. "They are possessed of no weapons either offensive or defensive, the satisfying of hunger is their only pursuit, they neither dig nor plant but eke out a miserable existence from the stores of the river and forest . . . they skirt the mangroves, huddled up in a small boat hardly measuring twenty feet in length; at one end the fire place, in the middle their few utensils and at the other end beneath a kadjang or mat their sleeping compartment . . . their deportment is lazy and slovenly, united to a great filthiness of body . . . one could not help being struck with the extreme squalidness of their appearance."[32] Undoubtedly there was not much chance of trade here.

Going north from the Johore Straits, however, up the east coast, the prospects of trade were much better. Until the late nineteenth century, until the advent of large scale tin workings and agricultural pursuits, such as coffee and rubber, the majority of the peninsula's population lived on the east coast. The banks of the long rivers, the Pahang, Kelantan and Trengganu Rivers in particular far surpassed in length anything the west coast had to offer, and between them by 1840 they boasted of 120,000 Malays and Chinese.[33] Their wants may have been few, and their lives primitive and sordid to a degree, but they worked tin and gold, and the northern states in particular were free of Dutch control or interference, so that when in 1787 the Sultan of Trengganu wrote to Light saying "I am very apprehensive that the Dutch have had for some time past a jealous eye on my kingdom, and mean before long to deprive me of it . . . send a gentleman of the Honorable East India Company's service to my kingdom to settle and to establish such commerce as may be advantageous to both parties,"[34] Light dispatched Captain Glass, and then later Lieutenant Blair, with 200 bags of rice. These were sold for $500; in addition the Sultan offered 5,000 pikuls of pepper for 200 chests of opium annually, which contract Bengal instructed Light to accept, "with a view to making such engagements the medium of remittances to Canton."[35] The trade with China: nearly always the dominant motive.

Light endeavored to follow up this promising commercial contact and in 1787, while dispatching to Bengal two Trengganu envoys, Orang Kia Siree Wangru and Nassul Ali Dim (a merchant), who had come across the peninsula overland empowered to negotiate for a Company factory, he recommended that Captain Glass be sent there as Resident. He stressed the closeness to China of Trengganu's pepper as well as its remoteness from the Dutch, and pointed to the possibility of it superseding expensive Bencoolen; but although Cornwallis met the two envoys in Calcutta, no resident was established. Fol-

---

[32]*Logan's Journal,* Vol. 1. (1847). J. T. Thompson: *Remarks on the Sletar and Sabimba Tribes.* pp. 341-352.

[33]*Newbold.* Vol. II. pp. 55-65.

[34]S. S. (F). R. Vol. 2. Sultan, Trengganu to Penang, 24 February, 1787.

[35]S. S. (F). R. Vol. 2. Bengal to Penang, 25 January, 1788. Bengal subsequently revoked this contract, giving it instead to a Calcutta firm, Messrs. Hope Senior and Junior, and Co., whose proposal 'for supplying the supra cargoes in China with tin, pepper and other Malay goods for the China market' was accepted. Bengal to Penang, 15 February, 1788.

lowing the Sultan's death, in 1794, the offer was not renewed, as the river slipped into the orbit of Siam.

These Malay rivers were not listed separately on any of the infrequent trade returns prepared by Light or his successors, indeed even when they were grouped together they were not named, but their produce was referred to generally as "imports by Malay praws." In 1791 for example, Light gave the imports by Malay *prahus* at $185,395, of which tin at $46,563 was the most important, followed by rice ($33,593), birds nests ($14,420), pepper ($12,840), gold dust ($10,125), and rattans ($9,677). It was exchanged in Penang for little else but opium and Indian piece goods.

For a few years an attempt was made to keep a tally of the prahus that brought this produce to Penang. Light in 1787 estimated "a hundred a month," and Leith records a steady rise between 1799 and 1802 from 1836 Malay *prahus* to 3328;[36] but it was an impossible task, as easy as counting a trail of ants, and the practice was discontinued. Yet without doubt, in the development of Penang these *prahus* played their part, particularly, it would seem, with the trade in tin.

By 1803, this tin, of which some quantity came also from Junk Ceylon or P'huket in the north, and Banka in the south, was estimated at 10,000 pikuls, valued in Penang by Leith at $130,000. As a commodity of trade it was excelled only by pepper ($400,000), opium ($300,000), and betelnut ($240,000), although as he said, "neither Bengal piece goods . . . nor many other articles of great value have been mentioned owing to the extreme difficulty of ascertaining anything like near the probable importations" . . .[37] In this he echoed Light, fifteen years previously, who commented "The merchants from the Coromandel will not readily give in upon their arrival a just account of the quantities of goods they have brought, from an apprehension that a knowledge of the quantity may injure them in their sales; and this principle has in a smaller degree an effect upon the European merchants trading here."[38] In circumstances such as this, and in the near absence of any official competent to record trade figures, statistics of commerce are to be regarded with reserve; particularly those that concern the produce that reached Penang from thousands of *prahus*, such as tin.

The tin figures, scanty and suspicious though they are, particularly in the early years of the settlement, nevertheless help explain the strange episode in 1818-1819 when the Company itself, contrary to its well established practice of leaving it well alone to the country traders, participated itself in the trade. Such a reversal of policy was brought about by a sudden drop in tin exports in 1817-1818, due to the dislocation of trade caused by the return of the Dutch.

[36]Leith, p. 53; S. S. (F). R. Vol. 2. Penang to Bengal, 17 September, 1787.

[37]Leith, pp. 52-54.

[38]C. D. Cowan; *Governor Bannerman and the Penang Tin Scheme, JMBRAS,* Vol. XXIII, Pt. 1, (Feb. 1950), deals with this episode in detail.

They came back to Banka, with greater powers than before and to Malacca as well. Trade also was dislocated by the Kedah attack on Perak. All this cut or strained the movement of tin to Penang, and whereas from 1806 to 1811 tin exports averaged $334,080, rising to $336,356 in 1816-1817, they dropped over $100,000 to $221,458 in 1818.[39]

Bannerman's predecessor, Petrie, had foreseen in 1814 that the return of Malacca to the Dutch would result in the loss of the Banka tin trade, and Bannerman was determined to ensure that the trade of the tin states on the peninsula, linked to Malacca by ancient contracts, did not follow suit. He appointed W. S. Cracroft, the Government Malay Translator, as Commissioner to negotiate commercial treaties with them. These were signed by Perak, then fighting the invaders from Kedah, on 30 July 1818 and by Selangor on 22 August. By these agreements and the subsequent purchases of tin by Anderson, re-created "Agent for Tin," Penang hoped that the Dutch would not be able to re-impose the measure of control they had exercised previous to their surrender in 1795; it is doubtful, however, if the agreements were necessary, for the pull of Penang was effective enough, the Chinese links strong enough, to withstand the faded attractions of Malacca.

At the same time, Bannerman, perturbed at the Dutch activity in Java and elsewhere, made two other attempts on the Company's behalf to secure a flow of tin to Penang. Farquhar, waiting for the Dutch to return to Malacca, sailed south in 1818, into the Dutch preserve, and concluded with Raja Muda Jaffir, the Bugis Under-king of Rhio, a tin treaty similar to that negotiated by Cracroft. In the dispatch that recorded this agreement he recommended the necessity of a permanent British post there, to safeguard its trading interests. Greater Carimon Island was his choice, the only island boasting a respectable mountain. The peak can be seen from Singapore, where a settlement was made a few months later early in the following year.

Bannerman moved not merely south but north as well, and attempted to reach an agreement with Patani, from which, down the winding Muda River, tin came overland to the west coast and so across to Penang. The headman of Kroh, the tin area, was agreeable to a tin contract, giving a monopoly of export to the Company. His suzerain, however, the Sultan of Patani, was determined to have his interests protected, and there were difficulties as well with the Chinese who controlled the Kedah tax farm on the Muda River; they also wanted a large percentage of the profits.

Finally the Sultan of Kedah interfered. He feared the gathering of Siam, and was singularly unwilling to have the Company commercially active across his territory and into Patani. He supported the Chinese tax farmers in their exorbitant demands and refused to budge. No tin from Kroh purchased by the Company reached Penang. With the invasion of Kedah by Siam in 1821 the scheme vanished.

[39]T. Braddell: *Statistics of the British Possessions in the Straits of Malacca.* (Penang, 1861). Appendix Table No. 8.

In the south, however, in Selangor, Bannerman was more successful, for despite the return of the Dutch, and their renewed interference there, Sultan Ibrahim sold a large quantity of tin to the Company. Although Bannerman and Anderson dropped momentarily their idea of securing Pangkor Island as a southern tin depot, nevertheless, as tin came north from Selangor and from Perak as well, Penang's tin position was improved considerably.

Bannerman had entered into this project with great enthusiasm. He had visualized the establishment on Pangkor and on Junk Ceylon of two tin depots, supplying the ore to Penang, which would become a great tin center. "To accomplish this important object," he wrote in December, 1818, "which may be ultimately the means of inducing H. C. China direct ships to touch at this port, I am well aware there are many difficulties yet to be surmounted. I shall have no objection to grapple with these . . . "[40] But alas, on 8 August, 1819, he died, and his whole scheme was abandoned.

Phillips, who assumed acting-office, sold the tin that had been collected at $18 per pikul to two Company ships bound for China. This yielded a profit of $5,396, of which Anderson, Malay translator again, took one third. The Company never again directly entered the commercial field.

After 1819, the flow of tin to Penang came in particular from three places. "Since 1819/1820 we have not had a pikul of Banka tin, the whole quantity brought here being principally procured from Poongah" (on the mainland, opposite P'huket), "Perak and Selangor."[41] And by 1826, as Chinese control of the working and the trade became consolidated, Penang could write confidently, "Tin has increased in importation one sixth, the exports are almost equally favourable, the ready sale which this article invariably meets with holds out a prospect that its importation will be much augmented, provided the ports of Pungah, Perak, and Salengore remain in a state of tranquility and uninterrupted by the Siamese."[42] By 1836 the export of tin from Penang was valued at approximately $334,743, excelled only by piece goods, ($540,382), opium, ($357,959) and pepper ($342,697), in a total export trade of $3,289,000; a little over a million of which was Straits produce, the collective name for the beche de mer, beeswax, betelnut, birdsnests, buffalo hides, camphor, cutch, dammer, dragon's blood, elephants teeth, fish maws, gold dust, pearl shell, rattans, sago, shark fins, spices, sticklac, tobacco leaf, tortoise shell and "Straits sundries" that came to Penang from the rivers and creeks of its Malaysian hinterland.[43]

Some of this was brought north by the Bugis, whose trade with Penang was not markedly dissimilar in content with that of Acheh, north Sumatra and the

[40]S. S. (F). R. Vol. A. 14. Penang Consultations, 17 December, 1818.

[41]S. S. (F). R. Vol. A. 18. Collector to Secretary, 16 July, 1825.

[42]S. S. (F). R. Vol. A. 28. Collector to Secretary, Penang, 31 July, 1826.

[43]Newbold, Vol. 1. pp. 80-81; where the figures were given in rupees; S. S. (F). R. Vol. 5. Penang to Bengal, June 28, 1793, which lists Sulu, Borneo, Java and eastwards, Siam and Manila as already trading with the settlement.

Malay States. Although the commodities bought and sold in Georgetown were similar, the vendors were not. The Malays, said Leith, "are indolent . . . When they procure a small quantity of rice, and some opium, no inducement, so long as those articles last, is sufficiently powerful to make them do any work." The Bugis, however, "are Bold, Independent and Enterprising . . . many of their Prows come here annually and exchange their gold dust and cloths for iron, opium, etc."[44]

They began coming north, past Malacca, in 1787,[45] and thereafter news of their annual fleets was waited for, like the arrival of the southwest monsoon, with great excitement.

They come annually to trade and remain two or three months on shore to the number of 1-2,000. They are Mahometins, proud, warlike, independent people, easily irritated and prone to revenge. Their vessels are always well provided with arms which they use with dexterity and vigour. They are the best merchants among the Eastern Islands. They are better governed by patient and mild exhortation than by force; if they commit a trespass they are easily made sensible and may be persuaded to render satisfaction, but they reluctantly yield to stern authority. They require to be carefully watched and cautiously ruled.

The great value of their cargoes either in bullion or in goods with the quantity of opium and piece goods they export make their arrival much wished for by all mercantile peoples.[46]

In late 1792, with a larger fleet than ever expected—thirty large *prahus* in sight and forty more understood to be a few days sail away, Penang wrote urgently for more opium, "it being the intention of the Company to increase the commerce of the port so as to be beneficial to our western settlements and to facilitate the annual remittance into our Treasury at Canton. This year the Bugis already have brought gold or silver to the amount of 2-300,000 dollars to purchase opium and piece goods."[47]

Few figures are available for this trade, which, while increasing, yet settled into a familiar pattern. "The Bugis Trade", wrote Penang in 1808, nearly a quarter of a century after Penang was founded, "which now forms so important and valuable a branch of the commerce of Penang, appears originally to have centred at Malacca." (This may well be so); "there were Bugis traders at Passier, Banjer Massier, but mostly from Baly, Man dar, and Sambawa, from which ports they leave at the commencement of the South West Monsoon, arriving in the Straits in July, more in August, September and October, declining towards the end of the year."[48]

[44]Leith, pp. 27-28.

[45]S. S. (F). R. Vol. 2. Penang to Bengal, 10 January, 1788. "The Buggesse Prows from the Island Celebes are waiting here for opium," Light said, "they have brought Spanish dollars and cloth to purchase 50 chests. The season for their return is far advanced . . . Their coming here will be of singular advantage, every prow bringing to the amount of $20,000, which they exchange for opium and piece goods." He regretted that he had sold all the opium.

[46]S. S. (F). R. Vol. 4. Penang to Bengal, 25 January, 1794.

[47]S. S. (F). R. Vol. 3. Penang to Bengal, 12 November, 1792.

[48]S. S. (F). R. Vol. 180. Penang to London, 31 October, 1808.

Their cargo remained the same as in 1787, "Bugis sarongs, mats, birdsnests, inferior spices, diamonds, gold dust and dollars; occasionally rice and tobacco." The whole fleet touched at Malacca, Penang recorded, "the wealthy and well equipped come on to Penang, where opium can be obtained at a better rate, although often the late-comers are driven back by the northwest winds that come in around September. On this they return, taking a cargo of opium and piece goods."[49]

Piece goods and opium: these figure in all the branches of Penang's trade. Long after the Bugis vanished (for the trade from the Celebes, which had been waning from 1811, when Java was occupied, disappeared completely with the foundation in 1819 of Singapore, 600 miles closer to Makassar), these two commodities were the mainstay of Penang's purchasing power. Southeast India concentrated on the manufacture of cotton textiles for sale in a faraway market with a singleness of purpose perhaps equalled only by nineteenth-century northwest England, which was soon to undercut it in those selfsame markets. With the occupation of Penang, the opening of an emporium close to the customer, business in piece-goods previously fed into Southeast Asia by country traders, boomed.

So too with Bengal opium. In 1786-1787 Penang sold 200 chests at $260 each. By 1790, 300 chests were being sold, and the demand was unfilled. Light thought that perhaps another 100 could have been sold that year at $350. By 1805 "the annual demand for the Malay Market may be estimated at 1,000 chests . . . yielding a profit of from 56 to 69 per cent . . . "[50]

Ample profit though it was, the export of opium remained secondary to that of Indian piece goods during this period. In 1830 while the chests of opium from Calcutta were valued in Penang at approximately $350,000, the rolls of Indian material from Madras reached double that figure, to $860,000.[51] In Malaysia, where opium smoking was far less of a habit among the indigenous population than among the Chinese, opium did not overtake cotton piece goods in value until Singapore, with its rapidly increasing Chinese thousands, had reached a respectable age by the 1830's.

Penang was involved in two other branches of trade that need to be considered, with England and China, of which that with the former was so rudimentary that it can be dismissed in a few sentences. When Penang was founded, and for some time after, there was no direct trade with England at all, and although some early exports from the new settlement, notably pepper, found their way via a transhipment in India to the United Kingdom, there was no sign of any import from Europe until the nineteenth century. Then, typical of the Industrial Revolution then well underway, one of the earliest signs of a British trade was the arrival of a steam engine; equally as typical was the

[49]S. S. (F). R. Vol. 180. Penang to London, 31 October, 1808.
[50]S. S. (F). R. Vol. B.1. Penang to London, 12 November, 1805.
[51]S. S. (F). R. Vol. K.15. Penang Public Consultation, 29 April, 1830.

intimation from Penang that as there was no one able to work it, the engine was being stowed away.

By the latter stages of the Napoleonic Wars the Company was sending occasional ships direct to Penang on their way to China. India had been opened to non-Company trade in 1813, but the Company still retained a monopoly of the tea trade, and ships directed to Canton would unload at Penang some of their cargo and would secure goods more suitable for sale in China. These ships were few, too few for Penang; for the Napoleonic Wars had not merely caused a shortage of ships, but of those that survived, most avoided Penang, either because they sailed fully loaded with cotton and opium from India, and had no reason to stop their sailing, or because after the capture of Java in 1811 they could sail, if coming from London or from Calcutta, directly and without fear through the Sunda Straits. But some did stop, and Penang was called on to sell, in particular, two English commodities unloaded from them; one useful, one useless.

The useless article was wool. "The woollens in store are considerably increased by the supply received by your ships *Alfred* and *Woodford* from England . . . and from the length of time many of the bales of woollens have remained in store they are not likely to be disposed of."[52] This was a general complaint. Wool kept coming despite its unsuitability, and was disposed of with the utmost difficulty, if at all. "We are unable to dispose of the large amount of broad cloth that has been in store for some time, which is in a very bad state and unmarketable."[53] It was usually sold at a loss and re-exported to a cooler climate.

The other staple from London was iron, preferably small flat bars that could be beaten, broken, and fashioned for a multitude of uses. It would appear as if until the nineteenth century the only metal in Southeast Asia was used exclusively for krises and other weapons, and there was thus a great unsatisfied demand for it. "The whole of your British iron received this season has been disposed of at an advance over the Invoice price of 33%, There remains an inconsiderable portion of Swedish iron."[54] This was a familiar refrain from the second decade of the nineteenth century onwards.

Almost as familiar, however, then as now, was the cry of anguish first recorded in 1814 against the unimaginative British producer. "The consignment of the year bears no resemblance to the quantity and descriptions of stores indented for . . . We indented for 500 tons of British iron, specified small, flat bars. We received 380 tons of rod and hoop. It is impossible to sell these large heavy hoops, we have in store a very considerable quantity, and the present addition quite precludes the possibility of effecting its sale. Indeed, of this

[52]S. S. (F). R. Vol. 180. Penang to London, 20 October, 1810.

[52]S. S. (F). R. Vol. 180. Penang to London, 13 December, 1815.

[54]S. S. (F). R. Vol. 179. Penang to London, 10 March, 1809.

description of Iron there has been no sale whatever for a number of years."[55] Such a protest has a very contemporary ring indeed. This trade from England by 1830 was valued at approximately $90,000.

Of more importance initially was the trade with China, the original reason for the founding of Penang. Tin and pepper were the two commodities most in demand in China, along with Straits produce. Minor items, still sold to China today, were the rhinoceros, buffalo and deer horns desired by Chinese apothecaries. For many years the export picture was similar to this early vignette; "of the China fleet from Bombay and Madras,—the *Besborough, Walpole, Lascelles, Royal Admiral, Rose Fowlis* and *Houghton*—which called at Penang, and received wood, water and refreshments, 2,500 pikuls of tin were loaded, besides canes and rattans for Canton."[56] By 1792 ships could sail directly south from Georgetown, following the discovery by Captain Popham of a deep passage between the island and the mainland, and save what was often a difficult leg northwards to round the northwest cape of the island. For most of the Napoleonic war this was the pattern.

As the war progressed, however, two factors already mentioned, the shortage of ships through capture or sinking, and the reluctance of those ships to call at Penang, affected the China trade most adversely. These factors were felt as early as 1801—in that year there was not one private English ship between Bengal and Canton for the whole season—but the adverse effects were not commented on at length in Penang itself until 1810. In that year Penang wrote to London, pointing out the great damage if ships were instructed, as had been contemplated, to sail not down the Straits of Malacca but through the Sunda Straits.

These instructions were not issued. "We have the satisfaction of communicating to your Honorable Court that your several ships of the present season, bound to China, arrived safe at this port at the different periods noted in the margin, and that having taken their respective supplies, proceeded on their voyage...as also the ship *Inglis,* built at this Presidency to engage at China in your regular service."[57]

This concern that the ships of the Company might not call, and the fulsome gratitude shown when they did, is most revealing. In the 1770's the Straits produce, above all the tin and pepper that was taken to China, was taken by country traders. By the 1810's this produce was going as the private speculation of Company officers. The country traders had disappeared. It is not that they had disappeared from India, for in Calcutta alone there were 18 private firms looking eastward by 1815, and 32 by 1820, while private trade with Europe began, and in Canton too an increasing number of firms were establishing themselves ashore, despite the restrictions still in force there. It was

---

[55] S. S. (F). R. Vol. 181. Penang to London, 24 September, 1814.

[56] S. S. (F). R. Vol. 2. Penang to Bengal, 7 October, 1787.

[57] S. S. (F). R. Vol. 180. Penang to London, 28 November, 1811.

simply that there was hardly any need for them to call at Penang.

As the detailed study of Greenberg has made clear, there was a glut of Straits produce in Canton, a "branch of the China trade (that) had always been precarious,"[58] and prices dropped calamitously; after 1819 Singapore replaced Penang as the entrepôt port where goods could be transhipped, or where bills of lading could be altered, for private trade to England; and finally with the opium demand rising steadily, private traders on country ships could sail direct from India with a full cargo.

The opium they carried was purchased from the Company at Calcutta, for although the Company retained a near monopoly of cultivation, and relied on the profits of the sales in Canton for its tea purchases, it did not participate in that trade, for fear of entanglement with the Chinese government. It was left entirely to the country ships. In 1803-1804 private traders carried 2,800 chests past Penang; by 1813-1814, ten years later, the figure had risen to nearly 4,800, and by 1824-25 over 12,000 chests went by country ships from India. In 1833-34, the year in which the agitation of these country traders finally brought about the abolition of the Company's monopoly of the tea trade, nearly 20,500 chests were sold.[59]

By this time the old pattern of trade had changed completely. The drain of silver to China which had so alarmed the Company in the 1780's, but which had been so necessary for the purchase of tea and which had led to the founding of Penang, had diminished and died away. Then, as the demand for opium became ever more insistent, the drain had been reversed. China by 1833 (the year the East India Company monopoly in Canton ended) was paying 6½ million silver dollars annually for the privilege of smoking itself into insensibility. No wonder that the bits of bamboo, the few pikuls of tin and the odd cargo of pepper waited in Penang for a ship to pause. In these changed circumstances Penang played no appreciable part whatever in the trade with China, its exports to Canton in 1830 amounting to less than $500,000, of which betelnut and edible birdsnests were the most important items. And as an ironic comment on a settlement founded to assist the country trade, "nearly the whole of the exports are made on the Hon. Company's ships by the Commanders."[60]

---

[58]Greenberg: p. 87.
[59]Greenberg: p. 221.
[60]S. S. (F). R. Vol. K.15. Penang Public Consultations, 29 April, 1830.

IX

PENANG AND THE
WAR WITH FRANCE

Penang was founded to assist the China trade. It participated in the Revolutionary War and the Napoleonic War with France largely to protect that trade. Whereas the war did not begin in Europe until 1793, there had been war in India with Tippoo Sultan, the ally of the French, and desultory skirmishing on the Indian Ocean, from 1789. This ended with the defeat of the Sultan on land in 1792, and the capture of Pondicherry by a scratch collection of British ships in August of the following year. Cornwallis, the naval commander in chief (and brother of the governor-general) by 1793 was an admiral without ships, as the East Indies station had been ignored during these years of peace in Europe, and Cornwallis had sent back those ships that were repairable. In 1792 all Cornwallis had was a small frigate, the *Minerva,* which escorted his brother home part of the way in September, a captured French vessel, the *Bien Aimé,* and a small ex-privateer, the *Concorde.* When the admiral too sailed home in 1793 on the *Minerva* to surprise his successor, Rainier, at Spithead in April, 1794, "India was almost without naval protection. To the directors of the East India Company it all seemed very odd indeed; and most, most undesirable."[1]

Throughout this period, when as Parkinson makes clear, Britain had maintained its position in the Indian Ocean mainly through the indecision and confusion of the French colonies reacting to the Revolution, and not through any naval supremacy, Penang had cowered on the flank, almost entirely defenceless. Light had begun the erection of a fort shortly after he arrived in 1786; and by October had built a wooden stockade that might have kept out an attack from Malay pirates, but little more. In January, 1788, Light began to double this stockade, and then to treble it, finally managing to hoist up a few guns. The wooden barricade soon collapsed. By 1790 he was writing "the fort is decayed ... the fort has rotted and whole faces are falling down",[2] and by 1793, when the war began, the commander of the troops had reported "Our Fort is nothing more than an old and rotten stockade, with decayed platforms that cannot hold guns."[3]

[1]Parkinson, *War in the Eastern Seas, 1793-1815.* (London, 1954). p. 69.

[2]S. S. (F). R. Vol. 2. Penang to Bengal, 20 June, 1790.

[3]S. S. (F). R. Vol. 3. Lt. Rabau to Cornwallis, 26 June, 1793.

Inside this fort, Light had a small European artillery detachment of seventeen men, thirty infantrymen (Lascars), and a Marine Force of 100 Sepoys, under the command of Lieutenant James Gray R.N. Anchored offshore was an ancient 400-ton Company ship, the best that Bombay could spare, designated as a patrol vessel by Bengal, but because of its unseaworthiness, used by Light as a store-ship. This was the extent of his defence; adequate enough, as he demonstrated, to beat off a threatened invasion in 1791 of over 5,000 Malays, but hopelessly inadequate against even one raiding French frigate or privateer, which could have bombarded the fort and destroyed the town with impunity.

Light, of course, had hoped, as had the Company in Bengal, that the Navy would come to Penang, and to encourage it the Governor-General recorded in December, 1786, shortly after his arrival, that it was "necessary to depute a person properly qualified to make an exact survey of island and harbour. The description of the harbour is favourable, but to justify the advance of such sums as would be necessary to prepare it for the reception and repair of ships of war, a more satisfactory description is required."[4]

Accordingly, Captain A. Kyd, of the Corps of Engineers, was instructed by Bengal in April, 1787, to proceed to Penang and there to obtain a precise and exact knowledge of the harbor. He was told to examine with great care the small island clinging to the landward side of Penang, Pulo Jeraja, of which Light had written, "between Pooloo Jaraju and Penang is a harbour fit for men of war to careen, being 7 and 8 fathoms close to Penang and the same close to Jaraja,"[5] and to prepare a plan for the most economical and effectual way of fortifying the harbor.

Kyd submitted a detailed report in September, 1787. After discussing the alternatives to Penang as a deep water port able to use the northeast monsoon and to protect the Bay of Bengal when the Navy had retired from Madras,—places such as the Chittagong River, the Arakan River, the Andamans, Nicobars, and others,—Kyd then gave specific reasons why Penang was preferable. His dispatch was ignored, and for his pains he was sent, a few years later, to report with Lieutenant Blair on the Andamans. It was not a particularly enthusiastic report—the islands were subjected to the full onslaught of the southwest monsoon, there was little food and there were 2,000 fierce inhabitants, and the islands and its inhabitants were extremely wild and wet—but it satisfied Admiral Cornwallis, who had the pleasure, before sailing home in the *Minerva,* of a rendezvous at newly established Port Cornwallis, named for him in 1791.[6] When war with France began in earnest then, in 1794, Penang was defenceless.

This, of course, is very largely the condition of most British possessions at

[4]S. S. (F). R. Vol. 2. Bengal Public Consultations, 13 December, 1786.

[5]S. S. (F). R. Vol. 2. Penang to Bengal, 25 December, 1786.

[6]A fine description of this is in Symes, *A Mission to Ava.* (London, 1800) pp. 126-138.

the outbreak of any war, and the position on Penang from this time on steadily improved. Late in 1793, although Bengal thought that the French at their base on Mauritius were too worried over their own safety to attack the island, Penang was re-inforced to the extent of a hundred European troops, artillery and infantry men, and then, as Light sent back dispatch after dispatch reporting the numerous captures of the French privateer *General Durnourier* and others, the Navy came again.

After the departure of Admiral Cornwallis, in September 1793, and before the arrival of Commodore Rainier, in the following September, the naval defence of India had rested with three armed Indiamen under the command of the senior Company captain, Mitchell. With a true sense of values, Mitchell concentrated on guarding that which was most important, the trade with China. In April, 1794, his squadron escorted a convoy, which refreshed and re-grouped itself at Penang, and then sailed to Canton. In the China Sea the convoy fell in with two French privateers, which it captured. Despite being attacked by four other French vessels, the convoy managed to sail them to Batavia. Subsequently it shepherded through the Sunda Straits the homeward-bound China fleet, formed in convoy; the French keeping clear. In this movement Penang had played a very useful role, supplying a harbor where the Indiamen could anchor and collect information, fresh provisions and further protection. Writing of the facility with which Mitchell had been supplied with stores, Rainier shortly after his arrival in 1794 said he "could not understand why the Andamans were put in competition with Prince of Wales Island."[7] Shortly after, the Andamans were abandoned, but before that Bengal had decided in 1794 that it would be desirable if another look was taken at Penang. Kyd, by this time a major, was sent off again.

He was given three instructions. He was told to report on the fortifications at Georgetown, and to advise whether any more were needed for the protection of the island, to examine the troops and to estimate whether they could defend Penang against a moderate attack, and if not how many more troops would be needed, and finally he was requested to "re-examine the harbour and report to what extent he thinks it may be employed as a place of equipment for His Majesty's ships."[8]

Before Kyd arrived Penang received convincing proof of the need for naval protection. In July, 1794, nine East Indiamen with cotton for Canton hurried into the harbor, and clustered near the point. Their guardian, the Bombay frigate *Commodore Pickett,* anchored only a little further away, while outside roamed the French privateer *Revenge,* which had narrowly missed this rich prize. To induce the Company frigate to venture out, Light loaned it every available man from the island, and sent a galley up the coast a few miles as lookout. Cautiously the Commodore Pickett stood out in search; but no sooner

[7]S. S. (F). R. Vol. 1. Commodore Rainier to Governor General, 31 December, 1794.   •

[8]S. S. (F). R. Vol. 6. Bengal to Penang, 10 July, 1794.

had it gone, than the China fleet, with typical lack of discipline, sailed south, hoping for the best. An American ship, the *Three Sisters,* was kept in port to safeguard the fleet as it was believed this ship had given information at Acheh to the *Revenge,* and the cotton ships reached Canton undisturbed. A narrow brush.

In the following year (1795) Kyd submitted his report. He described the small stone fort that Light had built to replace the rotten stockade.

The fort is a square of masonry of 500 ft. exterior side with a very inconsiderable ditch, with no covered way or out work of any kind, nor is there as yet even a parapet put upon it, and as the Chinese who contracted for the completion of it has failed in his undertaking, no other means has been taken to go on with it, so that the fort is as undefendable as it was at the beginning of the war when it was undertaken and at first carried on with great spirit.

It is exactly on the same spot, and of the same dimensions, as a stockade of trees that was constructed on first taking possession, intended merely as a security against the Malays, for which purpose then it was adequate . . . but now surrounded on all sides with buildings, many of them masonry, within a pistol shot of the walls. (He mentioned another defect, that it was) so close to the water's edge that ships can anchor 100-150 yards off, overlook it from the main mast, or even the poop of a large ship. It is hard to imagine a spot worse chosen, it can defend neither town nor harbour.[9]

This fort, built by Light at a cost of some $67,000 and without the prior approval of the Company in Bengal, had been hurriedly occupied at the outbreak of war. The fort was very largely a waste of money. It was clear from Kyd's report that extensive and expensive alterations and additions would be needed if it was to serve the purpose of defending the settlement from a European naval attack.

Kyd again praised the harbor, and compared the commercial development of Georgetown to the complete immobility of Fort Cornwallis on the Andamans. To this extent only he convinced Bengal. The Commander-in-Chief, Rainier, recorded in September that it was obvious that the fort was useless, and that it would be very expensive to repair, that there was little hope of the Company deriving much revenue from the settlement, and that as the excellent port of Trincomali was in British hands, no decision was necessary as to whether it should be made a naval base, but that "it may be a useful rendezvous for future expeditions to the eastward."[10] The Governor General agreed, and authorization for local repairs only was given. If Penang was to be defended, it would be by the wooden walls of the fleet, not by the crumbling stone of the fort.

Commodore Rainier, when he wrote of "future expeditions," presumably had in mind the utility already shown by Penang in the capture of Malacca. The French, by overrunning Holland in January, 1795, and by establishing the Republic of Batavia which concluded an alliance with France had brought a

[9] S. S. (F). R. Vol. 7. Major A. Kyd to Bengal, 2 August, 1795.

[10] S. S. (F). R. Vol. 6. Bengal Public Consultations. Minute of CIC to Captain Kyd's Report, 28 September, 1785.

new threat to the British in the east. The Dutch at the Cape of Good Hope, in Java and at Malacca, were at points of considerable strategic value. British trade with India and China could be attacked and possibly severed if an aggressive enemy was able to act from these points. The Navy moved swiftly.

From Madras for the attack on Malacca the Navy secured Major Archibald Brown and four European battalions, which the Commodore loaded onto transports escorted by the *Orpheus* and *Resistance*. Captain Henry Newcombe of the *Orpheus,* who was placed in charge, was instructed by Rainier to lose no time, that the China trade must be protected, and that Malacca must be captured.[11]

Malacca, most ancient and historic of the towns of the Malay Peninsula, lies at the head of a broad shallow bay, by the mouth of a small river. Originally perhaps it was the home of a few *orang sungei* or river people, primitive fishermen, but it rose to prominence, indeed it acquired an international reputation, during the great days of the Malacca Sultanate (1402-1511), when it became the center of Southeast Asian trade and the outstanding diffusion point for Islam in that area. After its capture by the Portuguese in 1511, a stone fort was built hard by the south bank of the river's mouth, and the Malay town sheltered on the opposite side. This the Dutch inherited when they came into possession in 1641. Malacca to them however was not the center of operations, not the core of their empire but the edge. The wealth of the town, derived very largely from its entrepôt trade slowly vanished (its hinterland, even when it became settled with Minangkabau migrants in the seventeenth century, had negligible attractions, and even most of its food came from overseas). Dutch trading policy, restrictive and regulatory, was opposed to the freedom on which an entrepôt trade could flourish. Tin treaties with the neighboring rivers, Perak in particular, sustained the settlement, but the Dutch were more concerned with Batavia and the Spice Islands, and when Newcombe anchored in the bay in August, 1795, and looked towards the little town, the great stone fort, with its nine solid bastions, was held by a mere 269 men, of whom over 200 were unenthusiastic Javanese, Amboinese, or other Malaysians, and there was no strong heart whatever left in Malacca.[12]

After some inconclusive parleying, a night landing ordered by Brown on August 17 on a strange beach south of the fort, miscarried. This was natural, the beach in question being lost in the darkness, and the troops encountering "jungle so thick as to render it impossible to land. The boats therefore drew off and stood to the northward, an officer walking in the surf abreast of the boats to inform us when we came opposite to the open ground, when the troops immediately landed."[13] The troops advanced through coconut trees towards

[11]Admiralty Records. 1/168. Commodore Rainier to Captain Newcombe, 19 July, 1795. (Quoted in Parkinson: p. 80.)

[12]This is dealt with by G. Irwin: *The Surrender of Malacca in 1795*. JMBRAS. Vol. XXIX. Pt. 3. (August, 1956). pp. 86-133.

[13]Col. J. Mackerras to A. Couperus, late Governor of Malacca, 1st April, 1805. Irwin: p. 112.

the fort. Their presence was discovered in the morning. A few shots were fired, so few that it was rumored (and later proven false, at least by the governor, Couperus) that Couperus and Koek, the leading burgher[14] (who had trading contacts with Scott in Penang), had collaborated with the enemy. With its honor presumably satisfied by the few volleys, the fort surrendered. Britain had acquired its second settlement in the Straits.

Brown and Newcombe were simple warriors, and they had little taste for the administration of a conquered territory. In addition there was the widespread feeling that the Dutch, whose Stadtholder was hiding from the French in England and had called on his territories to collaborate with the British, were merely the unwilling victims of a French conquest. The Dutch were not, at least in this struggle, it was felt, the enemy of the British. The Dutch administration was permitted to remain, and an official notice was issued, stating . . . "that the government shall continue so as it was, only that the Commanding Officer of the English troops will take seat as second in council."[15]

Penang had proved unexpectedly useful in this unheroic campaign. It had supplied the invasion force with powder, as the store-ship of the expedition had been captured by a French privateer. Bills and posters of a fifth-column character had percolated in from Penang before the invasion, and after the capture Penang was called upon to supply stores and fresh food to the *Orpheus* and the *Resistance.* Penang's utility continued, for subsequently, in 1804, an administrator was supplied to Malacca, and in 1805 it was incorporated within the Prince of Wales Island Presidency. Well before that, however, Penang had proved Rainier correct in being "a most useful rendezvous for future expeditions to the eastward."

By late 1795, the British Navy in the East was assuming a reputable size, and although the East Indies squadron led by Commodore Rainier had been placed under the command of an Admiral at the Cape, the force off Madras seemed so superior to anything that could threaten it, and the Admiral so distant, that a far southeastern venture against the Spice Islands seemed possible. Madras, which for centuries had peered into the Dutch preserves with the wistful air of a Sultan denied a harem, wrote to Rainier in late September, submitting for his consideration "the advantage that would result from an early possession of Amboyna, which we understand to be one of the most valuable"[16] of the Spice Islands.

Rainier, with two Companies of Europeans and a battalion of Sepoys loaded on to three transports, together with the two most powerful ships of his squadron, *Suffolk* and *Centurion,* and the smaller *Swift,* sailed on 15 October. He called first at Penang, then at Malacca. Here he swiftly sacked the Dutch governor, sending him to India for ten long years as a prisoner of war, and

---

[14]That is of Dutch-Malay blood.

[15]S. S. (F.) R. Vol. 47. Malacca Public Consultations, 21 August, 1795.

[16]Madras to Commodore Rainier, 29 September, 1795; in Parkinson, pp. 91-92.

directing that the town be governed by the Madras military; whence it lapsed into nonentity for nearly a decade. Rainier sailed on (one must infer with guides from the trading community of Malacca), into the eastern Java and Molucca Sea, where British ships, particularly of the Royal Navy, had seldom ventured before. Amboina was reached in February, 1796. It was quickly occupied, as was Banda, a neighboring island; but the collection of loot and the establishment of control (for this was intended to be no mere raid but a permanent occupation), together with revolts, insurrections and contrary winds, kept him there most irresponsibly, on the extreme limit of his command, throughout the year. He returned to Madras with much booty, again re-assembling his ships at Penang, in February, 1797,[17] leaving behind a British civil administration.

While he was away on this scavenging for spices, the French continued the war. Six powerful frigates sailed from Mauritius in July, 1796. Their object was to destroy Penang, and so to make easier their attacks on the China trade. The island was in no state to resist and no help could be expected from Rainier, far out of sight. Most providentially, the French frigates were encountered off Acheh, where they were refitting, by two British ships of the line that had been escorting a China convoy. An inconclusive battle followed (August 9, 1796) and although no victory was claimed nor won, the French squadron was damaged and diverted from Penang. The settlement was saved.

In 1797, for the third successive year, an expedition to the eastward was mounted by Madras, this time to Manila, and again, as with those to Malacca and the Moluccas, Penang served as the rendezvous. War with Spain had broken out in October, 1796, but news of it did not reach India until April, 1797. Rainier, by then an Admiral and in command of a considerable squadron, consorted immediately with the Governor-General for an invasion of the Philippines. By August the first eight transports had sailed for Penang, while others, from Calcutta and Madras, followed thereafter. On 3 September, with most of the 2,000 troops already stretching their legs on the island and the rear units of the naval element about to leave Madras, news came from Europe that peace had been concluded between France and the German States, and that France might endeavor, with the forces so freed, to invade India overland. The fear was premature, for Bonaparte did not sail for Egypt until 1798, but the expedition was cancelled. The troops under General Craig, including the 33rd Regiment commanded by Colonel Arthur Wesley (later the Duke of Wellington), were recalled to India.

For the next few years Penang played an important although unsensational role as a most convenient refreshment call and convoy assembly point for British ships going or coming from the east. A naval hospital, first requested by Rainier in 1795, was built, and the Navy called constantly for water and provisions. In November and December, 1800 and throughout January, 1801

[17]This is outlined by Capt. W. Lennon. *Journal of a Voyage through the Straits of Malacca, 1796-1797.* JSBRAS. Vol. VIII. Pt. 2. June, 1881.

a powerful force of eleven ships was based there, while orders from Dundas in London calling for the capture of Java were first rendered impossible of execution, by the lack of military support from India, and then postponed, later to be cancelled. When peace came, in March, 1802, no decisive step had been taken, against either the French on Mauritius or the Dutch on Java.

Lord Wellesley (elder brother to Wellington), who as Governor General had cancelled the Java expedition of 1800 through excessive fear of an invasion of India, swung back to aggressive plans in 1802. He decided that Penang and Malacca provided insufficient protection to the China convoys and that a further eastward base would have to be established. The Company in London had lost interest in its remote foothold among the cloves of Amboina, and it had written to Madras recommending that as measures were being taken on Penang and in India itself for the expansion of spice cultivation there, which would ensure that the Dutch would never have a world monopoly again, the British establishment on the Moluccas should be withdrawn. Both Robert Farquhar, the Resident,[18] and Wellesley agreed that the occupation of the islands was serving no useful purpose, commercially or strategically, and the Governor General decided to remove the administration and to install it on Balambangan.

Balambangan, the scene of the ill fated 1773-1775 expedition, was thought fit by Wellesley to be the center for naval operations against any European power that attempted to attack the lines of communication between Penang and Canton. Here the fleet in the eastern seas could shelter and provision, and, by its presence, here too might grow a trade emporium from which would radiate an increasing political influence. All these old hopes made new again were communicated to Robert Farquhar; how it was to be achieved was left to his discretion.

Collecting the 800 odd troops evacuated from the Moluccas, Farquhar sailed from Malacca, arriving at Balambangan on 29 September, 1803. A little over four months after arriving he wrote a long report in which his outline of the way in which a British settlement in Southeast Asia should be conducted echoed the free-trade sentiments of the founder of Penang. Farquhar, as Francis Light before him, held that "a great nation which imposes the fewest restraints upon and affords the most liberal encouragement to the exertions of the community, consults its own general benefit as much as the happiness and advantage of individuals."[19] By this time, February, 1804, Farquhar had left Balambangan and had taken over from Leith the Lieutenant Governorship of Penang, which in September, 1804, became responsible both for Balambangan and Malacca.

Farquhar urged on the authorities conducting the war with France and

---

[18]Robert Farquhar subsequently became Lt. Governor of Penang, 1804-1805, and then Governor of Mauritius.

[19]Bengal Secret and Political Consultations, 18 July, 1805. Farquhar to Bengal, 16 February, 1804, encl. report, same date; quoted in Willi, p. 126.

Holland that there should be a re-appraisal of the traditional British policy that avoided alliances and entanglements with the local powers. The rival European fleets, maneuvering on the waters of Southeast Asia, were ignoring very largely the indigenous inhabitants, and were neglecting to utilize what could be a very important element in the struggle. It was a war of the West in Asia. Let us, Farquhar argued, bring in Asia on our side. He suggested that Britain should conclude treaties of friendship and commerce with the numerous chiefs and rulers, and that from the broad base thus established, an empire of immense value to Britain could be erected. As with Raffles a few years later, however, who quoted Farquhar with approval,[20] this scheme had no attractions to either India or to the Company in London. It remained a naval war fought between European protagonists.

As with the scheme, so with Balambangan. When Dundas (Lord Melville), in London became aware that Wellesley had proceeded with the establishment of a base there, he was horrified. China ships were being but rarely attacked, the convoy system was providing adequate protection against two powers, Spain and Holland, whose fleets stayed in harbor, and a third, France, whose frigates had to sail one thousand miles to be within striking distance. At a time when Britain faced formidable foes inside India itself, as well as on the waters near its coast, and when major enemy bases were uncaptured, the founding of a remote outpost was a step too rash to be authorized. The base was ordered withdrawn.[21]

Although the troops languished on Balambangan throughout 1804 and most of 1805, Farquhar in Penang was called on in September of that year to clear land and hurriedly to repair the Sepoy lines "for the troops expected from Balambangan."[22] The detachment arrived and took up quarters on 16 December under the command of Lt. Col. Gales, whom Farquhar had left in charge of the island. Balambangan was abandoned, and Britain's next venture in North Borneo waters did not occur until the occupation of Labuan Island, near Brunei, in 1846.

In 1805 Penang was elevated to the status of a Presidency. The instructions from London to Dundas, the first President (the nephew of Lord Melville, the First Lord of the Admiralty), made it clear that the establishment of a naval base was to be his major objective. The Company commented as follows:

. . . a plan which has been lately laid before us, of which a copy and the paper accompanying it is enclosed at the desire of the First Lord of the Admiralty, for making the Island a Naval Arsenal for the building and repairing of His Majesty's Ships, gives a new

[20]See C. E. Wurtzburg: *Raffles of the Eastern Isles.* (London, 1954) p. 102. Memorandum by Raffles to Lord Minto, 1810.

[21]Possibly fortunately for Wellesley, a mission led by Roberts to Cochin China in 1805 seeking the cession of an island from the King also failed.

[22]S. S. (F). R. Vol. 11. Penang to Bengal, 27 September, 1805.

and high degree of importance to the subject. . . . We are fully impressed with the great national advantages of the object proposed by the First Lord of the Admiralty, entertain sanguine hopes of its practicability, at least to a certain extent, and have most willingly agreed to afford the utmost aid in our power in carrying into execution the measure proposed by His Majesty's Government. . . .

. . . the Island Jerejah, one side of which forms the inner harbour is the spot most proper for a Dock Yard for King's Ships. The forming of a Dock Yard will necessarily require the erection of Warehouses, Work-shops, and all the other appendages of such an establishment. . . . We find that something in the nature of a Fort has already been constructed in the Island, and whatever may be necessary to put the island in a tolerable state of defence we wish to be immediately executed, but as it is our wish that a regular Fortification for the permanent securing against a European force should be constructed, we therefore direct that you form and transmit to us a plan and estimate of such Work. . . .[23]

Penang was to have a naval dockyard and base; in addition it was to have a fleet. In January, 1805, Admiral Rainier came into Penang from China, sixteen sail of Indiamen under the strong escort of nine warships, there to find waiting for him his successor, Admiral Pellew. With much saluting and manning of yards, the two admirals met, conferred and departed, Rainier homeward bound, Pellew to prowl the Indian Ocean as commander-in-chief. He did not prowl for long. In August there arrived off Madras another admiral, Troubridge, junior to him, but with Admiralty orders that the command was to be split and that the eastern part, including Penang but excluding west India, from a line due south of Point de Galle in Ceylon, together with half the fleet, fourteen ships in all, was to be commanded by Troubridge, the new arrival.

The scheme was idiotic, presumably hatched by Dundas in London as part of his plan for a base at Penang. It ignored the monsoons, and the need all ships felt for Bombay. It overlooked the basic role of the fleet, the defense of the Bay of Bengal. It would have forced the western squadron to face the southwest monsoon, and similarly would have deprived the eastern squadron of the shelter of Bombay. Taking advantage of his seniority, and a saving clause in the instructions that permitted an over-all command whenever a superior force approached, Pellew kept control, and sailed to Penang, which was reached 23 September, 1805. While in Penang he divided the force, but the dividing line was 82½°E, which brought Madras and Trincomali into the western station, and so permitted the normal movement of the Madras squadron to Bombay before the northeast monsoon. By thus excluding Troubridge from India, Pellew gave Penang a squadron. It was the only one it was ever to have.

Pellew explained his decision to base Troubridge on Penang thus: "The protection of the rising Colony of Prince of Wales Island, and the security of the important and rapidly increasing trade carried on by the Country Ships between India and China, together with the observation of the Enemy's possessions in that quarter, would engage all the attention of a distinct command

---

[23]S. S. (F). R. Vol. 179. London to Penang, 18 April, 1805.

. . ."[24] The distinct command for the moment consisted of one sloop of eighteen guns, the *Rattlesnake,* on which Troubridge was forced to hoist his flag. With the remainder, Pellew sailed away.

Troubridge wrote "I am still shut up here by Sir E. Pellew . . . but I have not been idle . . . I have just returned from a thirteen hours row and sail along the Coast and up the River looking at Timber; by way of a treat, I took the Governor with me — the thermometer 93. I am so well seasoned that it does not effect me. I see nothing to hinder us from launching 74 gun ships, frigates and sloops . . ."[25] while at the same time Dundas, who had been dragged on the treat, informed London "of our intention of laying down the keel of a large Frigate without delay, and . . . we have so little doubt of being able about October or November next to begin also on a 74 Gun Ship that we are induced to request that you will order the whole copper and iron work for both, to be sent out by the earliest opportunity possible."[26]

This optimism soon was dissipated. Unexpected difficulties of a local nature soon arose over both the fort and the dockyard, the main responsibilities committed to the care of the Presidency. The attitude in London changed as well, either as a result of the resignation of Dundas, First Lord of the Admiralty, or of the battle of Trafalgar, or of both.

The newly appointed administration in 1805 had been told to prepare a plan and estimate of a fort sufficient to guard the settlement and proposed naval base against a European force. This was well-nigh impossible. Jeraja, where the base was planned, was six or seven miles down the eastern coast from Georgetown. A fort could be erected to guard that, or Fort Cornwallis could be adapted, perhaps, to defend the town; but no single fort could do both. From 1805 to 1811 the policy in fact adopted was the patching up of the fort in existence, while approval from London was sought, unavailingly, for the large expenditure needed for the construction of a major defense work at Jeraja.

In June, 1806, upon the arrival of Captain Robertson, the island's chief engineer and surveyor, Dundas, the President, directed him to submit plans for the defense of the town against a European naval attack, and also "for the more material point of permanently fortifying some strong position on the island,"[27] the site to be near the proposed base. Captain Robertson submitted a somewhat extensive scheme that called for the reinforcement of the forces to the strength of 2,000 men, the buying up, destruction and levelling of a large area of crowded Georgetown, and an estimated $20,000 expenditure in strengthening Fort Cornwallis. These plans for the temporary defense of the towns were rejected as far too expensive and grandiose by the Penang Coun-

[24]P.R.O. Adm. 1/176. Pellew to Admiralty, 30 September, 1805, in Parkinson, p. 283.
[25]Troubridge to Lord Sidmouth, 29 March, 1806, in Parkinson, pp. 290-291.
[26]S. S. (F). R. Vol. B. 1. Penang to London, 21 February, 1806.
[27]S. S. (F). R. Vol. 11. Penang to Bengal, 3 July, 1806.

cil, and the fort was left alone.

By early 1807, the arrival and departure of so many admirals, and the consequent firing of many ceremonial salutes, had so shaken the fort that part of the wall had broken down. The guns were regarded as the fort's worst enemy, and a large section of the rampart had to be taken apart and rebuilt.

Robertson submitted further plans in the hope of making the fort serve adequately the requirements as stated in the Court's instructions, but again his proposals called for such an expensive approach that they were rejected. He suggested that the old fort be allowed to slip into ruin, and that a strong pentagon eight times the size of the existing fort, be erected 120 yards further inland. As this would have necessitated the destruction of most of the town, a feat which its erection was intended to prevent, and which no French squadron had been able to accomplish, the Presidency Council had no hesitation in denying these proposals as impracticable. In any case, both London and the Council told him, expenditure for such a large project could be sanctioned only if it defended both dockyard and town; it did not appear as if this new scheme could do either.

Robertson was more successful on his third attempt. With the assistance of the Governor, Norman MacAlister, he submitted a more conservative plan in July, 1808, which was accepted by the Council, and the work proposed was built. Stone batteries, 600 feet in length, "well designed for the protection of our present Marine Yard and Harbour on both sides of the Point"[28] (that is Point Penagger), and costing a little over four and a half thousand dollars, were added to the existing Fort Cornwallis. They mounted seventeen heavy guns, were twenty feet thick, and were completed in January, 1809.

The work was added to during the year, when a battery was constructed extending out from the northwest bastion of the fort. It reached the edge of the beach, and held seven 32-pound guns which could command the harbor. For all its deficiencies, Penang had become by 1810 perhaps the best defended port in Asia, east of India. Eight years later, with peace in Europe, Fort Cornwallis was written off by the Council as no longer worthy of any further repairs. Some stones were laid at the foot of the battery on the point, to stop erosion by the sea, but that was all. It was adapted for use as a building rather than as a defensive work, and the preserved remnants of it in the Georgetown of today, encompassed by a most attractive Esplanade, bear witness to the 150 years of its defense by the distant Royal Navy, an absolute power that was never corrupted, and under which the island basked in peace, its highly polished 32-pounders useless and unnecessary.

Progress in the second commission entrusted by Dundas to his nephew was even slower than the first. There were numerous factors that tended to retard the construction of a naval dockyard and the building of ships, some of which

[28]S. S. (F). R. Vol. A. 3. Penang Public Consultations, 7 July, 1808.

had been present long before the Presidency was established and others which appeared after the scheme was officially sanctioned. Collectively these factors killed the project.

The most decisive factor was finance. Dundas, with power in both the Admiralty and the Company, had not considered it necessary to arrange the precise financial details. Whether Peter paid Paul, or vice versa, was not a matter of much moment to him. But with Dundas' departure it was important to each party that the other should pay. Naturally in the end neither did. In June, 1806, the Court proposed to the Admiralty that "one third of the cost of the Naval Arsenal containing the Docks, Warehouses and their Defences is to be defrayed by Government."[29] The Admiralty could not accept this, and said that although it was prepared to supply such machinery and equipment as was required by the Company for the building of the base, all expenses were to be borne by the Company "until such time as the Admiralty was convinced of the practicability and probable advantages of making Docks, Ships, etc. for a Naval Establishment."[30]

This reluctance by the Navy to accept any financial obligation made the Company look a second time at the scheme, fully impressed though it had been previously with its great national advantages. The Supreme Government in India in the previous year (1805) had directed Penang to restrict its drawing on Bengal to ordinary administrative expenditures. There was no money there, particularly as Wellesley was involving the government in a most costly war against the Marathas. In late 1806 the Navy further showed which way the wind was blowing by abolishing the absurd divided command, by reinstating Admiral Pellew as Commander-in-Chief of the East Indies, and by posting Troubridge, who since September, 1805, had been clinging to Penang, to South Africa. The island was no longer the headquarters of a squadron, and Pellew based himself for the most part on Trincomali. Penang was becoming rather a backwater, and the prospect of financing a naval base was dim.

In addition to this financial problem, there were local difficulties. Although Penang was (and is) an island covered in timber, on practical investigation it was found unsuitable for ship building. To undertake this project, timber had to be brought in from outside, from Burma, from Siak in Sumatra, and from Kedah. Most of it, teak, came from Rangoon under a contract made between the government and some country traders, Montgomery and Turner, they supplying the teak and the Company transporting it to Penang in the locally built 112-tonner *Margaret,* launched in 1806.

Several local contracts were given to European and Chinese firms in Georgetown to supplement the slow movement from Burma, 500 miles away, of timber. James Scott secured one, and added to the buildup in the Marine Yard with wood from Kedah. But these endeavors proceeded at a snail's pace, the

[29]S. S. (F). R. Vol. 179. London to Penang. 24 June, 1806.
[30]*Ibid.*

Superintendent of Marine commenting sadly on "the inability of Native contractors to fulfill at the stipulated prices the contracts in which they had hastily entered without well weighing the difficulty attending the conveyance of the Timber."[31]

To the lack of finance and the shortage of timber was added the dearth of skilled artisans so necessary for the establishment of a base and the repair and construction of ships. In 1806 a master builder had arrived, Joseph Seaton, but he came alone. As in Sydney, where similar shipbuilding attempts were beginning, the only labor available cheaply in Penang at that time was that of the transported convicts, but few of these possessed the specialized knowledge necessary for building a British man-of-war. Seaton found it impossible to recruit even a small core of technicians, for there were no smiths, shipwrights, or caulkers on the island.

This shortage of a skilled labor force was so severe that one project authorized in 1805, the building of marine docks, was never begun. An engineer to build them had arrived, Mr. Paul Tate, but, like Seaton, he was helpless. A steam engine had come too, and with the help of artificers and joiners from the aged *Blenheim* it had been assembled. But when the *Blenheim* sailed, in December, 1806, taking Troubridge and the entire ship's company to their death off Madagascar, where she foundered, all work stopped. Tate himself was somewhat suspect, for his plans for docks on Jeraja, together with a careening wharf, were not submitted until 1809, three years after his arrival. After scrutiny (of the costs in particular, the docks being estimated at $260,000 and the careening wharf at $36,000) it was decided that "it may be beneficial to the Public Service that Mr. Tate should proceed to Europe for the purpose of explaining his plans and report, with the view of affording such further information as may be required by the Honorable Court of Directors or any committee of professional men whom they may deem it expedient to appoint for the purpose of investigating this highly interesting subject."[32] Highly interesting it may have been, but this was the end of it. With Tate's disappearance, the whole idea was forgotten.

In one respect only were the 1805 hopes of the Directors achieved. In February 1806 Penang had written of its intention of laying down the keel of a large frigate without delay. In September, 1807, the Superintendent of Marine, having overcome to a certain extent the difficult timber situation, reported that "the quantity of timber already collected, and the measures that have been taken and successfully pursued warrants the opinion that ship building may be commenced with a fair measure of success."[33] It began just in time, for London already had ordered that all ship-building operations should cease and that no

[31]S. S. (F). R. Vol. A. 2. Penang Public Consultations, 24 July, 1807.

[32]S. S. (F). R. Vol. A. 5. Penang Public Consultations, 2 March, 1809.

[33]S. S. (F). R. Vol. 179. Penang to London, 11 September, 1807.

more contracts for timber should be let after sufficient had been secured for the frigate and the 74 ship of the line already planned. This dispatch reached Penang in December, 1807; it indicates clearly the abandonment of the 1805 naval base scheme.

The two ships, however, were built. As no ship or dock had been erected on Jeraja, shipbuilding was confined to the Marine Yard near the point in Georgetown. Tate, the engineer, in 1807 designed and in part constructed the slipway for the building and launching of the first, a frigate, but Seaton criticized both the construction and the basic plan, and a committee of ship owners, boat builders and public men ruled in his favor, and called on him to lay down his own slipway. This he did, and on it the 960-ton *Pinang* slowly took shape. In August, 1809, she was launched.

The experiment had not been a success. The labor costs had been very high, over $30,000, while the labor charges for the *Cornwallis,* a 44-gun ship built in 1800 at Bombay, amounted to no more than $15,000, half that of the 36-gun frigate. The *Pinang* was sailed to London and there sold to the Royal Navy.[34]

Meanwhile Seaton was busy building a "74," a most ambitious achievement. Doubts were entertained that the strengthened slipway would hold her, and that sufficient timber could be collected. Work proceeded steadily, however, and on 28 June, 1811, the 1,200-ton ship of the line *Inglis* was launched. An R.N. captain had arrived to commission her, she was fitted out and manned, and in September of that same year she escorted a convoy to China. In November, his work done, Seaton returned to England. I do not think that any other ship for the Royal Navy has ever been built in Malaya.[35]

By this time (late 1811) the retrenchment orders of the Court of Directors had disintegrated the Marine Department. The posts of civil engineer, master builder and superintendent of the marine yard were abolished, all marine stores were sold or sent to Trincomali, no contracts for timber were renewed, allowances were discontinued and expenditure drastically curtailed. The faint suggestion of a naval base vanished.

In 1805 there had been some logic behind the move to strengthen Penang. It was possible for the French from Mauritius to threaten the Bay of Bengal in the winter months when the East Indies squadron sheltered at Bombay, and a base to the eastward, such as Penang, therefore was desirable. It was also the assembly point for convoys and a strengthened Penang would give increased protection to the valuable trade that passed it on its way to or from China. Should the Dutch on Java become ambitious and aggressive, the more strength possessed by Penang the better would trade, and the Bay of Bengal,

[34]S. S. (F). R. Vol. C. 1. London to Penang, 29 June, 1810. (This *Cornwallis* is not to be confused with the *Cornwallis* (76) launched in 1813, the first teak ship ever built in India.)

[35]In May, 1955, as a Sub. Lt., M.R.N.V.R., I participated in the launching in Singapore of *H.M.S. Panglima,* but she was commissioned for the local defense of Singapore, then (in 1955) under the control of the Royal Malayan Navy. Subsequently she has come under the control of the Royal Navy.

be protected from them. And should the indolent Spaniards at Manila ever venture out, a striking force at Penang was that much closer than one at Madras or Bombay to send them back into Cavite Bay again. All this dictated a base at Penang.

Between 1805 and 1811, however, the war with France in the east turned dramatically, and by 1811, the logic in the case was all for a cancellation of the 1805 endeavor. Both France and Holland had been decisively beaten at sea in the East, and Spanish maritime pretensions had vanished, never to return. France had lost Mauritius, Holland had lost Java, and Britain in the east was supreme.

This supremacy was achieved by a remarkable governor-general of India who needs badly a biographer. Gilbert Elliot, first Earl of Minto, succeeded Sir G. Barlow in July, 1807. Under his active encouragement and sound policy, the main objectives of the British were realized and executed in a two-armed strategy that swept southwest and southeast from India to capture Mauritius and Java. During the previous sixteen years both had been raided at intervals (Pellew raiding Batavia in 1806 from Penang for example), but in 1810 as in 1793, India could have been attacked by either. Both, therefore, were seized.

In the campaign against Java, Minto used another remarkable man whom we noted briefly as arriving at Penang in 1805 in the entourage of President Dundas—Thomas Stamford Raffles. A gifted and thrusting individual, Raffles arrived direct from England. He had no Indian experience behind him, nor any future there to look forward to. He set to work, with all the acumen of a parvenue, to build a reputation in the east, and soon found that Penang was too small a place for his restless efforts and unsettled dreams. His chance came, the attention of the great was first attracted to him, in 1808, when he visited Malacca and was moved to protest over the policy being executed there.

From the time that it passed under the administration of Penang in 1803, Malacca had been governed by Captain William Farquhar (not to be confused with Robert Farquhar, his namesake), an engineer officer from Madras, who subsequently governed Singapore. He had been left very much to his own devices, and of necessity he had made use of the old Dutch civil machinery. The law for example remained the Dutch Law, and disputes were brought before the Court which under the name of the Dutch College of Justice consisted of the leading citizens. Farquhar gave this Court *carte blanche,* but stepped in merely to ameliorate the harshness of the Dutch criminal law.

Farquhar became a champion of Malacca and encouraged its trade with Penang. "He was a kindly and honourable man" Wurtzburg has commented, "but such a cautious and such a strictly orthodox civil servant that his ideas, in more than one respect the same as and perhaps even anticipating those of Raffles, never reached fruition."[36] Wurtzburg writes as the champion of

---

[36] Wurtzburg, p. 49.

Raffles, who used Farquhar abominably in Singapore, and this judgement perhaps is too patronizing. Without doubt, however, Farquhar was less arrogant and dominating than Raffles, and far less ambitious. Perhaps this is best reflected in his accommodation in Malacca. He had taken over the Dutch Government House, and saw no reason — presumably he felt he had no authority — to change it. Minto described its imperfections in a letter to his wife ". . . it stands at the foot of a steep hill which covers the whole tenement from the sea. Now, as the sea breeze is, in these climates, a true vital air and as delicious as the gas of Paradise, suffocation is our portion at the Government House."[37] To live in Malacca, or anywhere else in Malaya for that matter, at the foot of a hill, away from the sea, when one had the power to live at the top, or on the seaward slopes, is past comprehension. In other respects however, William Farquhar was sensible and far-sighted, and bitterly opposed his namesake, the lieutenant governor of Penang, Robert Farquhar, who advocated a policy of Malaccan destruction.

Robert Farquhar first belittled Malacca in August, 1803, while actually in the port on his way to Balambangan. He recommended to Bengal that there should be a reduction both in the garrison maintained there, and in the defenses. He advanced two reasons, first that the revenue of Malacca could not support the Sepoys quartered there, and second that the reduction of Malacca and the diminution of its position, would advance that of Penang. Were it reduced sufficiently, he argued, it might even persuade the Dutch not to return when peace came.

Early in 1804, the following year, newly arrived at Penang, he repeated his arguments, "after a more complete and minute enquiry into the internal and external state of Malacca."[38] This time he recommended a complete annihilation of all the fortifications and public works, and the transportation to Penang of all the inhabitants. In their wake would follow all the traders that were resorting to Malacca. In one swoop Malacca would change from being a competitor to a colleague. In 1805 Robert Farquhar again pressed his absurd argument of destruction. If the Dutch returned there would be hostility against Britain in the Straits, Penang badly needed to be strengthened, and all commerce should be concentrated at Georgetown.

London decided his arguments were logical. "We have signified to the Government of Madras our determination to withdraw our Garrison from Malacca and its Dependencies, and whatever other establishment may have been formed there on our account. But previous to the abandonment of the place, we have directed that the Fortifications, Arsenals and Public Works of all descriptions should be completely destroyed and demolished, so as to render it of the least possible value to the Enemy's Government in case the Batavians

[37]Minto (Ed.). *Lord Minto in India*. (London, 1880) p. 261.
[38]S. S. (F). R. Vol. 12. Penang to Bengal, 22 January, 1804.

should hereafter turn their attention to the occupation of that Station."[39]

It does not appear as if Penang ever consulted Malacca on the fate proposed for it, and William Farquhar was invited to give his views as to the practicability of implementing the Director's orders only in November, 1805. He sprang at once to the defense of the settlement, and vigorously opposed the suggested destruction. "There does not appear to be a single well grounded reason for adopting such a step . . . and I think very important objections may be urged against it."[40] He went on to list those objections, how it was regarded as the capital of the Straits, how traders from Sumatra and Rhio and elsewhere came there, but would not go northward to Penang, and how its commercial activity both stimulated and protected Penang, its merchants buying and selling to Penang and its ships keeping piracy from it.

This report reached Penang after Robert Farquhar had gone to Bourbon. It made the new Presidency, already dubious, reflect and pause. Demolition was deferred, and the arguments of Malacca supported by the doubts of Penang were forwarded to India. There were no second thoughts there . . . "you will proceed without delay to carry the orders of the Hon'ble Court with regard to that Settlement into effect, conformably to the instructions communicated to you by the Hon'ble Court under date 18 April, 1805."[41] Farquhar turned to the hateful idiotic task, for while it is permissible to contemplate the destruction of a powerful fort which if returned to the hands of the enemy might prove a threat in subsequent years, no logic could accept the reasons given for the uprooting of the old established settlement, its transference, lock, stock and barrel, far to the north, the severance of all its contacts, commercial and political that could never be renewed, and still expect it to thrive in its new surroundings. It was an act of incredible folly.

The massive walls of the historic old fort were attacked on 10 August, 1807. By 31 December, 1807, all the bastions and the connecting walls, the General Hospital, two granaries, the barracks and six store rooms either had been blasted with gunpowder or levelled with entrenching tools. The fort, apart from a few minor segments, had been completely broken up, and it was the intention of the administration that in 1808 the town would suffer likewise.[42] Then came Raffles. He had visited Malacca before, briefly. This time he stayed three months (August-October, 1808), as the guest of William Farquhar, and while there he wrote a celebrated dispatch. Eloquent, detailed, logical, scathing, it made abundantly clear that which Farquhar had failed to do, that the destruction of Malacca was absolutely wrong. It convinced Penang immediately, and on arrival in Bengal it convinced Minto too. Too late to save the

[39]S. S. (F). R. Vol. 12. London to Penang, 18 April, 1805.

[40]S. S. (F). R. Vol. 29. Malacca to Penang, 19 November, 1805.

[41]S. S. (F). R. Vol. 136. Bengal to Penang, 21 March, 1807.

[42]S. S. (F). R. Vol. 12. Penang to London, 31 December, 1807. An eyewitness account of this destruction is given in JMBRAS, Vol. XXVIII. 1955. A. H. Hill: *The Hikayat Abdullah.*

fort, but before the town or the citizens were subjected to further ordeals, Minto ordered the cancellation of the whole project.[43]

Raffles' reward came soon after. By 1810 there had been several changes at sea. In 1809 Pellew had sent Admiral Drury, with an expedition that assembled at Penang in October, 1808, the time when Raffles was at Malacca, to the capture of Portuguese Macao, in China. This had failed, but after assuming the command of the station from Pellew at Penang in December, 1809, Drury had gone east again and in April, 1810, had recaptured the Moluccas (Amboina and Banda to be precise); he had suggested to Minto that Raffles be sent to govern them, and Raffles, eager and ambitious, sailed to Calcutta to press his case. He discovered that the appointment was earmarked for someone else, but Minto, who had read his reports, and who was turning his mind from Mauritius, then on the point of capture, to Java, welcomed a timely memorandun on the subject from him. and accepted the suggestion that he proceed to Malacca as his agent and there investigate all possible sources of information and assistance for such an invasion.

Raffles returned to Malacca where Farquhar still was ruling. Raffles had never visited one Malay state while in Penang, but he had learned the language well. Sustained and animated now by a hatred of the Dutch, he turned to the organizing of a large fifth column, while in India the troops and transports were prepared for the task. Wurtzburg claims for Raffles the major credit of this campaign . . . "the success of the Java campaign as a combined operation, up to at least the first landing, including the route taken and the selected point of assault, together with a most accurate appreciation of such other vital military information as the strength and disposition of the enemies' forces, the attitude of the Dutch population and the reaction of the Javanese princes was, after due allowances for the specifically military details supplied by William Farquhar, the work of Raffles and no one else."[44]

This may be so; one searches in vain, however, for history to provide any other example of a civilian so brilliant that the success of a combined operation is attributed to him. India mustered for this campaign over fifty transports and nearly fifty men of war as escort, both Royal Navy and Bombay Marine, a total of nearly a hundred sail, conveying nearly 12,000 men. All this descended on Penang, fortunately in stages, the first division arriving on 18 May, and the second division three days later. With the town stripped bare, the fleet sailed on 24 May to rendezvous at Malacca, where Raffles met the governor-general, Lord Minto. On the fleet sailed, Minto, Seton (the Governor of Penang) and Raffles in the *Modeste* passing up the Straits of Singapore. On Thursday, 20 June, the ship's log read "Noon. The south end of St. John's Island north 1¼m. Fleet in convoy."[45] This probably was the first sight

[43]Wurtzburg: pp. 68-80, where the report is printed in full. See also D. C. Boulger: *The Life of Sir Stamford Raffles* (London, 1899) pp. 63-75.

[44]Wurtzburg, p. 116.

[45]Master's log, HMS *Modeste*. From the P.R.O. Admiralty Archives.

Raffles had of the island he later was to make famous, Singapore. On 4 August the force landed, ten miles from Batavia. The town surrendered on the 8th. The Dutch force was met and defeated on the 25th, and the Governor General, Janssens, surrendered on 18 September. The campaign had ended.[46]

So, too, in virtually all respects had the war in the east. Penang became useful once more, as a haven that sustained and succored the returning veterans, and Phillips, enjoying one of his acting governorships, was able to write that "it is most satisfactory to us to be enabled to report to you that the result (of the transports putting into Penang for fresh meat and water) has been the recovery of a very large body of valuable men who might otherwise have died at sea."[47] But apart from that, Penang suffered, rather than gained, by the capture of Java. The naval blockade of Java and the Moluccas, of which Penang had complained in 1810, was lifted, but the Bugis and other traders rather than beginning again the long haul north to Penang, began calling at Batavia, where the post-war administration of Raffles, installed as Lieutenant Governor, was far more lenient and less crippling to commerce than his Dutch predecessors. In addition, the capture of Java meant the opening of the Sunda Straits, and the East Indiamen that formerly convoyed to Penang and down the slow Straits of Malacca, took immediate advantage of this short clear route to the China Sea. Both local traders and Europeans then drifted away, and Penang found itself in the backwash of war.

To the British, the closing years of that war were irritated by the arrival of American privateers and the fear that many more were coming. In 1814, however, came peace, and with it the Anglo-Dutch Convention. By this Convention Castlereagh, the British foreign secretary, who was determined that a strong Netherland state capable of being a barrier to French aggression should be created, substantiated the promise he had made to William of Orange in 1813. To Holland, by 1814 under a king again, and free of the French, were returned all of its colonies and possessions captured by the British in the long war, except the Cape of Good Hope, Ceylon, and Guiana. The French were not so lucky, and by retaining Mauritius, Britain removed them for all time as a menace to India and to its eastern trade.

The Dutch did not return for some time. They came back to Java itself in 1816, and to Malacca, where Farquhar still was faithfully and quietly governing, in 1818. When they came, they constituted again another threat to British trade in the east. This threat, the inadequacies of Penang to meet it and its efforts to find another base, combined with the vigor of Raffles and the attitude of India and London, lead to the founding of Singapore in 1819.

---

[46]For this see Low: *History of the Indian Navy.* (London, 1877). Vol. 1. pp 227-238. Parkinson, pp. 412-417. This campaign is covered in detail in the East India Company's *Java Factory Records,* Vol. 11.

[47]S. S. (F). R. Vol. 180. Penang to London, 28 November, 1811.

X

SINGAPORE, 1819-1826

When the Dutch returned to Southeast Asia after the Napoleonic War they came back, phoenix-like, stronger than ever. The Dutch Company, the *Vereenigde Oost-Indische Compagnie,* had gone, bankrupt and discredited. But it was the Dutch Government itself that returned, and by 1818, its actions in resuming and then extending Dutch power in the archipelago were such as seriously to alarm the British on Penang. And not merely Penang; there was Raffles on Sumatra.

Raffles, who had been left on Java by Lord Minto as the lieutenant-governor, hated the Dutch. Opposition to them was the mainspring of his activity in Southeast Asia, and on his return to the arena in March 1818, as lieutenant-governor of Bencoolen, ancient but useless outpost of the East India Company on Sumatra, he initiated a number of moves aimed at checking them and at re-establishing some part of the British prominence abandoned by the withdrawal from Java.

By sending small forces to the Sumatran shore of the Sunda Straits — in April to Simanka Bay and in August to Forrest Bay — he endeavored to ensure that these straits, which provided a quick transit from the Indian Ocean to the South China Sea, could not be closed. The Company, however, mindful of the national interest that necessitated a strong Holland in Europe, acquiesced in Dutch claims to the region and forced him to abandon his disputed occupation. A further move that year, when in June-July, 1818 Raffles sent troops across Sumatra to hold Palembang against the Dutch, also received no support whatever, as it was viewed to be a clear infringement of Dutch rights. The troops were brought back to Bencoolen, most ignominiously, in a Dutch cruiser.

Although Raffles' actions had not received official support, and no sanction from India or London was ever given him to hold that which he had impulsively secured on his own initiative, he won more success with the campaign he waged with his pen. As soon as he arrived at Bencoolen he began writing lengthy but urgent dispatches to the Secret Committee of the Company in London. In dramatic, almost melodramatic, terms he described the crisis in the east, and urged that the rising tide of Dutch expansion should be checked. One of his main suggestions was that Britain, to protect its interests, should establish a chain of posts throughout the archipelago. Another, later to be included in the Anglo-Dutch Treaty of 1824, was that the equator should form the boundary of the Dutch-British interests.

Raffles was not alone in his comments on Dutch expansion. Penang too was writing, in terms more sober but perhaps more effective. Its merchants had become seriously alarmed. They feared that with the return of the Dutch to Malacca, their trade with the tin states of Perak and Selangor, with the Sumatran river stages, and with West Borneo and Rhio would be endangered. This segment of their circle of trade was considerable. Should the Dutch dominate it, Penang would suffer. In June 1818 a group of merchants addressed Bannerman, the governor, asking that he make such treaties, "as may effectively secure the freedom of Commerce with these countries."[1] This request, and the fear behind it, induced Bannerman in late 1818 to send a representative to Perak and Selangor, to seek tin agreements. At the same time William Farquhar, who was waiting to hand back Malacca to the Dutch, was instructed to secure free-trade treaties with the states of West Borneo, East Sumatra, and Rhio. He sailed on July 21, 1818, and although he was forestalled by the Dutch in Borneo, he concluded treaties with Rhio, Lingga, and Siak. In the outcome, they availed him little.

In India the governor-general, Hastings, had been the recipient of the dispatches both of Raffles and of Bannerman. Throughout 1818 both reiterated their fears that Dutch expansion was likely to jeopardize British trade, but whereas Bencoolen laid stress on the islands of the archipelago, Bannerman pointed to the trade with China. Both stressed the need for a further British base in Southeast Asia, and both by the middle of 1818, had come to recommend a post at the southern entrance to the Straits of Malacca, which not only would assist the East Indiamen on their way to China but which in addition would put Britain in among the islands.[2]

The inclination of Hastings to support this sensible suggestion was strengthened and confirmed by the visit of Raffles to Calcutta in October 1818. The meeting of Raffles with Hastings in 1818 was, if not as advantageous to his personal career as that he paid to Minto in 1810, at least as fruitful to his aims and objectives. Although Hastings had to write to the Dutch in that same month apologizing for, and disavowing the activities of Raffles in the Sunda Straits and at Palembang, nevertheless almost simultaneously he was instructing Raffles, without waiting for London approval (as was typical of the strong man on the spot), to conclude first a trade treaty with Acheh and next and of more moment, to have Farquhar establish a station beyond Penang. It had become most necessary, Hastings informed London, that the British should command all of the Straits of Malacca. His instructions to Raffles explain why.

---

[1] S. S. (F). R. Vol. 66. Penang Merchants to Governor, June 8, 1818.
[2] The relevant dispatches are in Wurtzburg. pp. 453-454.

If the activity of the Dutch were not checked, wrote Hastings to Raffles on November 28, it "would give them the entire command of the only channels for the direct trade between China and Europe." Therefore, with Penang able to guard only the northern entrance, Hastings regarded it essential "to secure the free passage of the Straits of Malacca, the only channel left to us" (by) "the establishment of a station ... such as may command the southern entrance.[3] As at the beginning of this narrative, so at the end: the trade with China remained a most important factor. Raffles was instructed to direct Farquhar to form a base at Rhio, exactly as Forrest had been ordered to do thirty-five years before; only in this case prudent foresight added an alternative: should the Dutch be back in Rhio, he was to have Farquhar also investigate Johore. This post script to his instructions, (added on December 5), saved the expedition.

Raffles sailed from Calcutta on December 7, 1818, just over thirty-two years after Francis Light. Much had occurred in those thirty-odd years. On Penang, in an area that had been visited before only by obscure country traders, and of which India scarcely knew, a settlement had been founded, with a radius of influence and a regular flow of trade that had established, for several decades, a definite British sphere of interest. A great island, Java, had been conquered; and a powerful trade had been steadily developed, passing Penang, to China. Now, borne on the crest of that China trade, there sailed south another expedition.

In Penang this expedition found Farquhar preparing for home leave. He was soon excited by the possibilities offered him, and readily abandoned his earlier plans. In Penang also was a frightened old soldier. Bannerman had become convinced that the Dutch controlled the entire area south of Penang, and that their reaction to any further meddlesome move by Raffles would be savage. Should the British move down the Straits of Malacca, Penang might be imperilled and its trade might vanish. In an effort to save his island, Bannerman endeavored to discourage the project. He was quite unsuccessful.

Throughout his career, Raffles was to engage in acrimonious correspondence with colleagues or superiors. Disputes over salary and allowances had marred his sojourn on Java, and spiteful inability to work through Farquhar became a sour feature of the early years of Singapore. In Penang too Raffles soon resorted to the pen, and we can capture today, on reading through this irritable correspondence, the strained atmosphere that prevailed upon Penang during the first few weeks of 1819.

Raffles had been instructed by Hastings to see that Farquhar established a base at Rhio, provided that the Dutch were not there. Penang knew, and Bannerman told Raffles, that the Dutch in fact were there. Raffles thereupon decided on January 16 to send Farquhar anyway, to reconnoitre and if possible to find a convenient site, either at Rhio, Johore, or Singapore, while he visited

[3] S. S. (F). R. Vol. 182A. Bengal to Raffles, November 28, 1818.

Acheh. Farquhar, with three small ships, sailed south immediately.[4]

Bannerman now attempted to hold fast to Raffles, and urged him to remain in Penang until Calcutta had replied to the dispatches in which he had stressed the inadvisability of this mission to Acheh. Raffles, in the face of this hostile attitude, decided to postpone the visit to Acheh, and to seek a treaty with that state later. He so informed Bannerman, whose delight however was short-lived; unknown to him, Raffles had slipped away after Farquhar, even before his letter was delivered.

Raffles came up with Farquhar on 26 January, after the latter, who had rendezvoused with an Admiralty surveying unit of two ships under the command of Captain Ross *(HMS Discovery),* had made a disappointing inspection of the Carimon Islands near the Straits of Singapore. The naval officers, together with Farquhar and his ship's captain W. Maxfield, came that evening on board the *Indiana,* Raffles' ship. Raffles had chartered this from his friend John Palmer in Calcutta, and had loaded it with a speculative and subsequently highly remunerative cargo of bricks. It was decided to proceed to the Johore River, but to inspect, on the way, the island of Singapore. Here Captain Ross had noted "a spot he considered more eligible in point of harbour, cleared of jungle and advantageous for trade."[5] This merely echoed the ideas of Raffles himself; a month previously, on 12 December, 1818, he had written to William Marsden, his scholarly friend. "My attention is principally turned to Johore, and you must not be surprised if my next letter to you is dated from the ancient city of Singapura."[6]

Nothing remained of the ancient city of Singapore except the ruins of a defensive wall, sixteen feet in width and eight to nine feet high, which ran for nearly a mile from the sea across the small plain to the jungle-covered hills. This in itself, although little commented on at the time,[7] was remarkable; no other archaeological ruin in Malaya can compare to this, not even the numerous sites of the ancient Indianized city in south Kedah. Singapura, or Tempasuk, must have been of considerable size and importance in Sri Vijayan days to warrant such a defense work. When Raffles and Farquhar landed however, early on 29 January, 1819, the island was almost as uninhabited as Penang had been in 1786.

They had come from the Carimons, up the Straits of Singapore, to debouch into and anchor in the broad bay of the island that faced those Straits. Near the mouth of a stream that flowed into that bay, the Sungei Singapore, was a small *kampong* of *orang laut* and Malays, ruled by the Temenggong of Johore, Daing Abdul Rahman. Behind it, amid the cluster of small irregular hills that are now

[4]S. S. (F). R. Vol. 182. Raffles to Farquhar, 18 January, 1819. This whole period is dealt with in *Wurtzburg,* pp. 478-501, who quotes the correspondence in detail.

[5]Diary, Captain Crawford, 27 January, 1819. Wurtzburg, p. 483.

[6]Raffles to Marsden, 12 December, 1818; Wurtzburg, p. 469.

[7]J. Crawfurd. *Embassy to Siam,* etc. Vol. 1., p. 70. The stream that ran alongside this wall, to serve the purposes of a moat, flows still today, in the drain by the side of Stamford Road.

suburbs of Singapore, a few wary Chinese grew gambier, a woody vine used for chewing with betel nut and for tanning and dyeing. On the other side of the island, fourteen or so impenetrable miles away, the few sluggish streams that ran into the Straits of Johore sheltered amid the mangrove a few more *orang laut,* primitive aborigines who live today, hard by the runway of an airdrome, exactly as they did centuries ago. The rest of the island's 220 square miles was empty of human life; littering the beach of the bay, however, were hundreds of human skulls, a mute explanation of the *kampong's* piratical livelihood.[8]

It was quickly established that Abdul Rahman was the *de facto* ruler of the river and the bay; and that there were no Dutch. The position seemed ideal for a trading post; a sheltered beach, flat land, water, all within close proximity to the Straits of Singapore. An agreement, the first of several, was concluded on 30 January. In return for an annual $3,000, the Temenggong ceded a site for a station and promised to have no relations with any other power.

The Temenggong, although the de facto ruler, was not, in theory, independent. He was one of the great men of state that owed homage to the Sultan of Johore. As in medieval Europe, where the personal allegiance of barons depended almost entirely on the great power of the overlord and where independent states arose as soon as that power was dissipated or diminished, the Temenggong, and the Bendahara, another great officer in Pahang, were in the process of establishing their own states. This process, part of the dissolution of the Johore Empire, had been underway for some time, at least since 1812. These leaders were Bugis, strong, politically minded, whereas the Malay Sultan of Johore at Rhio was almost a puppet, dominated before 1818 by his Bugis under-king, and after that by the Dutch. But was he the Sultan?

If Raffles was not to base his claim to Singapore purely on the right of conquest (which would not have surprised most people of that age, Asian or European), it was essential that he acquire a legal title to the island. The Company had not attempted to clarify its 1786 position in Penang with Siam, and although it came to realize that Kedah was not de jure independent, it had rested content in its agreement with that state. Raffles, however, anticipated serious disputes in the chancellories of Europe should his Singapore settlement be unsound in law. His flag raising in the Sunda Straits and at Palembang had failed due to his inability to secure a clear title to the disputed land. A treaty of cession therefore was deemed essential, and this he endeavored to secure.

The Johore Empire by 1819 was a collection of states virtually independent of each other. North of the Singapore Straits were Pahang, Johore and Singapore, while south there lay the Rhio and Lingga archipelagos. In 1812, when Sultan Mahmud died, the eldest son (Husain) was in Pahang, where he stayed; and in his absence from Rhio the Bugis power behind the throne, despite the refusal of the widow to part with the royal regalia, had appointed his younger

[8]*The Hikayat Abdullah.* An Annotated Translation by A. H. Hill. *JMBRAS,* Vol. XXVIII. Pt. 3 (June, 1955) is an eye witness account.

and more pliable brother, Abdul Rahman of Lingga. It was with this sultan that Farquhar concluded his 1818 trade treaty, and when the Dutch came back towards the end of that year they too recognized him and by a treaty signed 26 November, 1818, they sustained him in his position. In these troubled waters fished Raffles.

Shortly after his first discussions with the Temenggong, he sent Farquhar across the Straits to Rhio. Farquhar sailed on 29 January, with instructions to negotiate with Sultan Abdul Rahman and the Bugis Raja Muda Jafar for a treaty. This was impossible. The Dutch saw to it that no official business of any kind was conducted, and the Sultan made it clear that he was powerless. Farquhar returned empty handed.

This had been anticipated. While Farquhar was butting his head ostentatiously against a Dutch door, Raffles had sent secret ambassadors to Husain [or as he was known, Tungku Long], living in poverty in Rhio. Quietly and unobtrusively he slipped away in a small prahu. Guided by the *orang laut* chief, Batin Sapi, who knew best the most covered way, and escorted by two Malays of rank, Raja Embong and Inche Wan Abdullah, he reached Singapore on February 1. Here he was recognized by Raffles and by Temenggong Abdul Rahman as Sultan Husain Shah ibni Al-Marhum Sultan Mahmud, and with him on 6 February a further treaty was signed.

In return for $5,000 annually, he confirmed the cession of a site for a factory and agreed not to enter into any treaty with any other country, or to attack the British settlement. Two clauses that subsequently led to trouble were that the Temenggong was entitled to half the duty collected from native vessels, and that the method of administering justice was to be discussed and agreed upon later. Despite these flaws, Raffles had secured a cession of a site for a factory (although not of the entire island), from the man that he, as the British representative, and some at least of the Empire could be induced to recognize as Sultan. It might not be as clear cut as he had hoped for but if he had not obtained a legal right, it was at least an arguable right; and with that he had to be content. With his bricks unloaded and sold he sailed the following day (7 February), having been on Singapore just nine days in all.

He left behind him William Farquhar, the unsung hero of the first four years of Singapore. Farquhar set to work at once to implement his instructions. The memory of Palembang (where the Dutch had expelled the British the year before), and Balambangan (where the Suluks had destroyed an undefended factory), made him turn immediately to his first task; to throw up a fort under which the settlement could shelter. The bastion that he built on the nearest hill, unlike Fort Cornwallis in Penang, was well in from the sea. Like Fort Cornwallis, however, it was never needed.[9] Neither the Dutch nor other enemies ever came; Singapore was not to be attacked for 122 years.

---

[9]Singapore appears to have been that rare object, a Company settlement without a Company name. Singapore it was, Singapore it remained. Even the fort remained nameless until 1859, when it became Fort Canning.

Nevertheless, Farquhar had innumerable other worries as he faced up to the same problems as had Francis Light. Trade had to be encouraged, and a port helped to grow; law and order had to be established and a revenue secured. In addition Farquhar had an additional burden to carry in that Raffles, remote and almost unreachable in Bencoolen, regarded any deviation from instructions as insubordination and took it as a personal insult. In the handling of Farquhar, Raffles is shown at his worst; excellent at Malacca, where he had been furiously active in his solitary command, his sojourn on Java had been marked by arguments and discord among his subordinates. One of the clues to the character of this impetuous, ambitious, and clever man is in his size; he was small of stature. Like most small men, he endeavored to make up for what he lacked by a fierce watching of rights, by self assertion; he took umbrage very quickly.[10] Farquhar was to have a most difficult time, particularly after Raffles appointed as harbor master, in May, 1820, the incompetent but favored husband of his sister, Raffles Flint.

Singapore remained British, in the final outcome, because unlike the other settlements initiated by Raffles, it was found worth keeping; it saved itself by its own exertions. Its growth began that February, and has continued ever since. Captains Ross and Crawford, the naval survey unit, although not Raffles, had called at Malacca two days after leaving Singapore on February 7. The Dutch governor, who had been informed already by both Husain and Temenggong Abdul Rahman that the British had occupied Singapore, clearly was of the opinion that the island would not remain for long in their possession. His feeling was not shared by the Asian inhabitants of Malacca, and there began an immediate exodus of Malays and Chinese. Abdullah, the Malay writer from Malacca, has left us a vivid picture of this, and of the similar migration of the Chinese and Malays from Rhio.[11]

They were attracted to Singapore not merely because the British flag and the hundred or so troops suggested safety but also because it suggested freedom. This became the outstanding feature of Singapore. Whereas all the ports of the remainder of Southeast Asia exacted customs dues and levies, Singapore, despite numerous attempts by the Company in India to change it, began and remained a free port. Raffles should be given full credit for introducing it; that it remained so, however, unlike Penang, was due to the much more favorable locale of Singapore for trade, and to its very rapid growth.

Raffles introduced this free trade policy almost half-heartedly; it would not appear as if he imagined it would last for long, perhaps no longer than in Penang. As a temporary measure, to put the port on its feet, he instructed Farquhar:

[10]C. Gibson-Hill, in commenting on the relationship between Raffles and Farquhar at Malacca, says, "Raffles had had little contact with his father, and seemingly had never had to learn to tolerate the authority and assumed superiority of an older, less intelligent man: Farquhar, the father of his people at Malacca, must at times have come very near to giving him the experience when it was too late for him to profit by it." *JMBRAS*. Vol. XXVIII. Pt. 1 (1955) pp. 189-190.

[11]"Hikayat Abdullah," *JMBRAS*, Vol. XXVIII, Pt. 3, pp. 141-143.

"It is not necessary at present to subject the trade of the port to any duties – it is yet inconsiderable; and it would be impolitic to insur the risk of obstructing its advancement by any measure of this nature."[12] Scarcely a clarion call for free trade; yet it sufficed.

Unlike early Penang, where only one outstanding Company became established, (Scott and Co.), the growth of Singapore was assisted almost from its beginning by a number of European firms. The East India Company monopoly in India had gone in 1813, and in China, too, private traders were undermining the old Company position. The possibilities of Singapore were quickly apparent, and were utilized, not merely by the scores of small Chinese shop owners but also by Europeans possessed of some overseas contacts and with a little capital. As young James Matheson wrote, on his way to China in May, 1819 on the opium ship *Marquis of Hastings:*

> I have formed the highest opinion of Singapore as a place of trade. Its principal staple article at present is tin, for which there is a melting house belonging to the Sultan of Johore. It is procurable at $15 per picul. As yet, however, no trade can be carried on to any great extent there being no merchants to deal with; but this is a disadvantage which, as there are no duties or port charges, will soon vanish. I am of the opinion that a person settling here for a few months with a few thousand dollars as a circulating medium, (which they greatly want), might carry on business to great advantage . . . the situation of the settlement is purely delightful, being within 4 miles of the direct tract with China. . .[13]

James Matheson proceeded on to Canton, where his firm, Jardine Matheson and Co. was well established. His advice was followed. Early in 1820 the first European agency house was formed in Singapore by Alexander Johnston, who had landed there the previous year. This firm, A. L. Johnston and Co. became the Singapore agents for Jardine Matheson and Co. who began sending immediately goods from Canton for transhipment in Singapore for Europe, while accepting for disposal in China the tin and the Straits produce collected at the bustling new settlement.

The second notable merchant to arrive was Alexander Guthrie, who in 1821 began a business that has survived and prospered to this very day. Messrs. Syme and Co. was formed in 1823 by another daring young man with a few contacts and a little capital, while in 1826 an enterprising doctor who had left his Portuguese man-of-war to open a medical store expanded his activities into J. d'Almeida and Sons. Another flourishing twentieth century agency house, Paterson, Simons and Co. began in 1823; Boustead and Co. began in 1830. In 1837 these vigorous young men and many others formed themselves into the Singapore Chamber of Commerce.

The facilities of Singapore were found almost immediately to be of greater utility than those of Penang. In particular, it was convenient to three great

---

12S. S. (F). R. Vol. 182. Raffles to Farquhar, 6 February, 1819. Wurtzburg, pp. 495-500.
13Greenberg. p. 97.

areas of trade. It lay within a most satisfactory sailing distance of all lands lapped by the Java Sea. From South Sumatra, Java itself and all the lesser islands south of it, from the distant Spice Islands and the Celebes and from south and west Borneo, the southerly monsoon blew *prahus* steadily towards Singapore. In November the monsoon changed to the north, blowing these prahus equally as conveniently back to their home ports. By its situation Singapore could command all this vast area, greater in size than the U.S.A. In addition, it lay hard by a great tin area to its immediate south. As Matheson noted, tin from the Rhio and Lingga archipelagos found Singapore a most convenient port, where good prices and quick freights could be secured. And third, Singapore found a market to its north, with the east coast Malay rivers and, later, Bangkok, Cambodia, Indo-China, and China itself. As in the case of Penang, Singapore's pattern of trade was established within a few years. By 1824 its outline was clear, a three-quarter-open Chinese fan, from Bangkok in the north, swinging out eastwards and southwards round to the southwest, a trade area of greater strength than was ever seen before in Southeast Asia.

A possible fourth trading area was envisaged with China. Strategically Singapore's relevance to China had been seen. *The Times* reported on 31 July, 1820 that "our occupation of Sincapoor . . . is on the part of England a purely defensive position to cover her direct trade with China." The possibility of using Singapore as the major trading center with China was seen almost at the same time. The traders in Canton were experiencing innumerable difficulties. Should they be expelled, as seemed not unlikely, Singapore could become the opium base, as Chinese junks could reach it in a few days; their tea and silver could be traded here. This view, expressed before a Select Committee in the House of Lords in early 1821 appears to have commanded general East India Company support. Thus the possible opium utility of Singapore was, no doubt, one of the reasons why there grew an insistence that Britain retain it. Here again although the commodities had changed, was a variant on the old theme of a mart suitable for trade with China.[14]

This new settlement came at a most opportune time for Great Britain. The end of the Napoleonic Wars in 1815 had not opened the European market to it, as tariff walls were erected almost immediately to protect the infant industries that had sprung up under the shelter of Napoleon's continental system. In the United States also, tariffs rose up from 1815 onwards to protect U.S. industries against the British. Expansion in both these areas became increasingly difficult; with the establishment of Singapore, however, a new and most provident market in Asia came into being.

Assisted by new restrictions and tariffs in Java, as well as by increasing China trade and by its own geographical situation that brought new markets into existence, Singapore's trade grew rapidly. By 1821 at least 12,311 tons

---

[14]This is dealt with by Harry J. Marks: *The First Contest for Singapore, 1819-1824.* (The Hague, 1959), pp. 143-48.

of shipping, fully four-fifths of which was made up of country ships, sailed through the Straits to Canton, calling at Singapore on the way, while another 11,204 tons of country shipping slipped south from Singapore into the islands. The trade of Singapore from 1819-1822 inclusive was $18,661,139; it increased each year. It was a trade partly of European vessels, 208 of them trading with Singapore in those years, and of local Southeast Asian vessels, for example from Cambodia: in 1821 a timid 21 came to the port; it had grown to 70 by 1824. There had been no direct junk trade between China and a British settlement until Singapore was established. This had been one of Penang's misfortunes. In 1821, four large Chinese junks arrived, increasing to seven by 1824. The prahus from nearby rivers and islands could scarcely be counted, but it was estimated in 1822 that 2,500 at least had come, with a trade over the two and a half years of $5,000,000. As Dr. Wong Lin Ken says in his detailed study of Singapore's trade, "posterity is, therefore, not surprised that Great Britain should secure Dutch recognition of the British occupation of Singapore."[15]

Trade promotion presented no problem to early Singapore, but each year, as the polyglot population increased (by 1824 it had reached an estimated 10,000), the inadequacy of the administration of these people became more glaring. Raffles, in his initial arrangements with the Temenggong and the Sultan, had deferred the question of the administration of justice, and the situation was not stabilized until 1827. Until then the problem remained, to bedevil both Farquhar and Crawfurd, his successor.

A first step towards establishing a clear position was taken by Raffles in'a brief second visit to the island, from May 31 to 28 June, 1819. Disregarding the Sultan (an early indication of his outlived utility), he made an agreement with the Temenggong on 26 June. It stipulated that everyone within the settlement was under the authority of the Resident, who was to hear all important cases. He was given the authority of chief magistrate and commandant, together with the Sultan and the Temenggong. Minor cases, involving people of one nationality only, were to be heard by the capitans (if Chinese), by the heads of castes (if Indians), or pengulus (if Malays); so the agreement ran. It would not appear however as if these stipulations captured the realities of the situation. Certainly the court of the Sultan replaced immediately the pengulus, and they do not appear again in official correspondence, while the mention of Indian castes remains as but a faint suggestion of a development that perhaps fortunately did not occur.

Unrealistic in details, the decisions of this agreement also were illegal. No cession of territory had taken place, merely the right to establish a factory, and Farquhar had no legal right to exercise magisterial powers; nor had Raffles any right whatever to grant them. As a fundamental of British law, only the crown

[15]Wong Lin Ken: *A Study of the Trade of Singapore 1824-1869, JMBRAS*, Vol. XXXIV, Pt. 4.

was empowered to set up a judicature. This has been mentioned before, when dealing with Penang. For hundreds of years the legal anarchy of medieval Britain, where barons meted out each their own law, had been avoided by a rigid central control. Well meant though his intentions were, Raffles was usurping the powers of the crown. We have seen how long it took that crown to judicate for Penang; much the same was to happen to Singapore, which, quite illegally, accepted and acted upon these decisions of Raffles.

Farquhar endeavored to maintain order among the close-packed houses of the settlement, and on the shouting, active river, by means of a minute police force which he formed in 1820 to assist him in his administration of justice. In March, 1821, when a meeting of European merchants and traders agreed that it was inadequate to keep the peace, the total strength of this police force, including the one European in charge, amounted to a scant dozen men. The merchants decided to contribute to a night watch fund; this enabled a night force of another dozen to be employed. It can not be imagined that it was sufficient, even combined with the small military force, to keep law and order, yet authority was maintained, and European go-downs at least received some slight official protection.

Perhaps the most persistent irritant, if not the most dangerous threat to peace, was the Temenggong. The Malays or more correctly the Malaysians, were the majority ethnic group on the island for the first decade. The growth of Singapore made their undoubted leader a pirate within the law. He had the right to tax local prahus, and he had his own court. Unchecked tyranny was made too easy for him, and his undoubted strength was channeled into the wrong streams. His exactions and abuses of authority became notorious, and the first riot in Singapore's long riot history occurred against him, in 1823 when the Malacca Malays rose up in an armed clash with his followers. Military intervention was needed to restore order.[16]

Raffles returned to Singapore on his third and last visit, from October 1822 until June 1823; and following this riot he took several steps to check the Temenggong and to better the administration of justice. Farquhar had discovered at the end of Singapore Bay a sheltered strait, open at both ends, that had deep water close to the Singapore bank. Here, constantly scoured by the tides, a rare geological fault provided the island with an ideal harbor that was to become, by the late nineteenth century, the savior of Singapore, and was to grow into one of the greatest ocean terminals in the world.

Raffles, determined to move the Temenggong from the crowded center of the settlement, accepted the Temenggong's suggestion that he settle there. Although no doubt foreseen by the Temenggong, the result was not anticipated by either Raffles or Farquhar. By removing the Temenggong and his followers

---

[16]*The Hikayat Abdullah.* pp. 154-155. This was to be the only riot in Singapore in which Malays were involved until the Bertha Hertog riots of 1950.

from the river, it removed the irritant; but by depositing them in a sheltered, concealed inlet close to the port, where no padi could be grown, and where they could not be supervised, it increased their piratical pursuits and made them more of a sea-borne menace than before. It was not a wise move.[17]

Along with the shift of residence, Raffles removed both the Temenggong and the Sultan from the magistrates' court, and in their place he listed in his Regulation III of 1823, twelve prominent business men, who, three at a time, were to sit each quarter, with the authority of an English Justice of the Peace. The Resident would still hold a major court, but these civilians would hear most of the remaining cases. The capitans were held responsible, as before, for minor offenses within their community, and it still remained obligatory for cases involving the sentence of death to be transmitted to Bengal.

He instituted changes in the police force as well. The night watch fund was abolished, and the two forces were combined. The police chief was placed, as Assistant to the Magistrate, under the control of the court. Bernard, the officer in charge, was informed that he was not to institute any proceedings, or take any actions, without the prior consent of the magistrates. As a non-executive branch of the court, the police force entered a long period of stagnation, inefficiency and corruption, from which it was not to emerge until the 1840's. Until then, although Europeans suffered no bodily damages, the same cannot be said for the mass of the population; both body and property were in constant peril.

With the growth of Singapore in the 1820's, the menace of the Chinese secret societies, which have remained on the island ever since, first emerged. The lawlessness of the Chinese rapidly became of serious concern to the British administration. Were it not that these societies benefited from the growth of the administration and British connections, it seems quite beyond doubt that the Chinese could have easily overthrown them. In this they were not interested. It was the continuance of this administration that permitted the societies to flourish, so no direct challenge was made; nevertheless, it was in the Chinese secret societies where real power lay, and in the early period of Singapore their rule was virtually unchecked. They became, in effect, a second administration. In many ways they governed, not the British. Not until the 1870's was any determined effort made by the government to exercise any control over the Chinese; before the establishment of the Chinese Protectorate in 1877, they were left almost completely to their own devices and in this vacuum of authority the secret societies fought and clashed for power. The extent of that power may be seen by Munshi Abdullah's account of the large assembly and the initiation ceremonies of the Thian Tai Huey Society in the jungle of Tanglin; his conclusion that "at that time in the English settlement of Singapore the

---

[17]For this, see C. Gibson-Hill: *Singapore Old Strait and New Harbour, 1300-1870*. (Memoirs of the Raffles Museum, No. 3. Singapore, December, 1956). pp. 80-81.

Chinese robbed with unbridled licence in any quarter they pleased,"[18] seems a correct summary. Singapore would appear to have been an infinitely more lawless or more dynamic town than Penang; but Penang had no Abdullah.

The Company continued with its efforts to establish its occupation of the island on an agreed legal basis, and on 7 June, 1823, Raffles signed another convention with the Sultan and Temenggong. In exchange for $1500 and $800 per month for life (the prices were getting steeper), the rulers gave up their right to levy dues upon native trade and to act as judges. They had abused considerably both these powers, to the serious detriment of the settlement, their actions being scarcely distinguishable from their days of license and unbridled piracy before 1819. The convention stated that English law would be enforced, although due consideration would be paid to the Malay *adat* or custom, particularly in cases of marriage, inheritance, and religion. It was accepted that the whole island, excluding the land owned by the Sultan and Temenggong, was at the entire disposal of the British government.

During this final sojourn on Singapore, Raffles consistently found fault with Farquhar, and after numerous episodes of friction — over a land administration as chaotic as early Penang, over a town planned other than he desired and over a gambling revenue he found immoral — Farquhar was thrust into the background. Raffles resided with his brother-in-law, the master attendant, and carried on a humiliating and most unnecessarily hurtful correspondence with the Resident. Farquhar was forced to reply to the lieutenant-governor's secretary as Raffles refused all contact.

Raffles began to withdraw responsibilities from Farquhar and to transfer them to Raffles Flint. He reduced Farquhar's staff, at a time when the town had reached 10,000 people, and increased the staff of his brother-in-law. He gave to Flint a monopoly of the provisioning of ships and the lighterage trade in the harbor and river, and Farquhar was reprimanded when he endeavored to stop Flint, who by 1823 dealt directly with Raffles, from using the anchorage and clearance fees as his own particular perquisite.

Three years before, on October 23, 1820, Farquhar had tendered through Raffles his resignation to the governor-general. Subsequently however, he wrote on September 19, 1821, and on January 29, 1823 (again in each case correctly through his superior, Raffles), withdrawing his resignation. It would not appear as if the latter two letters ever reached Calcutta. Unknown to Farquhar, Raffles had suggested that Crawfurd, who had passed through Singapore in 1822 after his unsuccessful mission to Bangkok, should succeed him.

As a clear sign that Britain intended to keep the island, on May 1, 1823, Singapore passed out of the supervision of Bencoolen, and was placed at last directly under Bengal. A few days previous to this, however, on 28 April, Raffles had relieved Farquhar of all powers. Farquhar had challenged Raffles'

[18]*Hikayat Abdullah:* pp. 180-192.

right, as lieutenant governor, to act independently of the Resident on the numerous matters of detail entrusted by the Supreme Government to the local officer
in charge. Also Farquhar had challenged Raffles' right to criticize him directly
to the commander-in-chief in India on a military matter. Raffles could brook
no challenge to his conduct, and quite illegally Farquhar was dismissed. Worse
was to follow.

In the third week of May, Farquhar heard from Calcutta "with extreme surprise...of the appointment by the Supreme Government of Mr. Surgeon John
Crawfurd to relieve me as Resident of Singapore, without any official application having been made by me to resign my present situation..."[19] He suspected
this to have been organized by Raffles, who however gave him a bare-faced
denial. As a lieutenant-governor who ordered and acted over his head, as a
civilian who criticized the military actions of a soldier, as a superior who prac-
ticed nepotism and who imposed humiliations, Raffles in many ways must
have been an obnoxious and overbearing person. Clever and ambitious men
who fight hard for success often are.

Raffles left Singapore in June, 1823, and returned to England, there to quar-
rel with the Company over money matters and to found the London Zoological
Gardens. He took no part in the discussions with the Dutch then proceeding.
A sick man, he had finished with Asia. He died on July 5, 1826.

He had played an indispensable part in the founding of Singapore. With all
his faults it is impossible to imagine that Singapore would have been acquired
without him. He had not created the pressures that built up in 1818, he played
no part in the impersonal course of events that called for a new post; but it was
he who persistently and resourcefully, even at times in defiance of authority,
sought to act. His action in January, 1819 in taking Singapore was quite in
keeping with his bold, almost irresponsible but imaginative character. Penang
might well have been founded by someone other than Light—Forrest perhaps.
But without Raffles, it is difficult to see that any British move towards China
would have been made.

Yet as Marks makes clear, "taking Singapore was not the same as holding
it."[20] Raffles paid only three brief visits to Singapore. He played no part whatever in its retention, hardly any in its development. Historians have long
claimed for Raffles all the subsequent growth of the settlement. His master
touch has been everywhere. In fact, the credit for Singapore's growth must go
to those who made it grow, to the people who in defiance of all history built a
bustling port on the equator. Hong Kong was to grow into a similar city with
never a Raffles to claim posthumously the credit; similarly it should be appreciated that it was the vital élan of the Singapore community that saved the
settlement and made the British, despite the most dubious of legal entitlements,
determined to retain it. In this, Raffles played no part whatever.

[19]Farquhar to Raffles, 20 May, 1823; in *Wurtzburg*, p. 640.
[20]Harry J. Marks. p. 250.

Farquhar remained in the settlement for six months after the departure of Raffles, leaving in December. He called briefly at Malacca, where his twenty-year rule was remembered with affection and at Penang, where Phillips as usual was acting governor. In Calcutta his dismissal was judged illegal, and he sailed for London a vindicated man. Promoted to major-general, he died aged sixty-eight in 1839.

John Crawfurd, who succeeded William Farquhar as Resident of Singapore, negotiated a treaty with Sultan Husain and Temenggong Abdul Rahman, which was signed on August 2, 1824, and ratified in London on March 4, 1825; the third of the pieces of paper that Britain felt necessary for a comfortable retention of its settlement. The island of Singapore, together with the neighboring islets within a radius of ten miles, were ceded in full sovereignty to the British. In return for this cession the Sultan received $33,200 and $1,300 a month for life, while the Temenggong received $26,800 and $700 a month for life.

Crawfurd profited from the disputes that had marred Penang's early relations with Kedah, and by Article X he made it quite clear that at no time could the Company be expected to participate in the quarrels of the Sultan or the Temenggong. No defensive or offensive alliance with them would be entered into, although they were entitled to the protection offered by Singapore. Neither party would interfere in the internal affairs of the other. It was clear-cut cession of land from its owners in return for a money payment, with no strings attached to it whatever.[21]

From this time on the Sultan began to be neglected by the British as already he was ignored by the Malays, while the Temenggong developed his power in Johore and his descendants subsequently became the Sultans of Johore. Three months before this treaty was signed, the Dutch by the Anglo-Dutch treaty of March 1824, had accepted the inevitable and had agreed to the British possession. This acceptance, secured with little difficulty in 1824, would have been unthinkable in 1819, and for several years the Dutch objections to the settlement of Singapore had made many people fear for its existence.

The Dutch first heard of the settlement on Singapore at Malacca. The Temenggong and Sultan Husain wrote immediately after Raffles had landed, claiming that although they had signed a treaty they were powerless to do otherwise. Malacca sent the news to Batavia and the protests began. These Dutch protests however were not followed by force, largely because, it would appear, the letter written by Hastings in November 1818 disclaiming and apologizing for the actions of Raffles at Palembang and in the Sunda Straits was taken as the general official attitude to any further Rafflesian mischief. And, as the British by Farquhar's treaty of 1818 had recognized the other Sultan of Johore, it was considered that the settlement would soon be withdrawn. As a result, the

[21]This is printed in W. G. Maxwell & W. S. Gibson: *Treaties and Engagements Affecting the Malay States and Borneo.* (London, 1924).

newborn Singapore was permitted to draw breath and live.

At the outset, in fact, fiercer opposition came from Penang. Bannerman became terrified and in almost hysterical terms he ordered Raffles to instruct Farquhar to "evacuate the post at Singapore with his party (rather) than allow a drop of human blood to be shed in maintaining it."[22] His feeling was not so much for Singapore, however, as for Penang, and his intention to eliminate Singapore was confirmed by a dispatch from Hastings in India, written on 20 February, 1819, in ignorance of the founding of Singapore, instructing Raffles not to establish any such post. Feeling that he had official support then, he told Farquhar, who had written urgently for troops, that he could expect no reinforcements from Penang, merely an empty ship or two to help him evacuate the post.

Bannerman was quickly disillusioned. By March the news of Singapore had reached India. The *Calcutta Journal* came out in fulsome praise of the usefulness of the port, and Hastings wrote a somewhat guarded letter of congratulations to Raffles; together with a stern rap over the knuckles to Bannerman who was severely reprimanded for the stand he had taken. He died a few months later, of cholera, on 8 August, 1819.

Hastings made known to the Dutch in June that the Supreme Government supported the establishment of a settlement on Singapore, and as Bannerman's belated reinforcements poured into Singapore the Dutch decided not to provoke any armed clash in the area. They would not accept the legality of the settlement however, and the argument between the two moved to Europe. Here, although the Secret Committee of the Company had been most irritated on hearing that Raffles again had aroused and had antagonized the Dutch, the benefits of the settlement quickly were seen, not merely by the Company Tea Traders with China but by the growing body of opinion in London and Lancashire calling for free trade. Rarely united before, their combined pressure from the beginning secured strong government support.

Castlereagh, the foreign secretary, outlined the attitude of Britain by stating two principles of policy. The British government, he wrote to Holland, "cannot acquiesce in a practical exclusion, or in a mere permissive toleration, of British commerce throughout the immense extent of Eastern Archipelago; nor can they consent so far to expose the direct commerce of this country with China to all the obvious dangers and disadvantages which would result, especially in time of war, from all the military and naval keys of the Straits of Malacca being exclusively in the hands of the Netherlands Government."[23] These two principles, of support for the trade with China and encouragement of that among the islands, determined the British attitude to the Dutch. The Dutch attitude — although it was they who had initiated the discussions — was more negative; Holland itself was apathetic about eastern trade and provided no

[22]Bannerman to Raffles, 16 February, 1819; Wurtzburg. p. 505.

[23]Dutch Records, A. Vol. 13. Foreign Secretary to British Ambassador at The Hague, 13 August, 1819.

pressure on its leaders comparable to the British community. It sought merely to have clearly defined that which it held already and to dispose of commitments it found it no longer wanted, such as Malacca. Discussions between the two were postponed, after an initial exchange in July and August, 1820. Due partly to various legitimate excuses and partly to British vacillation and stalling they were not resumed until December, 1823. Nevertheless, the principles enunciated by Castlereagh were never seriously challenged, and were accepted in the March 1824 Anglo-Dutch Treaty.

A large part of the discussions, in 1820 and in 1823-24, had been devoted to haggling over money. Since 1816 a number of British accounts against the Dutch on Java had been unsettled. This thorny problem finally was cleared up by a lump sum payment of £100,000 by the Dutch. Singapore, and territorial arrangements generally, occupied less time. The realities of the situation were clear, particularly by 1824, and the location of power quite apparent. As Irwin notes in his brilliant study, the Dutch at these discussions "used Singapore more as a bargaining point than as a battle cry; they hoped that by giving way to the British here, they would stand a better chance of extracting concessions elsewhere." As a result, the British "were not pressed as closely as they expected about (their) title to Singapore."[24]

The Anglo-Dutch Treaty tacitly recognized the fields of interest that had become established since the late eighteenth century by the British move to China down the Straits of Malacca. The growth of Penang and its assured trading area of north Malaya, the dynamic erruption of Singapore with its sphere of interest and the British trade route to China were seen as part of one pattern. The Dutch on Java and its ancillary islands was seen as another. Amicably enough, these patterns were made more tidy. Holland ceded to Britain its few ancient outposts in India, while Britain exchanged its Bencoolen for Malacca. By so doing, the neglected foothold of each was withdrawn from the other's sphere of interest. Singapore was recognized as belonging to the British, who for their part agreed to make no further settlement on islands south of the equator.

At the conferences that preceded this treaty the territorial adjustments had not been considered worthy of prolonged discussion; yet nevertheless these arrangements decided the European map of Malaysia or island Southeast Asia for over a hundred years. Despite occasional friction, it produced a lack of clash and conflict for a longer period than most treaties.

In April, 1825, Cracroft from Penang took over from the Dutch the administration of Malacca, and in 1826, forty years after Penang was founded, it was brought together with Malacca and Singapore to become the Straits Settlements Presidency. Thus, after forty years of varied effort, the British were in possession of three posts down the peninsula. Past them sailed, in a steady stream, the British ships to China.

[24]G. Irwin: *Nineteenth Century Borneo. A Study in Diplomatic Rivalry.* (The Hague, 1955), p. 61.

CONCLUSION

The three ports that in 1826 were brought together into the new Presidency of the Straits Settlements were very different from one another. Their location, settlement, and history in each case had produced a city with a character of its own. They all shared a similar population, a mixed community of Chinese, Indians, and Malays, although the proportions differed somewhat. In Penang the Indian community from the very beginning was almost as large as the Chinese. Unlike the other two settlements, Penang was almost an Indian port. In Singapore on the other hand, the Malaysian population predominated. The Chinese immigrants from Malacca, Riau and China itself did not constitute a majority of the population until the 1840's, while the Indians were a small minority. In Malacca the mixture again was slightly different, with a Chinese population predominant. In each case in control of this mixed population were a few Europeans. There were other similarities. They shared a common flora and fauna, a common tongue, Malay, a common closeness to the Malay Peninsula. Between them they shared the Straits of Malacca and a common government. Straits produce was an article of trade common to all.

The similarities however did not disguise the differences. Agriculturally these were clear. Penang Island by 1826 had had forty years of development. Although largely mountainous, it possessed also a coastal plain facing the mainland. Several agricultural enterprises had brought about an early clearing of its thick jungle. Pepper was the first crop, initiated by Francis Light in 1790. He sent the Capitan China to Acheh to purchase plants and seed. Chinese gardeners responded quickly to his liberal disposal of land. Between 1795 and 1805 pepper plantations spread down the length of the plain, and pepper became the staple product of the island. Exports in 1804 were valued at $400,000, the next most valuable export being betelnut ($240,000). A traveler in 1805 describes how the plain "is well cultivated, and laid out in gardens, plantations of pepper, betel, areca, coconut trees, etc. intersected in all directions with pleasant carriage roads, the sides of which are lined with a variety of shrubs and trees that are in perpetual verdure".[1]

Little of this pepper found its way to China. Although sought constantly in the latter part of the eighteenth century, along with tin, as a commodity that would help the tea trade, most of this pepper went to Europe. Demand in

[1] J. Johnson. *The Oriental Voyager.* (London, 1807), p. 224.

China it appears was not sufficient by 1800 for ships to stop at Penang for a cargo. In Europe, when Napoleon slammed shut the doors of the continent in 1806 with his Berlin and Milan decrees, forbidding imports from British possessions, pepper on Penang suffered a severe decline. In London, cheap Malabar pepper undercut it and even when the war ended the shortage of ships and the cheapness of Indian pepper continued to hinder any revival. By 1830 its export was valued at a mere $5,000, and nearly all of that was Achinese pepper re-exported.

Spices were the crops that replaced pepper and these were given a major boost by the end of the war and the return of the Dutch. In 1790 Francis Light somehow secured plants of cinnamon, clove and nutmeg from Mauritius even though it was at war, and spices were encouraged from 1819 onwards by a British tariff which gave preference to spices from British possessions. In 1830 India permitted free entry to spices, provided they came from a British port. The British were not anxious to become dependent again on the Dutch. Spices took the place of pepper all down the coastal plain and remained the staple crop of the island until the middle of the nineteenth century.

A large part of this business had come under the control of James Scott and after him his partner, David Brown. Unlike Singapore, in the development of which a number of young European businessmen participated almost immediately, the business of Penang from its foundation had been almost monopolized by one man, James Scott. He had come to India as purser on the *Anson* in 1774. Taking his discharge, he became a country trader. By 1779 he was on P'huket, trading along the Malay Peninsula, the friend of Francis Light. He followed Light to Penang in 1786. They agreed that while one administered the island and accepted the inevitable financial loss that Company salary entailed, the other would make enough for both. This Scott did.

In 1795 Captain Kyd, the surveyor, commented that the Light-Scott combination had been "so great a bar to all free enterprise that no commercial house or merchant of any credit had ever attempted to form an establishment."[2] Scott maintained and improved his position as the years passed, even after Light had died. He established links with John Palmer in Calcutta and Beale and Magniac in Canton. He advanced money to secure mortgages on go-downs, estates, ships, and property. He built a large house, "Kelso." His company had "the virtual monopoly of the import and export trade of the settlement" according to Stevens, and were "sole bankers and money lenders to the community."[3]

After Scott's death, his business was conducted by David Brown, his former partner. The lands of the settlement continued to gravitate into Brown's hands. At Glugor, midway down the plain of spices, he built a large home, "Glugor."

[2]S. S. (F.) R. Vol. 7. Kyd to Bengal, 2 August, 1795.

[3]F. G. Stevens. "A Contribution to the Early History of Prince of Wales Island." *JMBRAS* Vol. VII. Pt. 3. (Oct., 1929), p. 381.

He died in 1825 having acquired great wealth and an amazing proportion of the cultivable land of the island. "Glugor" even today is still possessed by a descendant of David Brown.

From the arrival of Scott in 1786 to the death of Brown in 1825 is almost forty years, the period we are attempting to narrate. This period saw a great change in Georgetown, more pronounced in the second half perhaps than in the earlier period, and a cumulative development once the nineteenth century began. Here of course the transformation was dramatic enough, from a point covered by jungle and a completely uncultivated island densely packed with timber, to the clear signs of settlement and agriculture. All this was exciting and gratifying. Nevertheless the most extensive developments occurred after Penang had been established for twenty years, and one cannot help thinking that they were caused not merely by the growth of trade, but also by the expansion of agriculture.

On the outskirts of Georgetown from 1805 or so on, were new and graceful houses where a few years earlier had stood some attap huts on stilts. David Brown built "Glugor", Scott built "Kelso House", while in 1808-09 Raffles built "Runnymede," and, far more ambitiously came Scott's "Scotland House," two-storied, adapting the Malay style in a manner that was to become traditional in the Straits Settlements, a style which captured the coolness and elevation of the Malay house, but replaced the wood with stone. Outstanding among these great new homes was "Suffolk House," built between 1808 and 1811 by W. E. Phillips, the Englishman who was always acting governor but never confirmed, when Scottish governor after governor died after a short spell of duty.[4] "A very splendid mansion," as Wathen describes it, "with a very elegant and splendid withdrawing room."[5] Lord Minto, a tone of amazement creeping into his letter (for Phillips would not appear to have been a big man in any sense of the word), wrote that "Mr. Phillips is magnificently lodged; and his house, which he built himself, is one of the handsomest I have seen in India."[6]

In Georgetown itself there also were great changes. A town of brick and stone rose to replace the muddy lanes and crowded attap huts of the eighteenth century. In 1808 a tremendous fire, one of several, swept most of this away, and in 1814, six years later, there was another fire. After that date, no attap was permitted in the central part of the town.

The bricks that replaced the attap in Georgetown, and such public works as the widening and raising of the streets were made very largely by transported Indian convicts. So was the construction for Robert Farquhar in 1804 of a brick aqueduct to bring water for ships from the lovely 300-foot waterfall that is even today an object of delight. Slavery, a minor feature in the settle-

---

[4] Among the governors and other officials who died suddenly during this period were Dundas, who died in 1807; (1807 was a bad year. His wife, and John Hope Oliphant, 2nd member of Council, also died). Bruce, and Norman Macalister died in 1810; Caunter in 1812; W. Petrie in 1816; Bannerman in 1819.

[5] J. Wathen: *Journal of a Voyage in 1811 and 1812 to Madras and China, etc.* (London, 1814), p. 139.

[6] Minto: p. 256.

ment (there were 1,200 of them, all domestic slaves, in 1805) had been abolished in 1808, but the Indian convicts who dated from as early as 1790 were rarely detained in jail, even if convicted of the most terrible of crimes. Instead they were trained in various skills so that they could be employed for the benefit of the town. The earliest British Church in Malaya was built by them in 1808, on government funds derived largely from the opium and gambling farms, as were nearly all the public buildings of this period.

Turning to Malacca, it is easy enough to draw a contrast between it and the Penang of 1826, both in agriculture — a little padi is all that Malacca produced — and in the townships, but perhaps the sharpest contrast can be drawn by looking at the water in front of the two places. Both depended upon it for their sustenance, but whereas Finlayson (accompanying Crawfurd to Bangkok) found at Penang an endless variety of small craft as well as "a considerable number of ships of various descriptions and nations: English, American, Chinese junks, Siamese and Arab," when he reached Malacca he had to write "on entering this place we were forcibly struck with the contrast which it afforded with Prince of Wales Island. Here five or six vessels at the utmost lay scattered and straggling in an extensive bay. There hundreds of ships of all descriptions were seen crowded together... [here] the streets were solitary and deserted. A lonely inhabitant sauntering in his verandah, or idly lolling or smoking at his door, only served to render the scene more dreary, sad and melancholy. Even the Chinese of whom however but few remain, seemed to have forsaken their habits of industry. In Penang, all was activity and bustle and zeal."[7]

Although Penang had over thirty years start on Singapore, it is typical of the dynamism of the latter settlement that by the 1830's a very considerable part of the island already was covered with gambier and pepper plantations. The early European settlers had tried a variety of crops — sugar, coffee, cotton and nutmeg amongst them — all of which failed. The cultivation of gambier was a pre-Rafflesian industry monopolized by the Chinese. It spread rapidly after 1819.

Gambier needed an acreage of jungle next to it for fuel, while the refuse after the plant was boiled was invaluable manure for pepper. The processing was a technique brought across apparently by Chinese from Sumatra and the nearby islands. Cutting down the jungle for fuel and fighting off the tigers (a man a day was being lost by 1840), the Chinese advanced across Singapore island, reaching the Straits of Johore and moving into the peninsula by the late 1830's. Thus agriculturally the island presented a very different picture from that of the well-established, static estates on Penang, and also from that of the coconuts and padi plots of the Malays behind Malacca. Not even in the packed streets and the crowded harbor was there conveyed so clearly the passion for work

[7]Finlayson. p. 12; pp. 39-41.

and the fanatical efforts of the Chinese to earn money as in their savage defeat of the jungle.

Singapore town and harbor, however, also reflected this vigor. It was unprecedented for a port on the equator to flourish with such lusty life. Panama at one time may have seen similar vigor but nowhere in tropical Asia had the enervation and latitude of the equator been so ignored. If the heat and jungle of the equator were not sufficient, the ground chosen for the new settlement was a further handicap to growth. The anchorage was good but the townsite was swampy, with a river too narrow for ships, yet wide enough to split the area and to require bridges. The area was notoriously hostile yet defense was negligible. Singapore settlers had to be their own guardians, like men in the vigilance committees of the American frontier.

Here perhaps is the answer to the riddle of the enthusiasm and vigor that characterize the growth of Singapore and to a lesser extent of Penang. Perhaps to the Chinese this was the frontier, and their reaction to it was to work harder and live more boisterously than ever. The rude outpost was soon transformed into the dynamic and optimistic paramount city of the area. The few administrators — Raffles, Farquhar, Crawfurd and their successors — soon found that they could have little effect on the life and growth of the colony. It grew out of the exuberant effort of thousands, unaware of any halter restraining them. No community secured a trading monopoly, for although by the 1830's over half the leases of the best commercial sites were held by Chinese, there were also over twenty trading houses under British, Arab, Portuguese, German and American management. The independence of the frontier, the determination to succeed, animated them all.

The government by the British of these settlements — for forty years in Penang, for lesser periods in the others — had been marked throughout by a major characteristic, itself typical evidence of what we recognize as a colonial attitude. The British were firmly convinced of their superiority over their subjects, and governed always throughout this period with an unshakeable, unquestioning belief in their position.

The calm acceptance of their own leadership, direction, and decision went almost unchallenged by the communities they ruled. The Chinese did not bother to claim administrative leadership, but utilized the economic opportunities that existed, and grudgingly, when it seemed advisable, accepted the judicial decisions of the British. In his innermost being, the Chinese migrant leader felt — however dimly — that given the chance, he was just as good as the European. Neither he nor the Malay however was able or wished to dispute the assumption of leadership at this time, and it remained unchallenged for over a hundred years more, permitting the British in Malaya, with very little opposition, to establish British Malaya.

The British belief in their superiority over subject races had as a corollary a lack of curiosity, a lack of interest, in those races. It was curiosity, the questioning spirit, the seeking for truth, that had enabled Europe centuries earlier to break the deadlock of tradition and belief and to initiate a Renaissance. This in turn had led to an Industrial Revolution engendered and constantly developed by the rational enquiring mind that Europe had produced. Its goal, accepted as a dogma, was progress; and by 1826 Europe had progressed far ahead of Asia, still locked in tradition.

But with the British in Malaya for many years this curiosity had almost died. Raffles, with his plan for Malayan Studies, was an exception not to be encouraged. The three settlements thus made hardly any intellectual impact on the dark jungle of the peninsula. Here throughout most of the nineteenth century was a society bound by tradition, a convention-ridden society: unchanging, undeveloping.

In this the Malay Peninsula was as one with the rest of Southeast Asia. Vast differences though there were in government, from the mandarins of Vietnam to the head hunters of Borneo, all accepted the present forms. The mysteries and the miseries of life were never questioned, the problems of the past never investigated, the prospects of a future better than the present never envisaged. Progress was unheard of, and traditional thought and custom ruled supreme. The curiosity of Europe, the enquiring sceptical mind of the British could have brought a gradual shaking off of this all-embracing cloak of convention, but this sceptical curiosity was itself dampened by the assumption of complete colonial superiority. Interested largely only in themselves, unaware of any need to produce mental change, anxious merely for order and trade, the three settlements existed cheek by jowl with the traditional societies of the peninsula. The intellectual apathy inherent in the Malay States received little stimulus from the colonial settlements. The old continued to live alongside the new, separate and distinct.

The old way of life flourished also in China. This land, far more than the peninsula, was the object of sustained British curiosity. It was China which initiated these British settlements off the Malay Peninsula, and China at the end of this account is still the major attraction for the British east of India. The settlement on Penang was never seen as the one and only answer to the British problems in China even when first considered, and an embassy had been dispatched by London in 1787. The leader of the embassy died en route and it was abandoned. But in 1793, Lord Macartney reached China amid high hopes that the various difficulties faced by the British in Canton and unrelieved by the Penang settlement — problems of trade, of relations with the Chinese officials, and much else — would be removed. The Chinese however were indifferent to these difficulties, indifferent to the protests of the foreign merchants, and indifferent to the representations of Macartney. The western mind quite failed to grasp the outlook of the East. The problems remained.

China was convinced that it was the center of civilization. It regarded itself as self-sufficient. Trade was permitted, so Peking said in a famous royal announcement, as a concession.[8] The barbarian countries from beyond the seas could send tribute, and Lord Macartney was thanked for the tribute he brought, but he was told that the best way Britain could help its traders was by strengthening British loyalty to China by acting always according to China's wishes. His mission failed.

In 1816 another embassy was sent. The British were increasingly anxious to establish their footing in China on a more regular basis, and despite the failure of Macartney the desire to develop trade pulled them along. Lord Amherst however received none of the courtesy extended to Macartney and his failure and the flagrant discourtesy shown to him made the issue even more clear cut. As the British could not accept Chinese pretensions, and as the Chinese could not accept those of the British, there remained three alternatives.

The British by this time were east of India in strength. Throughout the world they were rising to a long plateau of global dominance. A realist surveying the scene would accept that in any Anglo-Chinese confrontation the British had the power. There remained the question of how that power was to be used. This was purely an Anglo-Chinese question. The British bases in the Malay Peninsula, which had been established as part of earlier movements associated with the British trade expansion, played little part in this expansion; only to the extent that some thought was given to the possible utility of Singapore as a port of trade with the Chinese, should the British be driven from Canton; a revival of the 18th-century idea of a base for Chinese trade not in China.

The alternatives facing the British by the 1830's were: to resort to arms to secure Chinese acceptance of Britain as a trader in China; to completely surrender to Oriental trading terms, such as permitted the Dutch to exist on Nagasaki; or to abandon China and retreat to Singapore.

As the second and third alternatives were rejected, being completely alien to the British temper of the 1830's, events drifted towards war. And yet it is worth noting that despite all the difficulties imposed by the Chinese, trade still slowly increased. Fostered by the merchants and aggravated by the increasing friction, it maintained a steady rise. In 1818, Morse estimates that Britain sold China $16 million worth of goods. By 1833 this had risen to $22 million.

In England the abolition in 1813 of the ancient East India Company's monopoly of trade to India was followed by petition after petition from the great new manufacturing towns to abolish its monopoly of trade in tea and the trade to China. It seemed an out-of-date constricting regulation, an old custom that was of no national utility at all. In 1830, both Houses of Parliament appointed committees to enquire into the East India Company. Their recom-

---

[8]For an excellent account of this, see J. Cranmer-Byng. "Lord Macartney's Embassy to Peking in 1793," in *Journal of Oriental Studies*. (Hong Kong), Vol. iv, No. 1-2, 1957/58, pp. 117-187.

mendations led the Reform Parliament to abolish the monopoly and from 1834 onwards, it became lawful for anyone to trade with China.

Immediately the pressure from Europe on China was increased; but very little increase in understanding followed, on either side. The Chinese maintained their classic theory of China as the center of civilization. Lord Napier, the British Chief Superintendent of Trade there, was hounded to his death, treated so contemptuously as to confirm the utter impossibility of establishing any other relation than by force. A head-on collision was bound to occur between Western ideas of trade and diplomacy, as conducted between sovereign states, and the Chinese concept of a world-state of which it was the center and in which all the rest were inferior. Such a collision had been avoided by the British in Southeast Asia, for despite all British assumption of superiority, neither they nor the other Asian powers had this traditional self-centered outlook. They could deal in diplomacy with the Emperor of Siam, or with the Sultans of Kedah and Johore and both sides could give and secure concessions in negotiations, and the recognition of superior power by one side was clear. But with China this was impossible.

In 1839 the English government then finally resorted to arms. Its forces showed a clear superiority and China, made dramatically aware of its military shortcomings by a British movement up the Yangtze Kiang, sought peace. By the Treaty of Nanking in 1842, most of the requests submitted by Macartney in 1793 were brought forward by the British and were agreed to by the Chinese. Of most importance was the acquisition by the British of a place to trade — a barren island off the mouth of the Canton River. At last a solution to the trade problem had been achieved. Here at Hong Kong the British were to establish what they had been seeking for over a hundred years. Not in Penang or in Singapore had they succeeded, nor in the many other attempts in Southeast Asia. Aware though they had been of the problem, their attempts to answer it had never been satisfactory. But in Hong Kong, at last, the British had secured a mart for trade with China. With the establishment of Hong Kong, the long move east from India had ended.

SELECT BIBLIOGRAPHY

In Section A of this bibliography are listed the primary sources available in Singapore, where research for this book was undertaken. In most cases this material is also in the India Office Library in London, although the nomenclature there may be different.

A. PRIMARY SOURCES

1. *Manuscripts* (National Library, Singapore)

   a. *Straits Settlements Factory Records*
   Vols. A 1-70 Penang, Singapore and Malacca Consultations, 1806-1830.
   Vols. B 1-10 Penang: Letters to London, 1805-1830.
   Vols. C 1-6 Penang: Letters from London, 1810-1829.
   Vols. D 1-11 Penang: Letters to India, 1800-1826.
   Vols. E 1-4 Penang: Letters from India, 1804-1831.
   Vols. F 1-5 Penang: Letters from native rulers, 1817-1837.
   Vols. G 1-5 Penang: Letters to native rulers, 1817-1835.
   Vols. H 1-14 Penang: Letters and Orders in Council, 1817-1825.
   Vols. I 1-41 Penang: Letters, Miscellaneous, 1806-1830.
   Vols. J 1-18 Penang: Index to Records, 1806-1830.
   Vols. K 1-18 Penang: Governor, Miscellaneous, 1805-1830.
   Vols. L 6-20 Singapore: Raffles Administration (1821-1823).

   b. *Straits Settlements Factory Records* (Library, University of Singapore)
   Vols. 1-7 Bengal Public Consultations, 1786-1795.
   Vols. 8-11 Miscellaneous, 1805-1823.
   Vols. 180-184 Penang: Letters to London, 1805-1820.
   Vols. 186-190 Penang: Letters from London, 1806-1816.

   c. *Miscellaneous Records* (Library, University of Singapore)
   Sumatra Factory Records. Vol. 15, 1771-1772.
   Java Factory Records. Vol. 11, 1811.
   Dutch Records A. Vols. 13, 26-30, 1784-1821.
   Raffles Collection, I-III, VIII, X.

2. *Printed Materials*

Burney, Henry	*The Burney Papers*. A collection of official records relating to the mission of Captain Henry Burney to the Court of Siam in the year 1826; reprinted from originals in the India Office. 5 Vols. (Bangkok, 1910-1914).
Crawfurd, John	*The Crawfurd Papers*. A Collection of official records relating to the mission of Dr. John Crawfurd, sent to Siam by the Government of India in the year 1821. 2 Vols. (Bangkok, 1915).
Cowan, C. D.	*Early Penang and the Rise of Singapore*. Documents from the Manuscript Records of the East India Company, selected and edited by

                                    C. D. Cowan. *JMBRAS,* Vol. XXIII. Pt. 2
                                    (March, 1950).
Elliot,
    Countess of Minto (ed)   *Lord Minto in India. Life and Letters of Gilbert*
                                    Elliot, First Earl of Minto, from 1807-1814.
                                    Journal of the Indian Archipelago, Logan's
                                    Journal: Notices of Penang. Letters from the
                                    East India Company settlement on Prince of
                                    Wales Island. Vols. IV, VI, (1849-1852, 1859).

Maxwell, W. G., and W. S.   *Treaties and Engagements Affecting the Ma-*
    Gibson   *lay States and Borneo.* (London, 1924).
Miller, H.   *Extracts from the Letters of Col. Nahuijs.*
                                    JMBRAS. Vol. XIX. Pt. II. (October, 1941).
Papendrecht, P. C. Hoynck van   Some Old Private Letters from the Cape, Bata-
                                    via, and Malacca (1778-1788). *JMBRAS.* Vol.
                                    II. Pt. 1, (June, 1924).
                                    Prince of Wales Island Gazette, 1805-1827.
Ross, C. (ed.)   *The Correspondence of Charles, the First Mar-*
                                    quis Cornwallis. 3 vols., (London, 1859).

B. SECONDARY SOURCES
    1. *Journals*
        a. *Journal, Straits Branch, Royal Asiatic Society:*
        I. H. Burkhill: "Jack's Letters to Wallich, 1819-1821." Vol.
                                        LXXIII. Pt. (1916).
        J. G. Koenig: "Journal of a Voyage from India to Siam and
                                        Malacca in 1779." Vol. XXVI. (Jan. 1894).
        W. C. Lennon: "Journal of a Voyage Through the Straits of
                                        Malacca..." Vol. VII. (1881).
        W. E. Maxwell: "The Dutch in Perak." Vol. X. (1882).
        A. M. Skinner: "Memoir of Captain Francis Light." Vol.
                                        XXVII. (1895).

        b. *Journal, Malayan Branch, Royal Asiatic Society:*
        D. K. Bassett: "Thomas Forrest, An Eighteenth Century Mar-
                                        iner." Vol. XXXIV. Pt. 2. (1961).
        J. Bastin: "Sir Stamford Raffles' and John Crawfurd's
                                        ideas of colonizing the Malayan Archipelago."
        ———   Vol. XXVI. Pt. 1. (July, 1953). "Raffles &
                                        British Policy in the Indian Archipelago, 1811-
                                        1816." Vol. XXVII. Pt. 1. (1954).
        C. D. Cowan: "Governor Bannerman and the Penang Tin
                                        Scheme, 1818-1819." Vol. XXIII. Pt. 1. (Feb-
                                        ruary, 1950).
        K. Garnier: "Early Days in Penang." Vol. 1. No. 87. (April,
                                        1923).
        C. Gibson-Hill: "The steamers employed in Asian Waters, 1819-
                                        1839." Vol. XXVII. Pt. 1. (May, 1954).
        ———   "Raffles, Acheh and the Order of the Golden
                                        Sword." Vol. XXIX. Pt. 3. (August, 1956).
        ———   "Raffles, Alexander Hare and Johanna van
                                        Hare." Vol. XXVIII. Pt. 1. (March, 1955).
        B. Harrison: "Trade in the Straits of Malacca in 1785; a
                                        Memorandum by P. G. de Bruijn, Governor of

	Malacca." Vol. XXVI. Pt. 1. (July, 1953). "Malacca in the Eighteenth Century; Two Dutch Governors' Reports." Vol. XXVII. Pt. 1. (May, 1954).
G. Irwin:	"Governor Couperus and the surrender of Malacca, 1795." Vol. XXIX. Pt. 3. (August, 1956).
A. Lamb	"British Missions to Cochin China, 1788-1822." Vol. XXXIV. Pts. 3 & 4. 1961.
F. G. Stevens:	"A Contribution to the early history of Prince of Wales Island." Vol. VII. Pt. 3. (October, 1929).
Tan Soon Chye:	"A Note on Early Legislation in Penang." Vol. XXIII. Pt. 1. (February, 1950).
N. Tarling:	"British Policy in the Malay Peninsula and Archipelago. 1824-1871." Vol. XXX. Pt. 3. (1960).
R. Winstedt:	"Kedah Laws." Vol. VI. Pt. II (June, 1928).
	"Notes on the History of Kedah." Vol. XIV. Pt. III (December, 1936).

c. *Journal, Siam Society:*

G. Gerini:	"Historical Retrospect of Junk Ceylon Island," Vol. II (1905).
D. G. E. Hall:	"From Mergui to Singapore, 1686-1819." Vol. XII (July, 1953).

d. *Journal of the Indian Archipelago: Logan's Journal:*

J. Balestier:	British Possessions in the Straits of Malacca. Vol. II (1848).
T. Braddell:	Gambling and Opium Smoking in the Straits of Malacca. Vol. 1 (New Series) (1856).
	On the History of Acheen, Vol. V. (1851). Concerning Col. Farquhar's going to look for a place to establish a settlement. Vol. VI (1852).
J. Low:	A Translation of the Kedah Annals. Vol. III. (1849).
	An Account of the Origin and Progress of the British Colonies in the Straits of Malacca. Vol. III. 1849, Vol. IV. (1850).
	Observations on Perak. Vol. IV. (1850).
	On the Ancient Connection between Kedah and Siam. Vol. V (1851).
Anonymous	"Translation of the Annals of Acheen," Vol. IV (1850).
	"Notices of Pinang," Vol. IV (1850). Vol. V (1851).
	Notes on the Chinese in Pinang. Vol. IX (1855).
T. Oxley:	"Some Account of the Nutmeg and its Cultivation," Vol. II (1848).
J. D. Vaughan:	"Notes on the Malays of Pinang and Province Wellesley," Vol. II *New Series* (1858).
J. B. Westerhout:	"Notes on Malacca," Vol. II (1848).

e. *Memoirs of the Raffles Museum:*

C. Gibson-Hill:	"Singapore Old Strait and New Harbour, 1300-

1870," No. 3. (1956).

2. *Books*
   a. *Contemporary:*

J. Anderson: *Political and Commercial Considerations Relative to the Malayan Peninsula and the British Settlements in the Straits of Malacca.* Penang, 1824.

————   *Mission to the East Coast of Sumatra in 1823, Under the Direction of the Government of Prince of Wales Island* ... London, 1826.

————   *Acheen,* and the Ports on the North and East Coasts of Sumatra, ... London, 1840.

C. Assey: *On the Trade to China and the Indian Archipelago* ... London, 1819.

J. Crawfurd: *Journal of an Embassy from the Governor-General of India to the Courts of Siam and Cochin China* ... 2 Vols. London, 1830.

————   *Descriptive Dictionary of the Indian Islands and Adjacent Countries.* London, 1856.

G. Finlayson: *The Mission to Siam and Hue, the Capital of Cochin-China, in the Year 1821-22. From the Journal of the Late George Finlayson, Esq., Surgeon and Naturalist to the Mission. With a Memoir of the Author, by Sir Thomas Stamford Raffles, F.R.S.,* London, 1826.

T. Forrest: *A Voyage from Calcutta to the Mergui Archipelago; also an Account of the Islands Jan Sylau, Pulo Pinang, and the Port of Queda; the Present State of Acheen* ... *to Which are Added an Account of the Island Celebes.* London, 1792.

Hickey: *Memoirs of William Hickey* (ed.) A. Spenser. 4 Vols. London, 1913-25.

J. Johnson: *The Oriental Voyager; or Descriptive Sketches and Cursory Remarks on a Voyage to India and China, in His Majesty's Ship Caroline, Performed in the Years 1803-4-5-6.* London, 1807.

G. Leith: *A Short Account of the Settlement, Produce and Commerce of Prince of Wales Island, in the Straits of Malacca.* London, 1804.

J. Low: *A Dissertation on the Soil and Agriculture of the British Settlement of Penang on Prince of Wales Island, in the Straits of Malacca.* Singapore, 1836.

N. Macalister: *Historical Memoir Relative to Prince of Wales Island in the Straits of Malacca, and the Importancę, Political and Commercial.* London, 1803.

W. Marsden: *A Grammar of the Malayan Language.* London, N.D.

W. G. Maxwell and   *Treaties and Engagements Affecting the Malay*
   W. S. Gibson: *States and Borneo.* London, 1880.

J. H. Moor: *Notices of the Indian Archipelago and Adjacent Countries.* Singapore, 1837.

T. S. Newbold: *Political and Statistical Account of the British Settlements in the Straits of Malacca; viz. Pinang, Malacca and Singapore, with a history of the Malayan States on the Peninsula of Malacca.* 2 Vols. London, 1839.

S. Osborn: *My Journal in Malayan Waters: Or, the Blockade of Quedah.* London, 1861.

Home Popham: *A Description of Prince of Wales Island, In the Straits of Malacca, with Its Real and Probable Advantages* and *Sources to Recommend It as a Marine Establishment.* London, 1805.

Lady S. Raffles: *Memoir of the Life and Public Services of the Late Sir Thomas Stamford Raffles.* London, 1830.

J. Stockdale: *Sketches, Civil and Military, of the Island of Java . . .* London, 1811.

M. Symes: *An Account of an Embassy to the Kingdom of Ava, Sent by the Governor-General of India in the year 1795.* London, 1800.

E. Trapaud: *A Short Account of the Prince of Wales Island, or Pulo Penang, in the East Indies; Given to Captain Light by the King of Quedah.* London, 1788.

J. Wathen: *Journal of a Voyage in 1811 and 1812 to Madras and China . . .* London, 1814.

J. Welsh: *Military Reminiscences.* 2 Vols. London, 1830.

b. *Recent Studies:*

A. Aspinall: *Cornwallis in Bengal . . . Together With Accounts of the Commercial Expansion of the East India Company, 1786-1793, and of the Foundation of Penang, 1786-1793.* Manchester, 1931.

P. Bannerjea: *Indian Finance: In the Days of the Company.* London, 1928.

D. C. Boulger: *The Life of Sir Stamford Raffles.* London, 1897.

C. C. Buckley: *An Anecdotal History of Old Times in Singapore.* 2 Vols. London, 1903.

H. P. Clodd: *Malaya's First British Pioneer.* London, 1955.

W. C. Costin: *Great Britain and China, 1833-1860.* Oxford, 1937.

R. Coupland: *Raffles, 1781-1826.* Oxford, 1926.

H. Dodwell: *The Straits Settlements, 1815-1863, The Growth of the New Empire, 1783-1870, of the Cambridge History of the British Empire.* Cambridge, 1940. *The Nabobs of Madras.* London, 1926.

C. Fawcett (ed.):   *East Indiamen. The East India Company's Maritime Service,* by Sir E. Cotton. London, 1949.

H. Furber:	*Henry Dundas, First Viscount Melville, 1742-1811*. Oxford, 1931.
———	*John Company at Work*. Harvard, 1948.
M. Greenberg:	*British Trade and the Opening of China, 1800-1842*. Cambridge, 1951.
D. G. E. Hall:	*A History of South East Asia*. London, 1955.
———	*Michael Symes. Journal of His Second Mission to the Court of Ava in 1802*. London, 1955.
V. Harlow:	*The Founding of the Second British Empire, 1763-1793*. Vol. I. *Discovery and Revolution*. London, 1952.
B. Harrison:	*Southeast Asia*. London, 1954.
G. Irwin:	*Nineteenth Century Borneo, A Study in Diplomatic Rivalry*. Holland, 1954.
C. R. Low:	*History of the Indian Navy*. 2 Vols. London, 1877.
L. A. Mills:	*British Malaya, 1824-1867*. Singapore, 1925.
H. B. Morse:	*The Chronicles of the East India Company Trading to China, 1635-1834*. 5 Vols. Oxford, 1926-29.
C. N. Parkinson:	*Trade in the Eastern Seas, 1793-1813*. Cambridge, 1937.
———	*War in the Eastern Seas, 1793-1815*. London, 1954.
C. H. Phillips:	*The East India Company, 1784-1834*. Manchester, 1940.
Earl H. Pritchard:	*Anglo-Chinese Relations During the Seventeenth and Eighteenth Centuries*. Illinois, 1930.
———	*The Crucial Years of Early Anglo-Chinese Relations, 1750-1800*. Washington, 1936.
V. Purcell:	*Early Penang*. Penang, 1928.
———	*The Chinese in Malaya*. London, 1948.
———	*The Chinese in Southeast Asia*. London, 1951.
H. W. Richmond:	*The Navy in India, 1763-1783*. London, 1931.
R. Rost (ed.):	*Miscellaneous Papers Relating to Indo-China*. 2 Vols. London, 1886.
A. Francis Stewart:	*A Short Sketch of the Lives of Francis and William Light, the Founders of Penang and Adelaide*. London, 1901.
F. Swettenham:	*British Malaya*. London, 1948.
W. F. Vella:	*Siam Under Rama III, 1824-1851*. N.Y., 1957.
R. Winstedt:	*A History of Malaya*. Singapore, 1935.
W. Wood:	*A History of Siam*. London, 1926.
A. Wright and T. H. Reid:	*The Malay Peninsula*. London, 1912.
C. E. Wurtzburg:	*Raffles of the Eastern Isles*. London, 1954.

INDEX